THE
NEGOTIATION PROCESS

THE NEGOTIATION PROCESS
Theories and Applications

Editor
I. William Zartman

SAGE PUBLICATIONS   Beverly Hills   London

JX
4473
.N43

Copyright © 1978, 1977 by Sage Publications, Inc.

All rights reserved. No part of this book may be reproduced or utilized in any form or by any means, electronic or mechanical, including photocopying, recording, or by any information storage and retrieval system, without permission in writing from the publisher.

For information address:

SAGE PUBLICATIONS, INC.
275 South Beverly Drive
Beverly Hills, California 90212

SAGE PUBLICATIONS LTD
28 Banner Street
London EC1Y 8QE

Printed in the United States of America

International Standard Book Number 0-8039-1034-7

Library of Congress Catalog Card No. 78-19536

SECOND PRINTING

CONTENTS

Introduction
    I. WILLIAM ZARTMAN   7

Part I: THEORIES

1. Simple Model of Negotiation: *A Sociological Point of View*
    OTOMAR J. BARTOS   13

2. Negotiation as a Learning Process
    JOHN G. CROSS   29

3. Negotiation as a Psychological Process
    BERTRAM I. SPECTOR   55

4. Negotiation as a Joint Decision-Making Process
    I. WILLIAM ZARTMAN   67

5. Boundary Role Conflict: *Negotiation as Dual Responsiveness*
    DANIEL DRUCKMAN   87

Part II: APPLICATIONS

6. A Game-Theoretic Analysis of the Vietnam Negotiations: *Preferences and Strategies 1968-1973*
    FRANK C. ZAGARE   111

7. Tactical Advantages of Opening Positioning Strategies: *Lessons from the Seabed Arms Control Talks 1967-1970*
    BENNETT RAMBERG   133

8. An Application of a Richardson Process Model: *Soviet-American Interactions in the Test Ban Negotiations 1962-1963*
    P. TERRENCE HOPMANN and THERESA C. SMITH   149

9. Argumentation in Foreign Policy Settings: *Britain in 1918, Munich in 1938, and Japan in 1970*
    ROBERT AXELROD   175

10. Bargaining as Trial and Error: *The Case of the Spanish Base Negotiations 1963-1970*
    BRIAN H. TRACY   193

References   225

Index   237

INTRODUCTION

It is an exciting development in scientific inquiry when the study of a subject suddenly blossoms to the point where an internal debate on competing paradigms becomes possible. Twenty years ago, there was no body of literature on negotiation as a social process, although there were plenty of works on specific negotiations, and more generally on international diplomacy. Since then, not only has negotiation emerged as a field of study but it has given rise to a fruitful debate among competing approaches. Since these approaches all recognize a common subject defined in similar terms, the debate on differences reinforces the integrity of the new field of study. Furthermore, in the discussion, competing arguments are drawn not only from the level of theoretical logic but also from experimental evidence and from case studies about the real world, providing tests of relevance and reality for the intellectual constructs. In the course of this confrontation, a new concern has now arisen over the nature of the process itself, and the enlarged debate on this topic has begun to provide a fuller comprehension of one of the basic modes of decision-making in society. This collection of ten chapters by leading participants in the current study of negotiation is a snapshot of these multiple debates in action. The study of diplomacy begins with de Callieres (1963; first published in 1714), and ends with Nicolson (1964; first published in 1939 and revised in 1950 and 1963). The study of negotiation begins with Schelling (1960), who brought the insights from recent methodological advances—notably from game theory—to bear on the analysis of joint decision-making under conditions of partial information. Schelling is an economist with a penchant for strategies as well as utilities, and his discipline has had the longest history of concern over negotiation, seen particularly in earlier works such as Zeuthen (1930) and Hicks (1932) on wage determination under conditions of bilateral monopoly. Later, economists began to see wage bargaining as part of a larger field of social processes, with a variety of outcomes and types, rather than simply an economic determination. It is interesting, in the light of the current debate, to note that Douglas

(1962) found phases involving range-making and decision-making in the rich data of actual bargaining cases which she studied, Stevens (1963) outlined a convergence model based on approach and avoidance behavior, and in between the two approaches Walton and McKersie (1965) identified the strategies and tactics associated with different types of goal or outcome structures. Within the study of wage bargaining, the initial search for a single mechanism governing concession rates toward a *juste milieu* was thus being challenged by other analyses of outcomes or bargaining phases determined by the social context of the negotiation. The study of concession rates was not exhausted by its longer history, however, and found its most perceptive expression in the work of Cross (1969), who viewed concession behavior as a learning process in which both stable and unstable patterns and expectations were established and acted upon to determine outcomes theoretically.

As the methodology of economics was giving impetus to the study of negotiations, new formulations were being formed in sociology. At the same time as Schelling's work appeared, Homans (1960) provided a better appreciation of the mechanisms of distribution and satisfaction. Assiduous collection of data through repeated experimentation and statistical methods of analysis were combined to test sociological models of the negotiation process in the major study of Bartos (1974) as he attempted to identify the normal patterns of concession behavior among negotiators. Deutsch (1973) also brought together his own series of experiments in conflict resolution to produce a number of maxims relating to trust and other social-psychological aspects of cooperative behavior in the presence of conflict.

The political study of international negotiations has not shown the same evidence of landmark studies, but, like the subject matter itself, has been eclectic in the absorption of insights from other disciplines. Three works which provided a synthesis of postwar diplomatic experiences reflect this eclectic nature: Ikle (1964) brought together concepts from related studies in economics and sociology along with international relations literature to analyze diplomatic behavior both as a process of choice and as a typology of outcomes, Lall (1966) drew inductive maxims from a range of diplomatic experience, and Young (1968) similarly produced a series of propositions for comparison with historic cases.

The renewal of scholarly attention to negotiation produced an avalanche of theoretical, conceptual, experimental, and critical articles and shorter studies as well as the landmark books and collections already noted, and thus called for new works of synthesis and evaluation, and new collections by groups of authors complementing each other's work on the same subject. The first—and for a long time the best—of these syntheses came early, from Sawyer and Guetzkow (1965), and it served as a basis for a later update by Druckman (1973). More recently, a skillful integration of primarily social-psychology work has been provided by Rubin and Brown (1975), an area where synthesis is needed to bring together a wealth of small studies into the broader evaluations and conclusions which the authors provide.

The major collections available provide the same sort of stock-taking. Young (1975) has brought together half a century of the leading theoretical writings on bargaining, confronting deterministic explanations based on process (through calculus) or on outcome structures (through game theory) with the need to take into account the "undetermining" effects of manipulation or strategic interaction (power). Zartman (1976) has focused his collection on different ways of analyzing current—primarily international—cases of negotiation, emphasizing explanations based on structure and on process but also regarding it as a permanent situation rather than a single encounter. Druckman (1977) has provided a series of studies which illuminate aspects of the general negotiation process from the point of view of social psychology and related disciplines in an attempt to bring new findings to bear on different parts of the same process.

Thus, a new field of study in two decades has produced a significant body of literature in many forms—a number of major works, collections of studies cutting across the topic from several angles, different disciplinary and methodological contributions to the conceptualization of the subject and to the analysis of data, and a growing commonality in the definition of the central process and its most important questions. In this situation, it is time for a different type of collective effort, one that confronts these very elements and, capitalizing on the common understanding of the subjects, invites leading analysts to enter into a competitive exposition of their particular approach to the explanation of outcomes, first in theoretical and epistemological terms and then in application to specific cases. A confrontation of competitive paradigms of this sort can provide critical tests along a number of different dimensions: on the theoretical level among the conceptual approaches themselves, on the practical level among their applications to real cases, and between the two as the case analysts put the conceptual models to the test.

The five chapters of part I in this work block out the major disciplinary approaches to the subject. Bartos presents a parsimonious model that ingeniously turns the famous Nash (1950) solution from a static outcome into a dynamic process. The chapter is a distillation of its author's previous work in sociological analysis but refined to the point where it represents a new departure in evaluating negotiating behavior. Cross' economic model is somewhat more complex, but it also departs from a static game-theory analysis to examine bargaining as a learning process involving reponsive changes in concession rate behavior. Whereas parties in Bartos' model move within discernable limits toward an anticipated midpoint of justice, parties in Cross' model use their movement to induce more rapid movement of the other party toward a desired point, both parties bargaining at the same time against the costs which passing time imposes on them. The model is again a more general formulation of the earlier ramifications developed by the author and encompasses other similar patterns as well. Spector's psychological analysis relates bargaining behavior to personality predispositions and their reaction to other personalities in dyadic interaction. This interpretation challenges the various concession models in that it ascribes different behaviors (including concession behaviors) to different interaction pairs of personalities, and also shows different outcome preferences to be dependent on specific personality types. Zartman's interpretation, in turn, challenges the simple concessionary models and claims instead that negotiation involves first joint agreement on a formula defining the part of the problem to be resolved, identifying the agreed perception of it, establishing a criterion of justice for settling details, and only then resolving those details which fit within the formula. As an analysis derived from political science and related to a specific mode of decision-making, the approach includes a place for the exercise of power in altering expectations and acceptances. Finally, Druckman as a social-psychologist analyzes the negotiator as an intermediary between his constituency and his opponent, involved in dual negotiations and hence the double adjustment of values. Thus, the neatness of previous models comes apart in the real world, and more complex models are needed to encompass both the process of the responsive adjustment of expectations (and hence behaviors) and the collective alignment of perceptions: conceding and packaging both are part of negotiating.

It should be noted in this spectrum of approaches that in all cases essential elements of a common process are basic to the analyses: two-party interaction, responsive behavior, joint determination of outcomes, common establishment of terms of reference for evaluating outcomes, positive-sum and zero-sum aspects, and above all a process which is the key to understanding specific outcomes.

The articles in part II have the common characteristic of using theoretical models—including many of those expounded in part I—for testing and application in current instances of diplomatic negotiations. Strategies determining whether to negotiate, strategies governing the choice of opening moves, patterns of interaction determining outcomes, choices among subroutines and negotiating set-structuring moves, and forms of persuasive power for influencing negotiating behavior are the ingredients of the models discussed. The methods of analysis are drawn from game theory, strategic analysis, linear multiple regression analysis, communications analysis, and content analysis, in each case using recent historical data on events and discourse. These papers seek both to employ and to evaluate the models and methods on which they are based, in an attempt to explain their particular outcomes but also to comprehend better the complexity of the negotiating process.

Zagare undertakes a structural analysis of the Vietnam negotiations at Paris using game-theoretic protrayals to show how preferences combined to prevent a solution and then either diverged or were manipulated to permit an agreed outcome. It does not deal with the determination of specific details but rather with the decision to accept foreseeable points of agreement and their payoffs. Ramberg enters into the next stage of negotiations and examines the effects of different opening strategies as illustrated by the Seabed arms control talks. Following competing theoretical claims, he explores the value of opening high, fair, or broad, and concludes that fair openers (equitable positioning) are the most advantageous in arriving at an early and acceptable agreement. Hopmann and Smith are concerned with the effectiveness of reactive behavior models in explaining negotiation behavior, as seen in the case of the nuclear test ban talks, against criticisms that the negotiating process is basically integrative rather than reactive. Using a Richardson model tested in several forms, the analysis supports the understanding of negotiation as a forward-oriented reactive process determined by the other party's moves within the negotiatory exchange. Axelrod, in an innovative study, looks at the type of argument that carry the greatest persuasive power in different negotiating settings. Instead of finding aggressive debating, overwhelming evidence, or causal demonstrations to be the clincher, it showed that novel arguments and innovative reformulations are likely to be the winning forms of persuasion, as supported by three different foreign policy discussions. Finally, Tracy studies the Spanish-American base negotiations in order to determine the most effective paradigm for comprehending the process, and finds that a two-stage model of structuring and conceding is needed to take all types of moves into account. Movement can be back and forth between the two phases, and different types of concession behavior are found on different structures and different issues.

Again, all of these case studies have incorporated the same process elements, even if sometimes implicitly or under different terms, and all of them are critical and selective in their utilization of the more general models which inform their analysis. In each case, the conceptual models and different approaches have shown their relevance and usefulness but have received some refinement in the process.

This would be payoff enough if it represented the sum of the ten-part exercise, but in the process of combining the various contributions a further advantage appeared. Not only have various approaches been expounded and tested, but an underlying debate has also appeared which was not evident in the earlier collections on the subject. Beneath the attempts to capture the process of integration and concession lies the greater question: is negotiation a process of integrative or reactive behavior? Or perhaps more caricaturally: does one best understand negotiation by coming at it from its positive-sum or its zero-sum component? Taken alone, each approach carries some rather strong implications, but as the arguments develop it begins to appear that the greatest error lies in taking each approach alone. While the relation between the two components is still not fully elucidated, and certainly not captured in a single mathematical model, it becomes clear that both the definition of a terrain for government and a structuring of issues, on one hand, and then the resolution of disagreement through convergence and other responsive strategies are the necessary components of the negotiating process, one or the other being more important in terms of time and effort according to the particular case. In both parts of this collection, the final chapter not only provides its own approach and analysis but in the process shows the need for bringing together the two aspects or phases of the subject. In each part the preceding chapters, instead of providing incompatibly alternate explanations, support one aspect or the other as an ingredient in the process. The development of this broader understanding of negotiations through these studies now not only permits further investigation into the mechanisms and the application of a number of coherent approaches to analysis. It also opens the way for more comprehensive models that rise to the complexity shown in the process and that spell out the relationship between its components.

—*I.W.Z.*

Part 1: Theories

1. Simple Model of Negotiation

A SOCIOLOGICAL POINT OF VIEW

OTOMAR J. BARTOS
Department of Sociology
University of Colorado

The objective of the paper is to state a simple theory of negotiation, one that is both realistic and testable. The basis of this theory is the notion, stated most clearly by sociologist George Homans, that men strive to create and maintain the conditions of justice. To this notion is added the fact that the well-known Nash solution to bargaining games not only is consistent with Homan's notion of justice but also is reached frequently in experimental negotiations. Given these ingredients, the paper hypothesizes that negotiators view the midpoint between their past demands and offers as just and strive to achieve it. Various implications of this hypothesis are explored.

Most rigorous theories of negotiation start from the assumption of *individual* rationality: each negotiator is trying to maximize his own payoff (utility).[1] As a result, an agreement is seen as an equilibrium point in which the opposing interests are balanced.

While this approach leads to various elegant solutions, we feel that it is based on some (to us) unresolved conceptual difficulties (see Bartos, 1967a). In the course of our own investigations (see Bartos, 1974), we came to believe that negotiations ought to be seen as a process involving *dual* and mostly conflicting motivations: the individual (competitive) desire to maximize one's own utility *and* the collectivistic (cooperative) desire to reach a fair solution. In fact, we believe that negotiations proceed smoothly only as long as they are guided by the collectivistic desire for fairness; that problems arise whenever the individualistic motivations take over. We shall outline a theory that is based on these beliefs.

1. For a good summary of such theories see Stahl, 1972: 213-252

THE THEORY

Our theory is quite simple and basically nonmathematical. We believe that simplicity is beneficial to most purposes we might want to use such a theory. We shall return to this point in the last part of this paper. Right now, let us consider some of the essential notions of our theory.

SOCIAL SIGNIFICANCE OF FAIRNESS

Volumes have been written in defense or in criticism of equality as an essential ingredient of justice—and we have no intention to add to this purely speculative literature. Still, some rather interesting observations that bear on this question have been made by anthropologists and sociologists.

The basic observation is that, hierarchical as many preliterate societies may be, the equalitarian norm of reciprocity nevertheless plays a crucial role in them. Although early anthropologists such as Frazer (1919) focused on the economic function of reciprocity, later anthropologists such as Malinowski (1922), Maus (1925), and Levy-Strauss (1949) emphasized that reciprocity has significance that goes beyond the mere exchange of material goods: reciprocal exchanges create bonds of friendship that hold the society together. In fact, many exchanges in primitive societies are purely ritual, without securing economic gain for anybody.

Sociologist Homans (1961) formulated the so-called rule of distributive justice that, in his opinion, is a universal human rule. Although the specific formulation of this rule is rather complicated, the essential notion is that men view as fair, rewards that are *proportional* to the recipient's contribution to society. Note that this rule implies that men ought to be rewarded equally if and only if their contributions are equal.

Why would men ever abide by a rule of fairness? Such obedience is amazing considering that we are talking about men who are motivated to get as much as possible. Some behavioral scientists, notably economists, might suggest that this obedience comes because—and whenever— a norm of fairness represents a state of equilibrium: and any deviation from this state generates forces that restore it. But a sociologist will point out that much more than that is happening. True, a norm of fairness may be established because it represents a state of equilibrium, and such an equilibrium may contribute to maintaining it. Still, the main burden of maintaining the norm comes from everybody's realization that it *is* a norm and *as such must be maintained*. And from the fact that society institutionalizes sanctions that are above and beyond those provided by the equilibrating forces that lead to the formulation of the norm in the first place.

All this may be very elementary and well known. Still, when we study negotiation we should keep these observations in mind, for they might help us understand why some negotiated settlements fall apart while others last. Or, on an even more basic level, they suggest why one ought to be interested in such matters as fair agreements and reciprocation.

FAIR AGREEMENTS

According to popular wisdom, in many bargaining situations it is fair to split the difference and agree on a point that lies midway between the two sides' last bids. We shall give more precise meaning to this adage, showing that it is consistent with a well-known and empirically supported bargaining theory.

In order to provide a framework within which we can clarify the phrase split the difference, let us consider a possible (although greatly simplified) conflict of interests between the United States and the Soviet Union. As is customary, we shall represent it as a payoff matrix:

TABLE 1

	USA	USSR
(1) Universal disarmament	−3	2
(2) Inspection stations	5	−1
(3) Destruction of all nuclear weapons	−3	−1

One may wish to resolve this conflict of interests in one masterly stroke, by identifying a fair agreement and by inducing the two parties to accept it. We shall focus on one solution (type of agreement) that is particularly prominent in the game-theoretical literature, both because it is mathematically elegant and empirically supported:[2] the Nash (1950)

---

2. For evidence showing that the Nash solution often occurs in experimental negotiations see Bartos, 1974: ch. 8.

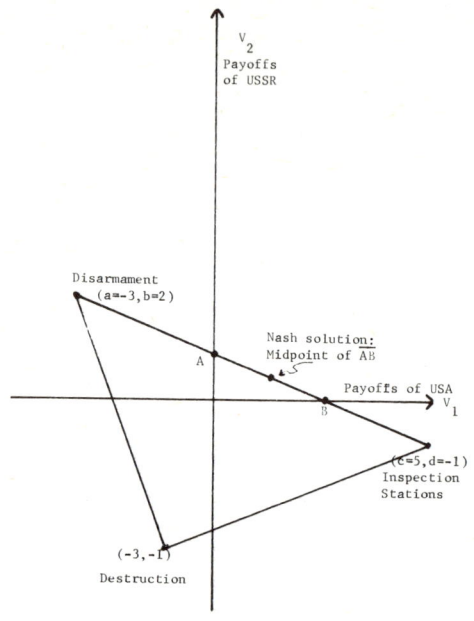

Figure 1: The Game of Table 1 and its Nash Solution.

solution. It is convenient to represent this solution graphically, as shown in Figure 1. Observe that the game given in Table 1 is represented as a triangle the corners of which have the coordinates corresponding to the two nations' payoffs from the three proposals. Nash solution is the midpoint between the points A and B. It can be shown that if the first two issues have coordinates a, b, c, and d (as indicated in Figure 1) then the payoffs provided by the Nash solution will always be:[3]

$$\text{First negotiator:} \quad v_1 = \frac{ad-bc}{2(d-b)}$$

$$\text{Second negotiator:} \quad v_2 = \frac{ad-bc}{2(a-c)} \tag{1}$$

Since in our example a = –3, b = 2, and d = –1, it follows that the Nash payoff to the first party (U.S.) is about 1.17 and to the second party. (USSR) about .44.

3. For a more complete discussion of Nash solution see Bartos, 1967b: ch. 13.

It should be added that this presumably fair result is accomplished by reaching an agreement that results when general disarmament is assigned the weight of .48 (instead of a weight of 1, as it would be were it accepted in its orginal form) and inspection stations the weight of .52.[4] The general formula for computing these weights is

$$\text{First proposal:} \quad P_1 = \frac{ad+bc-2cd}{2(a-c)(d-b)}$$

$$\text{Second proposal:} \quad P_2 = 1 - P_1 \qquad (2)$$

By applying these weights we can compute Nash payoffs in a manner different from that given in equation 1:

$$v_1 = P_1 a + P_2 C = .48*(-3) + .52*5 = 1.16$$

$$v_2 = P_1 b + P_2 d = .48*2 + .52*(-1) = .44$$

Note that, although the method of computation is different, the results are close enough to the payoffs computed by equation 1.

Determining the payoffs for a specific case may be illuminating; still, we may ask why Nash feels that his agreement is fair. In addition to various reasonable arguments, Nash points out that his solution (agreement) puts the two players in a symmetrical position. This symmetry is shown in Figure 1 by the fact that the solution lies at the *midpoint* between points A and B. Note that A and B represent the absolute maximum since it has positive payoff for them and zero payoff for the United States; B is the Americans' maximum since it has positive payoff for them and zero payoff for USSR.[5] Thus the Nash solution is fair in the sense that it gives to each side *exactly one-half* of the maximum payoff it can rationally expect to get. But, of course, the solution does *not* give the two sides the same *payoff*: The United States receives 1.17, while the USSR gets only .44.

4. For this elementary discussion it is preferable to think of weights rather than probabilities (see Bartos, 1967b: ch. 13).
5. Since points A and B both have nonnegative profits, they might conceivably be accepted by both parties. Any solution that has a negative payoff for at least one party is, by definition, unacceptable to a rational player.

It should be noted that Nash solution is analogous to Homans' rule of distributive justice. Homans maintains that the rewards a man receives ought to be proportional to the contributions he makes to his society; in effect Nash maintains that a negotiator ought to receive a payoff that is proportional to his "feasible maximum" payoff (as illustrated by points A and B in Figure 1).

Suppose that everybody were to agree that Nash's solution is fair; would it follow that the give-and-take that characterizes negotiations would disappear? And that negotiations would be transformed into brief sessions involving assessment of the two parties' payoffs and computation of the Nash solution? Far from it. The catch is that it is in each negotiator's interest to misrepresent his payoffs. To see this, imagine that the Americans would say that their payoff for disarmament is less than their actual payoff of –3 shown in Table 1. If all remaining payoffs were revealed truthfully, this single lie would have the effect of increasing the payoff the United States would receive from the Nash solution. To see this, suppose that the misrepresented payoff is a' = –10. Then, if (as before) b = 2, c = 5, and d = –1, the Nash weights computed by (2) would be $P_1 = 1/3$ and $P_2 = 2/3$. Applying these weights to the *true* payoffs (i.e., to a = –3) and using equation 1 would get the United States' payoff as

$$v_1 = P_1 a + P_2 c = \frac{1}{3}(-3) + \frac{2}{3}(5) = 2.33$$

which, of course, is a considerable increase from the original Nash payoff of 1.17.

Thus we see that, although agreeing on how to determine a fair agreement is important for negotiation, it is by no means sufficient: one needs also to determine reliably the payoffs of the two parties. The question then is: what should one do if one *cannot* determine them?

THE IMPORTANCE OF OPENING BIDS

Any professional negotiator knows that certain conflicts simply are not as yet ripe for negotiation. What he means is that to go to the negotiation table is futile under some circumstances since one cannot reasonably expect that an agreement will be reached. Can we give this intuitive feeling a more precise form?

Let us return to Figure 1. Note that the Nash solution has nonnegative payoff for both sides and as such is, by definition, acceptable to rational negotiators.[6] But, of course, there is no reason why all conflicts of interest must be of this kind: some, when represented graphically, form a triangle (or some such image) that is entirely below the origin 0. In those cases it is impossible to find an agreement that has nonnegative payoffs for everybody.

Let us consider how one may proceed to determine whether a conflict is ripe for negotiation. Suppose that the Americans extend feelers to the Russians asking them to make a proposal that could be a subject of negotiation, and that the Russians ask the Americans to do the same. Now, although neither negotiator knows his opponent's payoffs, he can determine whether he finds his opponent's position minimally acceptable.[7] Specifically, suppose that the Soviet Union responds by suggesting that universal disarmament be adopted. We know from Table 1 that this proposal has negative payoff ($a = -3$) for the United States and hence is not acceptable. Similarly, if the United States insists on the acceptance of large-scale systems of inspection stations, the Russians will refuse to enter the negotiation since their payoff from that proposal is also negative ($d = -1$). Since these opening bids are unacceptable, we conclude that the conflict is not ripe for negotiation and no further action is taken.

But suppose that instead of insisting on universal disarmament, the Russians indicate that they might be able to accept less than that. In fact, suppose that they happen to dilute their disarmament proposal so that it now coincides with or lies to the right of point A of Figure 1, i.e., that it is now acceptable to the Americans (has no negative payoff for them). Suppose, furthermore, that the Americans in turn soften their insistence on fool-proof inspection stations, again going so far that, graphically, their new (diluted) proposal coincides with or lies to the left of point B in Figure 1. Then both sides find each other reasonable and the conflict is ready for negotiation.

Let us consider the significance of the opening bids. In the first place, it is in each negotiator's interest to make his opening bid as close to having zero payoff for his opponent as possible. In practice,

---

6. A negotiator is rational if he agrees to anything that does not worsen his situation. Games like that represented in Figure 1 are so constructed that failure to reach an agreement brings both sides the payoff of 0. Hence the acceptance of any agreement that has a nonnegative payoff is, by definition, rational (see Bartos, 1967b: ch. 13).

7. Observe that we need not assume that the negotiator's own payoffs are defined precisely.

each negotiator must search for an opening bid that will be accepted by the opponent *only with the greatest reluctance*, since only then can he assume that the opening bid is as close to point A (or B) as possible. Second, having obtained a reluctant acceptance from the opponent, the negotiator may assume that this bid actually does have zero payoff for the opponent.

Thus, as a result of having an opening bid accepted reluctantly, each negotiator has an idea of what agreement to expect. Suppose that the two opening bids are in fact the points A and B in Figure 1, and that both sides accept Nash solution as fair. Then, even though neither side knows the opponent's payoffs, each can determine what to expect: each negotiator should expect to get the payoff that is *exactly the midpoint* between his payoff from his own opening bid and his payoff from the opponent's opening bid.

We see then that the opening bids (the original positions) are of crucial importance: they determine jointly what is viewed as a fair agreement. It is therefore not surprising that skilled negotiators will take extreme care in formulating their opening bids.

IMPORTANCE OF
THE OPENING CONCESSION

We just noted that once the opening bids are accepted, each negotiator has (or, at least, ought to have) a fairly clear idea where the negotiation is going to end. Why, then, should the two parties not reach the agreement right away and avoid prolonged bickering that characterizes most real-life negotiations? There are a number of reasons, some of them intrinsic to the negotiation process itself, others dictated by the setting within which negotiations occur.

To understand the reasons that are inherent in the process itself, we must correct the impression we might have created inadvertently. In pursuing our sociological orientation, we have emphasized the motivation to be fair so much that we might have created the impression that negotiation is all sweetness, reasonableness, and cooperation. Far from it. Far from suggesting that negotiation is purely a group-oriented process, we feel that the true conflict in all negotiations is that between competitive individualism and cooperative collectivism. If you will, the negotiators cooperate (by being fair) only if and to the extent to which they must; if they feel that they can get away with it, they will be ruthlessly competitive and try to take advantage of the opponent as much as possible.

This fact helps us to understand why negotiators seldom agree right away on what both (ought to) view as the eventual solution. Suppose that one of them—foolishly enough—proposes that they split the difference and the other gleefully takes advantage of him by making a counter-proposal that is more advantageous to him; what would be the consequences? Precisely because both negotiators (presumably) believe that to split the difference is fair, this situation would effectively move the agreement to a location that is a midpoint between these two second bids—and this location is much more favorable to the opponent!

Thus, after having agreed that the opening bids are acceptable, both negotiators are in a quandary: just how large a concession should they make? They are torn between the desire to make a large concession and get a quick agreement and the fear of being taken advantage of.

It is our belief that the dilemma of deciding on how large the first concession ought to be cannot be decided without reference to some factors extraneous to the negotiation process itself. At the very least they are psychological, such as the negotiator's propensity to be a trusting person (in which case his first concession will be large). Or they may be social, such as his knowing the opponent's reputation for being tough (in which case his concession will be very small indeed);[8] he may speak for a very tough constituency (in which case he can afford only the smallest concessions); he may be under pressure to reach agreement quickly (and be forced to make a large concession); and so on.

FAIR CONCESSIONS

Implicit in our discussion is the idea that a rational negotiator will expect that his concessions will be reciprocated, that his opponent will make concessions that are as large as his own. Since we are assuming that he does not know his opponent's payoffs, how can he determine whether his opponent's concessions match his own?

It turns out that, at least in our conceptualization (as represented in Figure 1), such a determination is quite easy. We noted that once the points A and B are established, both negotiators can determine the midpoint between these two points and thus formulate fairly clear-cut expectations about what the fair agreement is. By the same token, it is

---

8. We found in our experiments that a negotiator's toughness (i.e., his tendency to make only small concessions) was related to a variety of background factors: women tended to be tougher than men, and both sexes tended to be tough against opponents who were young, male, non-Caucasian (Chinese, Japanese, or Hawaiian), or poorly adjusted psychologically (Bartos, 1974: 286).

possible to compare any two smaller segments on the line AB and determine whether they are of equal length. Since such two small segments (one located close to A, the other close to B) represent possible concessions, the determination of whether the concessions match is in principle possible.

In practice, of course, the determination will be less precise and more difficult. Suppose that the Americans express their willingness to curtail their production of nuclear submarines by 20% in exchange for the Russians' agreeing in principle to have manned inspection stations on their soil, while the Russians state that they are willing to accept unmanned inspection stations provided that the United States curtails the production of nuclear submarines by 50%. Can one decide whether these two concessions are comparable?

We merely observe that such comparisons *are* being made constantly by the negotiators. Moreover, Jensen (1963) reports that when he weighted the size of the concessions made by the Americans and the Russians during the disarmament talks, his weights were quite similar to those made independently by another coder.

Moreover, our theory really does not require the negotiator to assess explicitly the relative size of each pair of concessions—he has a much simpler method of determining whether the opponent is fair. It is perhaps clear from Figure 1 that *the concessions are fair as long as the negotiators have no need to revise their original expectations about what the ultimate agreement will be.* This is so because if the midpoint between the current pair of bids is the same as the midpoint between the opening bids, then each negotiator's current bid must be the same distance from his opening bid.

Thus all a negotiator has to do when he hears his opponent's last bid is to monitor his own expectations. If they did not undergo a change, the negotiation is proceeding fairly. If they must be modified, then a red light should flash in his mind—the opponent may be unfair.

We say that the opponent *may* be unfair because the failure to match concessions is necessary but not sufficient evidence of unfairness. Such a failure is unfair if and only if the opponent's payoffs have not changed. Thus as soon as an unexpectedly small concession is experienced, the negotiator should examine carefully whether the opponent's preferences have changed. If he discovers that they have and that, given the changed circumstances, the concession *is* fair, then he should revise his expectations. And, as long as the newly expected agreement is still favorable to him, he should continue negotiating.

RESPONSE TO UNFAIRNESS

It is perhaps obvious that our theory states that a rational negotiator will behave in such a fashion as to maintain his expectation about the probable outcome (unless he has evidence that the payoffs have changed). If the opponent makes an unfairly small concession, then he should stop making further concessions until the opponent catches up.

We feel that the unfairly treated negotiator should stop making further concessions rather than retract his last concession, for a good reason: most negotiators honor the code that maintains that an offer, once made, should never be withdrawn. Thus withdrawing a bid, even if this is done in response to unfairness, brings sanctions just as does a violation of any code.

This raises the question whether an unfairly small concession—which also violates a code—brings forth sanctions, beyond and above the cessation of further concessions. Homans' theory of distributive justice provides us with a clue: "The more to an individual's disadvantage the rule of distributive justice fails of realization, the more likely he is to display the emotional behavior we call anger" (Homans, 1961: 75). In plain English, the negotiator who is treated unfairly not only will stop making further concessions, but he will get mad as well. And whatever bonds of friendship and good will might have been created as a result of having negotiated fairly are weakened and perhaps dissipated altogether. And the fate of the negotiation is put into jeopardy.

If it is true that an unfairly small concession will bring forth anger, will an unexpectedly large concession make the negotiator happy? Homans does not think so. He seems to feel that a reward beyond what is viewed as fair makes men embarrassed. To remove their embarrassment, they begin to convince themselves that they really deserved the large reward in the first place. That is, they revise their idea of what is consistent with the principle of distributive justice (1961: 75).

Consequently, we feel that unexpectly large concessions are always risky, since the negotiator always can conclude that he misjudged the midpoint and revise his expectations upwards. We also feel that the only safe course is making fair concessions, without rocking the boat in any way.

SUMMARY OF THE THEORY

As promised, our theory is simple and nonmathematical. It starts from the customary definition that negotiation is a process whereby a compromise is reached by parties whose interest are in conflict. Unlike many theories, it applies to cases in which the negotiators are ignorant of their opponent's (true) interests and may even be vague about their own.

It postulates that most men will find Nash solution fair and will strive to bring it into effect. It considers how men actually *can* accomplish this in view of their imperfect knowledge of payoffs. The theory proposes that each negotiator should search for a proposal that is favorable to him but barely acceptable to the opponent. Once a pair of such proposals is found, the negotiation can start and the two proposals are viewed as opening bids. Moreover, if there is a series of bids before an agreement is reached, each negotiator ought to view his opponent's last bid as fair if (and only if) it does not alter his expectations about what the ultimate agreement will be.

We argued that there is a good reason why negotiators do not begin by zeroing in on the agreement they expect to reach ultimately: to suggest that agreement right away amounts to asking for being exploited by the opponent. It is therefore rational to begin the negotiation process by making only a small concession. We felt, however, that no purely rational considerations can determine the size of the first concession; instead it must be determined by such background factors as negotiators' personalities, reputation, and institutional constraints.

Finally, we noted that making a *fair* concession is an optimal strategy in negotiation. An unfairly low concession not only will stall the negotiations, but it will make the opponent angry. An unexpectedly high concession may cause the opponent to increase his level of expectation, thus making it likely that the negotiator will have to settle for a less desirable outcome.

APPLICATION OF THE THEORY

As any theory, a theory of negotiation ought to be subjected to the acid test that determines its usefulness: what predictions does it generate? How does it explain some puzzling events? What strategies does it suggest?

PREDICTION

A good theory of negotiation should permit us to take a specific case—such as the SALT talks—and make fairly specific predictions. How large is the Russians' next concession going to be? Will the talks reach an agreement? When? On what? Needless to say, our theory cannot generate such specific predictions, but then neither can any theory we are familiar with.

There are two main reasons for this failure, one that cannot be remedied, the other that can. The incurable problem has to do with discovering the (true) payoffs of the participants: as we have argued, in most real-life situations to do so with precision is impossible. The potentially curable problem is that, at present, we do not know what factors are linked with the propensity to make concessions. It is possible, however, to perform statistical analyses that would give us the necessary clues. Such analyses would treat a nation's propensity to make concessions as a dependent variable and systemic variables such as level of industrialization, wealth, power, political stability, degree of centralization, and degree of democracy as independent variables.[9]

In the absence of the needed data we cannot do better than the practitioners of the art of negotiation are doing already. If we were to make predictions about the SALT talks, we would attempt to get some indications of the Russian's true interests, relying on their public statements, intelligence reports, and, above all, on their past bids (if any). If we succeeded in obtaining a pair of bids that were mutually acceptable, we would simply predict that the midpoint between these bids is the most likely outcome. We would, however, be alert to note any large change in the political climate that might indicate a significant shift in Russians' preferences or propensity to make concessions. For example, the nuclear test ban treaty of 1963 hit a snag in 1960 when the Russians suddenly lost interest in reaching an agreement because (as it turned out later) a high level decision to resume testing was taken (Jensen, 1963). Such changes would naturally call for a revision of our predictions.

We would also observe that the Russians have the propensity to make their main concessions late while the Americans make them early

---

9. We showed (in Bartos, 1974) that such an analysis is possible and profitable. However, our analysis involved experimental negotiations with individuals as units. What is needed now is an analysis of real-life data with larger units such as nations.

(Jensen, 1963). We would predict that—unless Americans learn from this and synchronize their concessions with those of the Russians—the Americans will be very frustrated in the early rounds and might even break off negotiations on the grounds that the Russians are not making fair concessions. Thus they might lose twice in the eyes of world public opinion: in the early rounds because they broke off the negotiations; in the late rounds, because they did not match the Russians' generosity.

EXPLANATION

Our theory helps us explain why some negotiations succeed while others fail. A successful negotiation in all probability started when the conflict was ripe for settlement, i.e., when the parties were able to formulate mutually acceptable first bids. It probably was in the hands of skillful professionals who were interested in being fair and hence were scrupulously matching their opponent's concessions. If a shift in political climate occurred during the negotiations, it probably was a shift for the better, one which increased the parties' payoffs for proposal(s) being discussed, or one that made them more conciliatory.

By the same token, negotiations that failed lacked some or all of the above ingredients. Negotiations in which no progress is made and which are characterized by mutual recrimination (such as the United States-North Korean negotiations) in all likelihood lack real basis for agreement and are conducted for the sake of public opinion. Some negotiations (such as the early U.S.-USSR disarmament talks) might be in the hands of representatives who are either too trusting (the Americans) or too suspicious (the Russians) to assure a smooth progress toward an agreement. Still other negotiations might have failed because of a political shift that made the expected agreement less desirable or that dictated a tougher stance.

RECOMMENDATIONS

As the reader may suspect, the main recommendation we can make for prospective negotiators is to be scrupulously fair and avoid the temptation to take advantage of the opponent. For example, adopting a tough stance might induce the opponent to respond with larger concessions, but this advantage will be short-lived and expensive. Sooner or later the opponent will discover that he is being treated unfairly and become tough too. And the negotiations will become deadlocked or break down completely. Even if an unfair agreement were reached, the unfairly treated side would soon become resentful and attack the agreement. The current criticism of our past agreements resulting from the SALT talks is a good example of this.

The corollary of this recommendation is that neither incurable trust nor chronic suspicion are desirable. A certain degree of trust is essential—otherwise the first concession would never be made—but it must be tempered with realism: if the opponent does not respond to a trusting gesture in a fair fashion, then one ought to stop making further concessions until the opponent reciprocates.

At the same time, the negotiator must be sufficiently flexible and perceptive to distinguish true unfairness from one that is only apparent. At times the opponent's concession may seem too small when in fact the problem may be a wrong assessment of what splitting the difference means. In that case, one should revise one's expectations to a more realistic level.

More difficult problems arise when the opponent's concession is smaller than expected due to a change in his interests. If this change is real, then the negotiator ought to accept it as long as the prospect for a favorable agreement is still good, even though the terms are less favorable than originally expected.

In short, we see a good negotiator as being to some extent fatalistic, realizing that he cannot perform miracles. He meets setbacks with equanimity, assessing any unexpected developments with cool detachment and fairness. At the same time, he is aware of the fact we mentioned at the very beginning of this paper: negotiation is an example of *social* exchange, and as such it has strong potential for creating lasting bonds of friendship. Thus an ideal negotiator combines the cool detachment of a scientist with the charm and warmth of a person most of us would like to have as a personal friend. A very tall order, indeed.

Otomar J. Bartos is Professor of Sociology at the University of Colorado. His primary interest is computer application to theory construction. Among his publications are Simple Models of Group Behavior *(1972) and* Process and Outcome of Negotiations *(1974), both by Columbia University Press.*

2. Negotiation as a Learning Process

JOHN G. CROSS
Department of Economics
University of Michigan

This paper presents a discussion of the role of adapting expectations in the bargaining process. Negotiators are characterized as persons who choose bargaining strategies in their attempt to optimize their payoffs from the situation. These strategies are contingent on each party's perception of the strategy of his opponent, and if these perceptions contain errors, expectations will change and this will lead in turn to a modification of each party's strategy choice. The payoff demands and manipulative moves which characterize the bargaining process are seen as combinations of actions which are specified in the original bargaining plans of the parties and of changes in the plans themselves. The influence of the learning process on the settlement point is described as well as some empirical implications of the theory in general.

SOME ALTERNATIVE PERSPECTIVES ON BARGAINING

The most cursory survey of the literature devoted to the bargaining problem is sufficient to impress one with the enormous diversity of opinion on the nature and function of bargaining processes. The breadth of this diversity is partially demonstrated by the variety of titles which have been assigned to papers in this journal. Evidently, one event which we all may agree to call a negotiation may nevertheless be described by several different scientists almost as though it were as many different kinds of event. The comparison and evaluation of existing theories has become a severe challenge because the aspects of bargaining of most concern to a commentator are so often different from those stressed by the formulator. The author who describes the division of an established joint benefit is criticized for neglecting the strategic or manipulative nature of bargaining; the theory of manipulation is rejected because it stresses "dirty tricks" which are inappropriate in the context of a problem in cooperative decision-making; and a model which describes the value of cooperative ventures is easily condemned for overlooking the crucial problem of how the fruits of cooperation are to be divided up. The old story of the blind men describing an elephant could not be more to the point.

This state of affairs has doubtless arisen as a natural consequence of our limited understanding of an extremely complicated phenomenon. Nevertheless, if we are to describe the elephant piecemeal, it is doubly important that each of us take care to define the limits of his own area of concern. In an effort to provide such a focus for this paper, I would like to begin by outlining what I see to be the most significant properties of our common problem, so that I can indicate where in subsequent arguments these properties become relevant.

From statements of negotiators themselves and from descriptions of both professional and journalistic observers, we may distinguish at least four fundamentally different characterizations of the function of bargaining processes.

(1) Most simply, bargaining may be nothing more than a charade. According to this view, the parties have a common (although unstated) understanding of what the final agreement will be, and the elaborate sequence of bids and counterbids, threats, strikes, and other uses of force has as its sole purpose the gratification (or appeasement) of third parties. This interpretation is often applied to labor negotiations in industries which have long histories of experience with unionism. In 1947, Lemuel Boulware, negotiating opposite the Electrical Workers Union on behalf of the General Electric Company, argued that both parties fully understood what the final settlement would be, and maintained that all of the intervening bargaining was nothing more than an expensive fraud.[1] During that negotiation, and subsequently during the 1950s and the early 1960s, General Electric outlined to the union what it expected the agreement to be and refused to move from that position unless the union succeeded in presenting previously unknown "facts" which altered GE's forecast of the course of an ordinary

---

1. See, for example, Stevens (1963), pp. 34-35.

negotiation. During this period, General Electric suffered a series of long and expensive strikes, and many observers believed these to have been occasioned by the disappointment and hostility which this policy generated among union members who were not granted the concessions from initial positions which had become traditional. Indeed, Boulwarism has often been characterized as an unfair labor practice, not because of any obvious bias in the estimated agreement points (the proposed settlements were often generous), but because it is seen as an attempt to discredit union leaders in the eyes of the membership. In effect, it denies to these leaders the opportunity to appear to their constituents as having squeezed concessions out of reluctant employers, thus resulting in a severe political liability for them.

The characterization of a negotiation as a charade often accompanies a belief that the range of possible agreements is actually very narrow. Suppose that we describe a two-person negotiation in terms of the set of possible outcomes. We define $x_A \equiv x_{a1}, \ldots, x_{an}$ as the payoff to party A at the time of settlement, where x_{ai} is the quantity of good i contained in that payoff. Similarly, $x_B \equiv x_{b1}, \ldots, x_{bn}$ is the vector of quantities in the payoff to be received by party B. Corresponding to any payoff x_A, there are limits to the available payoff to B, where these limits may be represented by the relations $x_B \leq H(x_A)$. The possible payoffs to each party are given a lower bound by the fact that one always has the option of abandoning the negotiation if the settlement falls below some minimum (which may correspond to the potential return from establishing a cooperative agreement with someone else). In the case of a single good, these boundaries are commonly described in a two-dimensional diagram as in Figure 1.

The settlement point can only appear somewhere in the area abc of Figure 1. There is no reason to expect the length ab to cover a large portion of the function $x_B = H(x_A)$, however. Indeed, returning to the example of wage negotiations, it is often possible for economists to disregard the bargaining process entirely and use ordinary market variables to explain the bulk of empirical variations in wage settlements, suggesting that the indeterminancy left to be resolved through negotiations is so small as to be neglected entirely. Such empirically based suggestions that the range ab is very small lends considerable support to the Boulware view that the elaborate negotiations which seem to take place are only staged for the sake of appearances.

(2) According to a second view, bargaining is a game of chance and skill, something like chess or poker. It may even be played for fun. A

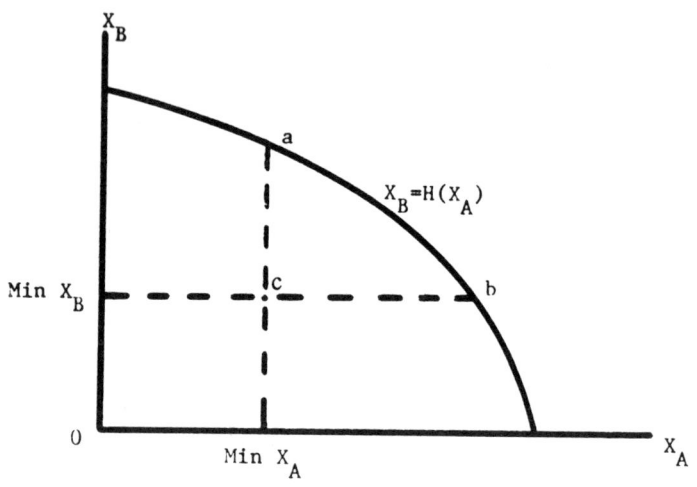

Figure 1

skillful negotiator is someone who makes good moves in the same sense that a chess master makes good moves. One could aptly describe the negotiation as the process whereby a tourist establishes prices to be paid to a middle eastern curio dealer.

This second view of bargaining should place great stress on the rules on which the game is to be played. Any game must be governed by some system of rules, and since the bargaining game is not described by Hoyle or any other acknowledged authority, these rules must be established by tradition, or perhaps even by the parties themselves. Naturally, they may vary from place to place. The sophisticated tourist will learn these rules before entering the curio shop; otherwise he may lose the game merely because he does not know how to play. By inadvertantly breaking an unwritten rule, he may even terminate the negotiation altogether if the other party interprets his action as evidence of bad faith and an unwillingness to play the game fairly.

It is in recognition that all negotiations contain some elements of this game process, that many of us may be suspicious of Thomas Schelling's (1960) proposed strategies for dealing with what he calls "mixed-motive" situations. Many of his "pre-commitments," threats, and uses of force or randomized force require the introduction of unorthodox elements to circumstances in which negotiation, or some implicit process very like negotiation is taking place. These unconventional actions may easily be seen as rule-breaking acts and therefore as evidence of bad faith. This interpretation in turn can disrupt the process, delay the settlement, and perhaps even destroy the possibility that an agreement of any kind will ever be reached. Examples of this problem are readily found in the area of labor-management disputes. In particular, first-time negotiations with newly formed unions are often accompanied with great bitterness, strikes, and even violence as tactics are employed which do not enjoy mutual acceptance as fair plays. It is not until after the parties have developed commonly understood (although perhaps unwritten) ground rules that the bitterness and violence subsides. Indeed, once this understanding has been achieved, even strikes may occur in an atmosphere of business as usual.

The point is that it is a mistake to treat negotiation as though it was a special case of warfare. The two may have points in common, but the objective of negotiation is always cooperation. The agreement is the beginning of a relationship rather than the end of one, and the few-holds-barred character of open conflict is simply inappropriate to such a situation. To my mind, the important question is not how force may be used, or why it works, but how it is that certain tactics come to be seen as legitimate moves in a negotiation while others do not.

(3) The aspect of the bargaining process which receives the greatest stress in formal analyses is, of course, its mechanism for dividing the fruits of cooperation among two or more participants. The emphasis is on division rather than cooperation, however, in that the dimensions of the benefits to be allocated to the parties are assumed to have been well established already, and the range of possible settlements is taken to be relatively large. Referring again to Figure 1, each point in the area bounded by abc is beneficial to both parties. Both sides are assumed to have full knowledge as to the elements of this set, with the exception that each party may be unaware of the extent of the benefit (or utility) which an agreement would confer upon the other, and the problem is reduced to that of selecting one agreement point from all the possibilities. Since the elements in the vectors x_A and x_B have been defined so that more is always preferred to less, one can reasonably confine the analysis to the line ab on the boundary.

It is usual for analyses of this problem to take advantage of the full-information assumption, and to express the payoffs in terms of utility functions: $U_A(x_A)$ and $U_B(x_B)$. The line segment ab is then shown as a comparable segment of a utility possibility set. The advantage in this procedure lies in the reduction of payoff vectors to single-valued utility indices. In effect, no matter how complicated the original situation may be and no matter how many dimensions may be required to define an agreement point, we can state the problem in only one dimension: the selection of a settlement point along the boundary of the utility-possibility set.

Invariably, these utility functions are written on the assumption that each party gains satisfaction only from his own payoff so that he is essentially indifferent as to the payoffs which may be received by anyone else. For the purposes of many kinds of analysis, this assumption seems unobjectionable, but it does weaken any characterization of a negotiation as a game. The satisfaction which one receives from playing a game may be as much a matter of relative as of absolute performance, and if Arthur is pleased because he has driven a hard bargain with Bill, the traditional utility formulation will not be adequate.

(4) Each of the foregoing three interpretations of the bargaining process presumes, more or less, that the set of all possible agreements $x_A \leqslant H(x_B)$ is known to both parties. It is obvious, however, that in most well-publicized negotiations this is far from the truth, and that in fact much of what is happening centers around a search for mutually beneficial agreements. Indeed, negotiators themselves frequently describe bargaining primarily as a search process. In the face of an imperfect understanding of one another's preferences, each party is exploring a list of issues, some of which are already under discussion and some of which will have to be introduced for pairs of items on which concessions may be profitably exchanged. An issue of small importance to Arthur but of great significance to Bill may be granted to Bill, in exchange for a concession from Bill which is of relatively greater importance to Arthur. There is no reason for the issues to be related in any way other than that they are of mutual concern to the parties. A union may agree to take steps to reduce absenteeism in exchange for an employer's commitment to increase plant security, or the Soviet Union may agree to on-site inspections in exchange for a reduction in some specific American warhead delivery system. Conceivably, the issues need not arise even in the same negotiation. The Soviet Union may make a concession in the Strategic Arms Limitations Talks after closing a large wheat deal with the United States.

In all cases of traded concessions, the division problem is still important in that the terms of trade must be agreed on, but the major effort lies in finding such mutually beneficial exchanges in the first place. The negotiation as a whole may actually consist of a series of component bargains in each of which (1) the parties discover that two issues afford possible exchanges, (2) terms of trade are settled on, and (3) an agreement is struck (initialled) before the next pair of tradeable issues has even been discovered.

Unfortunately, the literature on negotiation is almost silent on this searching and settling-in-sequence aspect of the process. Most models of bargaining (my own included) stress the full-information, one-dimensional problem, and rely on a paradigm in which the two parties concern themselves with the division of a sum of money, or the determination of an hourly wage. It is particularly distressing to observe that when some counterpart of this paradigm actually arises in practice, the bargaining process as we usually think of it either changes its character or ceases altogether. If it is only the division of an established sum of money which is at issue, most people seem to resort to simple ethical rules such as fair division, or they take advantage of some division rule which has been established in a previous (perhaps even expired) contract. If labor-management negotiations are finally reduced to only one issue (such as wages), the dialogue often seems to stop, mediators and other third parties may be called in to assist, and sometimes strikes occur; all of these being evidence of a failure in the negotiating process. In short, the searching and trading which takes place in a negotiation may be more than simply an interesting dimension of the problem, and may actually be essential to its effective operation.

The searching process may even play a part in solving the division problem. To the extent that the large negotiation is composed of a sequence of smaller parts, the resolution of early issues may set patterns and precedents to be followed by subsequent exchanges among the parties. The disposition of major issues in the final agreement may be conditioned in large part by information and expectations which are established early in the process.

THE FOCUS OF THIS PAPER

We have described a negotiation as a combination of searching, dividing, game-playing, and fraud. To put all these together into one paper is certainly more than we can accomplish, and, indeed, the emphasis here will remain on the traditional question of division. The best we will be able to do with respect to these other elements is point out their relevance from time to time in the discussion, leaving, reluctantly, the broader questions to another time.

Since we are to concentrate on the question of division, we will accept the usual assumption that the set of potential agreements (such as the area bounded by abc in Figure 1) is known to both parties, and we will put aside the interesting problem of how the payoff possibility set $x_A \leqslant H(x_B)$ was discovered in the first place. Moreover, although we do not intend the theory to be so restricted, the diagrams will have to be constructed for the case of only one payoff good.

If we were to ask a witness of a negotiation to describe precisely what he has seen and heard, we would be given a list of dated events. At a time which we might for concreteness call day 1, one party, Arthur, made a public statement as to the firmness of his resolve in the forthcoming negotiation. On day 2, his counterpart, Bill, published a response. On day 3, Arthur made a persuasive case and Bill responded with a threat; an actual offer (which amounts to a demand) was put on the table by Arthur on day 4, and so on. This went on until some date at which the two sides reached agreement.

We may divide these events into two classes: actual payoff demands, and a series of statements, threats, and coercive actions which are not directly related to the payoff, but which are intended to influence the ultimate settlement. These latter we may term manipulative moves. Although they are not a part of the agreement themselves, they do affect the overall value of the negotiation, partly because they may be successful in influencing the settlement point, and partly because they may impose costs of their own. A threat, for example, may be expensive to make and expensive to carry out, and if it were not for its potential impact on the settlement, both parties would prefer that it did not occur. In general, we will treat manipulative moves as potentially costly actions which may change outcomes but which never directly provide positive utility to either party.

Both payoff demands and manipulative actions are dated. We might describe Arthur's behavior for example with a vector $X_A \equiv x_{A1}, x_{A2}, \ldots x_{At}*$ which represents his payoff demand on day 1, day 2, day 3, and so on until day t* when the settlement is achieved, and a vector $T_A \equiv t_1, t_2, \ldots, t_m$ which represents the particular dates on which Arthur chose to employ the various manipulative moves which are available to him. A value in this vector of $t_i > t*$ is taken to mean that move i was never used. All of this may be described by a diagram such as Figure 2.

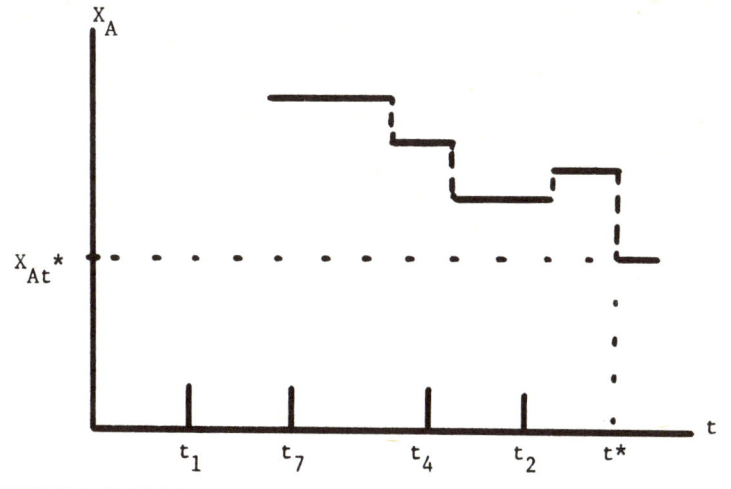

Figure 2

Figure 2 represents Arthur as employing only manipulative moves numbered 1, 2, 4, and 7, his first demand not occurring until well after the negotiation has started, and actually retracting an offer during the course of the bargaining.

The points on Figure 2 represent only those overt demands and moves which are obvious to our disinterested witness. They may actually be a reflection of a much more elaborate and subtle game plan which Arthur has chosen to employ. Arthur may have outlined for himself a whole array of contingency plans which will provide responses to Bill's behavior: "If Bill reduces his demand, then I will reduce mine," or "If Bill makes a threat, then I will reduce my concessions." There may even be random elements in these plans: "If Bill makes a large concession, I will flip a coin in order to determine my own next move." In order to distinguish the behavior we observe from the game plan which may underlie it, we will use the expression r_A to represent the vector of actual observations $[T_A, X_A]$, and a variable S_A to represent a choice of game plans. S_A, in effect, is nothing more than a list of possible r_A-vectors, each of which is conditional upon some pattern of behavior from Bill.

In a similar fashion, we may distinguish a vector r_B of overt demands and manipulative moves made by Bill in the course of the negotiation and define a variable S_B to represent the strategy which underlies this behavior.

It is tempting to regard the values of X_A and X_B as the actual demands of the two parties. On day 3, the demand x_{A3} is on the table, so to speak, and immediate agreement would be possible if Bill were to accede to it. In fact, Bill may be able to achieve immediate settlement on much more favorable terms. The demand x_{A3} may be an exaggeration, a bluff, and both parties may know it. Moreover, as we have already mentioned, established-bargaining situations are filled with conventional, if unwritten, rules of play, and many of these have to do with the end game. Final resolution of a negotiation may be achieved by splitting the difference on all remaining issues, trading the remaining issues in some more or less arbitrary way, or calling in some authoritative final arbiter. Both parties know of these rules and will automatically subtract the value of their influence from an opponent's stated demand. Even though our independent witness may observe a demand of x_{A3}, both Arthur and Bill may know the real demand to be smaller.

A GAME THEORY ANALYSIS

The formal theory of games was originally formulated for the purpose of treating just such a situation as we have described. If the two parties choose game plans (strategies) S_A and S_B, and if these plans are unchanged throughout the course of the negotiation, then knowledge of the rules of play and S_A and S_B themselves would enable one to predict the entire course of events without having to observe the process at all. S_A and S_B together are sufficient to determine the date of settlement, t^*, the nature of the agreement, and the choice and timing of the various manipulative activities.

The value of the total negotiation to each party is determined by three things: (1) the actual payoff received from the settlement, (2) the date of settlement (a settlement long delayed may be worth considerably less than it would have been had it come more promptly), and (3) the costs incurred from the various manipulative actions which have been taken during the course of the negotiation. Since these may all be determined from S_A and S_B together, we may write the utility functions in the form $U_A(S_A, S_B)$ and $U_B(S_A, S_B)$. Based on the assumption that the two parties are fully informed as to the payoff possibilities, the problem becomes the ordinary one of expected utility maximization, and each party will wish to choose a strategy, S, which will maximize his expected payoff given the strategy choice taken by his competitor.

A fundamental presumption of the theory under discussion is that delays in settlement reduce the value of agreement. In fact, the mechanism of adjustment to be described in the next section uses this time factor as a major motivating force, but here let us argue only that an agreement indefinitely delayed is regarded by both parties as essentially worthless. This means that the strategy choices are only concerned with dates earlier than some upper-bound K. Under this assumption, it is possible to prove that our specification of the problem guarantees the existence of at least one equilibrium pair of strategies $S_A{}^*$, $S_B{}^*$ where $S_A{}^*$ maximizes $U_A(S_A, S_B{}^*)$ and $S_B{}^*$ maximizes $U_B(S_A{}^*, S_B)$.[2]

We certainly do not believe that practicing negotiators are so knowledgeable, so single-minded, or so adept at mathematics as this game-theoretic view suggests; nevertheless, as a point of departure for the analysis of bargaining, this paradigm is very useful. Even though we cannot maintain that the parties actually succeed in discovering their optimal strategies, we can argue that they would like to, and that any party who knew the strategy choice of his competitor and possessed the knowledge and ability necessary to exploit this information would see himself as enjoying a distinct advantage. Moreover, a negotiator with this orientation would be aware of the general properties which might characterize the equilibrium of the idealized model, and he would expect these same properties to be relevant also to his own imperfect efforts to achieve this ideal. There are in fact three characteristics of the game-theoretic equilibrium which are of concern to him and to us:

(1) Corresponding to $S_A{}^*$ and $S_B{}^*$, there will be a pattern of overt demands and manipulative actions $r_A{}^*$ and $r_B{}^*$. The demand components of these vectors are given by X_A^* and X_B^* where the final elements in these vectors, x_{At}^* and x_{Bt}^*, represent settlement payoffs. These settlement payoffs are the only payoff elements which enter into the utility functions. The others, representing demands which are not met, are irrelevant, and in fact, so long as they do not fall so low as to bring about an inadvertant agreement, they may take on practically any values so far as the payoff utilities of the bargainers are concerned.

---

2. The strategies S are essentially lists of vectors. S_A, for example, has lists of dates for the use of manipulative moves $t_1 \ldots, t_m$ where for every i, $0 \leqslant t_i \leqslant K$, and lists of payoff demand sequences X_A, where each element in a sequence is positive but limited by the conditions of the game. The strategy space is therefore closed, bounded, and convex. If the utility functions are everywhere continuous in all of the elements of S_A and S_B, the possibility of randomized choices within the strategies makes the dependence of Arthur's choice on Bill's strategy selection a continuous relation (and vice versa). The Kakutani Fixed Point theorem may then be used to guarantee a solution.

This does not mean that they are entirely inessential, because they may play an important part in the determination of the equilibrium strategy pair. It does mean, however, that payoff demands made early in a negotiation may bear no direct relationship to the parties' equilibrium-payoff expectations.

(2) The equilibrium is generally not Pareto optimal. Because the manipulative actions require time to be put into place and to have their effects, the settlement date, t^*, is normally substantially greater than zero. This is only to say that the negotiation takes time. However, since manipulative activities are costly in themselves, and delays in agreement always reduce the value of a settlement, values of t^* greater than zero represent a cost, and both parties would be better off if the manipulations never took place and if the settlement payoffs $x_{A_t}^*$ and $x_{B_t}^*$ were received immediately at day 0.

Some game theorists have argued that in a full information, cooperative situation, it would be unreasonable to allow for any outcome which is not Pareto optimal. For example, when Nash (1953) introduced the possibility of force and other manipulative actions into his bargaining model, he defined all such actions to be "threats" which influence the outcome, but which need never be carried out, because fully informed negotiators can take them into account without having to bear the cost of actually using them. To follow such a course in practice, however, is clearly beyond the abilities of most negotiators. It would require not only that they have the analytical capacity to solve for the pair S_A^*, S_B^*, but that they be able to implement the implied settlement agreement without actually experiencing many of the events on which that equilibrium depends. On the other hand, negotiators with long experience with one another can be expected to have learned a great deal about one another's bargaining strategies and to have used this knowledge in planning their own behaviors. In recurrent bargaining situations such as the two- or three-year cycles common to labor negotiations, the parties may eventually become so familiar with the situation and with one another that accurate prediction of the final settlement point becomes a realistic possibility. This is just the argument that was described as Boulwareism earlier in this paper. Boulware was arguing, in effect, that the equilibrium pair S_A^*, S_B^* was known to both General Electric and the Union, and that both parties would be better off if they acknowledged that fact and saved themselves the trouble and expense of acting out the game. Of course, the problem in this case was that the union did not see this as a proposal to restore

Pareto optimality, but as a new manipulative move in a more subtle bargaining strategy—and they may have been right.

(3) The equilibrium pair S_A^*, S_B^* is generally not unique. We have already mentioned the fact that from the point of view of the parties' payoff utilities, demands made before the settlement date are irrelevant, and it is likely that a variety of different demand patterns could ultimately lead to the same settlement. Of greater importance is the fact that there may be many different equilibrium strategy pairs which will lead to different settlement points. In the extreme case of a situation in which no manipulative actions are permitted, every payoff pair on the frontier of the utility-possibility set can be shown to be the outcome of a possible equilibrium strategy pair.[3] In effect, the game-theoretic model has failed to identify a solution. In practice, the presence of possible manipulative actions may reduce this range of indeterminancy by giving each party some defense against very poor payoffs, but the likelihood of some indeterminancy still remains. One possible way of dealing with this indeterminancy in the theory is to impose more restrictions on the fundamental game-theoretic structure. This is the purpose of arbitration schemes such as those which have been proposed by Nash (1950) and others.[4] Rather than following this procedure, our theory here will be that negotiators themselves deal with the indeterminancy simply by acting out the process, letting the negotiation come out wherever it will.

IMPERFECT KNOWLEDGE AND LEARNING

We cannot assume that actual bargainers correspond to the idealizations found in the theory of games, but we have argued that they will use such idealizations as models for their own behavior. They seek bargaining strategies which will maximize the expected return to themselves. They recognize that time delay and intervening acts of coercion

---

3. For example, if settlement occurs whenever $x_A + x_B = Q$, then Arthur may decide to demand some x'_A at every date until K, when he quits. In the face of this strategy, Bill's utility maximizing choice is to accede and demand x'_B at all dates short of K where $x'_B = Q - x'_A$. Given this strategy Arthur's utility maximizing strategy is still to demand x'_A at all points in time. Thus we have an equilibrium. Such an equilibrium exists for any a'_A greater than zero and less than Q.

4. See Luce and Raiffa (1957): 121-145.

are inferior to immediate acceptance of the settlement point, although their lack of information as to the nature of that settlement requires that they engage in the process anyway. Finally, they recognize that payoff demands at dates earlier than t^* have very little practical significance so far as the value of the settlement itself is concerned. Instead, presettlement demands may be used as instruments for influencing a competitor's bargaining behavior. (The effectiveness of such instruments will be considered later.)

Suppose that at the start of a negotiation, Arthur has developed some estimate of what Bill's strategy is going to be. We will call this estimate R_B. R_B is subject to some uncertainty depending on the extent of Arthur's experience in negotiating with Bill, and we will represent this uncertainty with an index V_B. V_B may in fact be composed of a vector of terms (e.g., standard deviations) which describe possible errors in each of the dimensions of R_B, but for our purposes it is sufficient to treat it as a single-dimensioned variable which approaches zero as uncertainty is reduced. Given R_B and V_B, Arthur chooses a strategy, S_A, which maximizes the expected benefit which he will receive from the negotiation. Since here we wish to focus on the influence of the variable R_B, we will assume that Arthur does possess the ability to calculate an optimal S_A to correspond to any particular R_B, V_B combination. In a similar fashion, Bill forms an estimate of Arthur's plan, R_A, together with an uncertainty variable V_A, and then selects a strategy S_B which maximizes his own expected utility. Of course, if it should happen that the estimates are correct so that $R_A = S_A$ and $R_B = S_B$, then the parties' strategy choices would already be near equilibrium, and the negotiation would proceed, mechanically, as planned. The two parties might even find some means for short-circuiting the process and jump to an immediate agreement.

We are concerned primarily with cases in which the estimates R_A and R_B are not perfectly accurate. If there are errors in these expectations, this will be discovered over the course of the negotiation, and the parties will feel compelled to revise them. Revisions in R_A and R_B and in V_A and V_B will lead in turn to revisions in strategy choices, and a series of adjustments and readjustments will begin to occur. Naturally, the explicit concessions and overt attempts at outcome manipulation which occur during the course of a negotiation do not reflect only these changes in expectations. The strategies themselves incorporate demand changes and manipulative actions which are dated, and what we observe as the dynamic progress of bargaining may be a mixture of

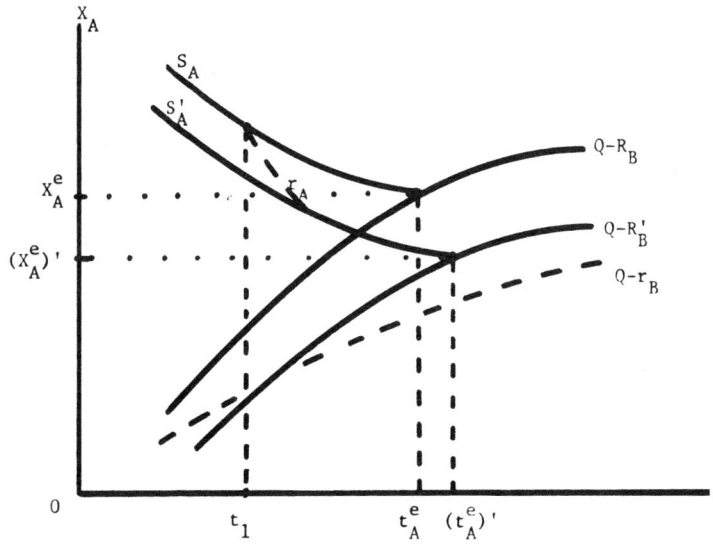

Figure 3

these planned stages in unchanged strategies and of changes in the strategy choices themselves.

An example of the process which we have in mind is given in Figure 3. Suppose the two parties are to divide a homogenous good which is available in a fixed quantity Q. Arthur has made an estimate, R_B, of Bill's strategy throughout the negotiation and has devised an optimal counterstrategy, S_A, in response. Given S_A and R_B, Arthur expects an agreement at time t_A^e and a settlement share x_A^e. Suppose that R_B is too optimistic, and that Bill's overt demands are following a pattern r_B which is incompatible with that expectation. Eventually, Arthur will have to modify R_B to be more consistent with r_B. On the diagram, this occurs at a time t_1, when R_B is changed to R'_B. Arthur now must choose a new optimal counterstrategy S'_A where S'_A maximizes $U_A(S_A, R'_B, V_B)$, and where U_A is defined at the point in time t_1.[5] Since this learning and

---

5. Note that the original strategy was chosen at a date $t = 0$ and that S'_A is chosen at a *different* time t_1. If the utility function is influenced by the calendar date, this fact must be taken into account. It is also important to consider the possibility that with R_B unchanged, the changing calendar date might lead to a change in S_A. Normally, utility functions are constructed so that this will not occur. This general problem is discussed in Strotz (1956).

adjustment mechanism has taken time to operate, it may be impossible for Arthur to implement S'_A fully because some elements in this strategy would have required application at dates earlier than that at which S'_A was decided on (this possibility is one reason why the presence of uncertainty, V_B, has an influence over Arthur's original strategy choice S_A.) The best Arthur can do now is make a utility-maximizing transition from S_A to S'_A. Arthur's observable bargaining behavior, r_A, is then obtained from S_A, S'_A and the transition between them. On the diagram, $(t_A^e)'$ and $(X_A^e)'$ are Arthur's new expected date of settlement and settlement share, respectively.

For the sake of clarity, two important details have been omitted from Figure 3. First, we have represented only the actual payoff demands, and have left off the various manipulative activities which are a part of S_A and r_B. Second, we have mentioned the possibility that explicit payoff demands are routinely reinterpreted by experienced negotiators to take account of various conventional end-game procedures. If it is normal practice to conclude a negotiation by splitting remaining differences or trading-off unresolved issues, then stated demands will always differ from true demands, but in ways which are readily taken into account. The diagram in Figure 3 abstracts from this possibility and is drawn to represent what each party would understand to be the settlement offers.

We intend that the parties in this theory see themselves in symmetric roles. That is, if Arthur finds that his own bargaining behavior is determined in part by adjustments in his own expectations, then he will attribute that same kind of learning to Bill, and conclude that r_B is a reflection both of S_B and of changes in S_B which have occurred as a consequence of adjustments in Bill's expectations. If we may paraphrase the bargaining attitude we mean to represent, Arthur might argue to himself:

(1) "Bill is too optimistic: he have to learn that S_A is not so favorable to him as he thought. As he does learn, this will be reflected in r_B, and I will be able to get a better settlement than I could now."

(2) "Even though Bill is learning, it is not going so fast as I expected, and I will have to revise my own expectations downward."

Thus our negotiator is attributing the *same* kind of learning behavior both to himself and to his competitor. There is no suggestion that he expects to behave one way while his competitor behaves another.

Given the awareness which our theory attributes to the bargainers, it is natural to expect them to attempt to manipulate one another's expectations. However, that same awareness would lead them to expect such attempts from their competitors and to discount behavior which might be so interpreted. In my view, the sequence of moves and counter-moves or bluffs and counterbluffs which this might produce will have as its major effect an increase in the values of the uncertainty variables V_A and V_B. Increases in V_A and V_B will in turn have two consequences. First, as already noted, strategy choices are affected by uncertainty: large amounts of uncertainty may, for example, encourage very large, initial payoff demands as a kind of insurance against making an unnecessarily generous offer. Thus, bluffing may induce counter-bluffing. Second, by reducing the confidence which one party may place in his own estimate of his competitor's behavior, large values of V_A and V_B will slow the learning process and increase the persistence of initial expectations. We have already discussed the fact that payoff demands which are made before the settlement date have no significance apart from their impact on the dynamic progress of the bargaining. If Arthur plans to settle at time t_A^e for payoff x_A^e, a very large preliminary demand may still be tried, for purely strategic reasons, without endangering that settlement. However, he will discount, quite properly, all such demands which might be put forward by Bill, recognizing them to be similarly costless bluffs. Thus, the information value of these early demands will be seen to be negligible, and the learning process will proceed slowly at best.

As the anticipated settlement dates t_A^e and t_B^e approach, uncertainty will decline and payoff demands will become more reliable indicators of expectations. In the extreme case, the date t_A^e might acutally arrive before Arthur learns of his overoptimism. At t_A^e, however, Arthur will try for his expected payoff x_A^e, and when he is rebuffed, then it will be obvious to him that R_B was in error, and adjustments in it will take place. Furthermore, in trying to obtain x_A^e, Arthur will make an unambiguous statement of his own demands, and so long as Bill recognizes it as such, he can use this information to improve his own estimate R_A, whether or not the date t_B^e has arrived. We expect this pattern of bluff and attempted manipulation to be a typical one: early in a negotiation, a great deal of strategic maneuvering may occur, uncertainty will be high, and as a consequence, the parties will be reluctant to draw inferences concerning the future course of the bargaining. As anticipated settlement dates approach, however, the parties will get down to business, and the information flows will become much more reliable.

THE BARGAINING PROCESS

The model, as we have outlined it, is very general and would require several further restrictions before any explicit solutions could be obtained. We would have to specify the forms of the utility functions, the dependence of strategy choices on uncertainty, the nature of the learning process, and the rules which determine the availability of various manipulative actions. Nevertheless, even from this general model, we may draw some conclusions regarding the relationship between payoff demands and expectations, and hence about the character of the dynamic course of the bargaining.

Suppose that we describe as the general case of bargaining a situation in which each party entertains overoptimistic expectations. (If expectations are realistic in the sense that $R_A = S_A$ and $R_B = S_B$, the negotiation is reduced to a charade, and if one party is extremely pessimistic, the negotiation may reach a settlement before the learning mechanism has any effect at all.) In this case, the diagram in Figure 3 and a similar one drawn from the point of view of Bill can be used to describe the course of negotiation.

The learning mechanism establishes a dynamic interaction between the two parties' behaviors. Arthur's strategy S_A determines the current course of r_A, which is used by Bill in the formation of R_A. In response to R_A, Bill selects strategy S_B which determines the course of r_B, and this in turn is the basis for Author's estimate R_B. It is important to bear in mind that as a consequence of learning, S_A and R_B may be continually changing, so that what is learned in the form of R_A or R_B is a composite of a sequence of strategies rather than a single one. From either negotiator's point of view, there is no way to distinguish changing strategies from the mechanisms of an invariant one. Arthur may observe r_B, but he cannot know whether r_B is the outgrowth of learning (he hopes that it is), or the manifestations of some subtle strategy of Bill's.

The choice of bargaining strategy S_A is motivated by a desire to maximize $U_A(S_A, S_B)$. This utility value is not dependent solely on the settlement payoff, however, for it also reflects the costs of time delay before a settlement is reached, and the losses which may be suffered because of various attempts to use force or coercion. The selection S_A reflects a trade-off between these opposing values. If the cost of time delay is small, S_A will reflect a willingness to wait in the interests of achieving a large settlement; if the cost is large, S_A will reflect a willingness to sacrifice some payoff for the sake of early agreement. Thus if Arthur views his prospects optimistically (Bill is seen to be conceding rapidly, or to be making small demands), the anticipated time cost of negotiating is reduced (because the delay will be shorter) and S_A will be designed to achieve a larger payoff at settlement time. If R_B is seen to include the use of force, even if the date for that force has not yet arrived, s_A will be designed to reduce the cost of that force, partly through the use of countermeasures, but also partly through reductions in the final payoff expectations.

Even in this most general model, a number of conclusions may be drawn immediately.

(1) The negotiation will take more time than either party initially expected.

(2) High time costs, or vulnerability to coercion will reduce a party's settlement payoff.

(3) The use of force or coercion which increases the cost of delays in agreement will reduce the duration of the negotiation.

(4) If a party's learning rate is high, for whatever reason, the duration of the negotiation will be reduced.

(5) If a party's learning rate is high, for whatever reason, that party will receive a smaller payoff at settlement time than he would otherwise.

(6) There is a central tendency in the bargaining process which reduces any asymmetries in the parties' expectations which are not reflections of differences in learning rates, utility functions, or in the availability of means for altering the outcome through the use of force.

Some of these six conclusions are not very startling. Conclusion 1 is obtained directly from our discussion of Figure 3 and is no more than a reflection of our description of the general case of bargaining as one in which both parties are overoptimistic. Conclusions 2 and 3 are equally straightforward and are obtained from our description of the utility function. If, due to high bargaining costs, a party lowers his payoff expectations whatever the value of R_B, then, even with the learning process, r_A as drawn in Figure 3 will be lower at every point in time, and Arthur's final payoff wll be reduced. Conclusion 4 is an obvious consequence of the fact that a high learning rate will lead to a more rapid downward shift in expectations, which will lead in turn to a more rapid downward fall in r_A. Conclusion 5 is obtained from the same observation. If Arthur finds that his estimate of Bill's behavior was overoptimistic, and if he reacts strongly to this discovery, r_A will reflect a substantial decline in expectations. If, on the other hand, Bill is slow to react to similar information, r_B will not include such a decline, and the agreement will occur after Arthur has made most of the concessions.

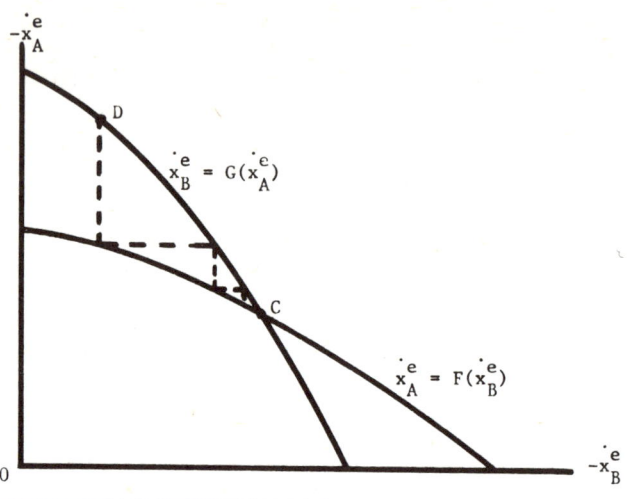

Figure 4

The central tendency described in Conclusion 6 is an important property in that it reduces the dependence of the outcome on the unspecified initial expectations of the two parties. It comes about because of interactions between the two learning mechanisms. Suppose that the two negotiators are approximately equal in learning ability, but that Arthur enters the negotiation with expectations which are substantially more optimistic than those of Bill. Compared to Bill, Arthur has more to learn so to speak, and as time passes, Arthur will have to make several adjustments in S_A. These same adjustments in S_A, however, will be reflected in an r_A which is quite favorable from Bill's point of view and which will therefore slow adjustments in S_B. Arthur's optimism and the discovery of it force him to modify his behavior, and these modifications in turn interfere with changes in Bill's expectations, even though these, also, may be too optimistic. Thus the degrees of optimism of the two parties are inclined to converge.

An example of this process is shown in Figure 4. For the sake of a simple case, let us represent the parties' expectations with only the two variables x_A^e and x_B^e. Rates of change in expectations are represented by $\dot{x}_A^e$ and $\dot{x}_B^e$. According to our proposition that learning is responsible for these changes, $\dot{x}_A^e$ and $\dot{x}_B^e$ are interdependent. Bill's expectations affect Bill's own bargaining behavior, but this behavior in turn determines Arthur's expectations. We can write this relationship as $\dot{x}_A^e =$

$F(\dot{x}_B^c)$, and without being too specific as to the precise form of this function, recognize that $\dot{x}_A^c$ and $\dot{x}_B^c$ vary inversely with one another. The more rapidly Bill learns, the larger is $\dot{x}_B^c$, hence the more justified is Arthur's optimism, and the smaller is $\dot{x}_A^c$. Similarly, $\dot{x}_B^c$ is dependent on Arthur's bargaining behavior and hence on $\dot{x}_A^c$, and we will write this relation as $\dot{x}_B^c = G(\dot{x}_A^c)$. These two functions are represented in Figure 4, where $-\dot{x}_A^c$ and $-\dot{x}_B^c$ have been put on the axes (with the minus signs, the axes may be thought of as representing rates of concession). Point C on the Figure represents an equilibrium in that the two concession rates are mutually consistent, and other pairs of $\dot{x}_A^c$ and $\dot{x}_B^c$ will tend to converge on C (at least in stable cases). Beginning at any point such as D, the sequence $\dot{x}_A^c = F(\dot{x}_B^c)$, $\dot{x}_B^c = G(\dot{x}_A^c)$, ... follows the dashed path to C.

Except for the restrictions used to draw Figure 4, we have described a theory rather than a model, and in order to provide explicit solutions to particular bargaining situations we would have to provide specific forms for the relations which are involved. In fact, a great many models (and hence a great many empirical possibilities) can be represented along the lines of the theory which has been described. One such example is my own earlier bargaining model (Cross, 1965) in which each party's strategy was simply to demand the expected settlement payoff at each point in time ($\dot{x}_{At} = \dot{x}_A^c$ for all $t \leqslant t_A^c$). In this model, R_A and R_B were estimates of $\dot{x}_A^c$ and $\dot{x}_B^c$ respectively, and the learning function made changes in these estimates' linear functions of the differences $(R_A - \dot{x}_A^c)$ and $(R_B - \dot{x}_B^c)$. This particular formulation was quite properly criticized for the restrictiveness of these assumptions, particularly for the unrealistic specification of the strategy choices. In the general theory, it is always in the interest of a negotiator to conceal changes in his own expectations (because such changes are encouraging to the other party and slow his learning), and a strategy choice known to have the form $x_{At} = x_A^c$ for all $t \leqslant t_A^c$ maximizes the information content of every stated demand. Coddington (1966) has provided a model at another extreme in which each party's strategy is to demand some arbitrarily large payoff until the expected settlement date at which time the true settlement offer is made. Strategies of somewhat more realism than either of these can be introduced without great difficulty. For example, Arthur may plan to demand $x_{At} = x_A^c + P(t_A^c - t)$, where P is a positive constant, so that some concessions can occur whether x_A^c is changing or not. Such a strategy combines an appearance of cooperative negotiation with a useful element of concealment. Perhaps the most realistic representation of a strategy would be to make demands which can be traded away for concessions from the other party, making explicit the possibility that the parties' strategy choices contain conditional elements. Unfortunately, the mathematics of such a model would be far more difficult than those associated with our more naive formulations.

SYMMETRY

Central to our theory is the proposition that negotiators are similar in their understanding and insight into the bargaining process and into one another's behavior. If Arthur finds that his expectations are too optimistic, he may at least hope that Bill is also having to revise his own. If Arthur uses some strategic bluffs in an attempt to influence Bill's expectations, he expects some similar attempts from Bill. Under these circumstances, as we have already argued, bluffing activities may not have a significant effect on the outcome. Inflated demands will be expected and discounted, and their most important consequence will be a reduction in the parties' rates of learning rather than alteration of the ultimate settlement.

In fact, a bargaining pattern may develop in which each party makes initially inflated demands himself, disregards the demands of his competitor, and then gradually relinquishes these exaggerations, expecting his competitor to do the same. This may become such an established routine that it would actually be dangerous to do anything else. The concessions which are made possible by the initial exaggerations may become an unwritten rule of the game, and any party who abandons this course may then be seen to be negotiating in bad faith with the result that the negotiation is seriously disrupted. Earlier in this chapter, we suggested this to be a possible explanation for the hostility which Boulware's approach apparently engendered in negotiations between General Electric and its employees.

Apart from these unwritten laws and the occasional need to impress constituents with a public display of bargaining prowess, there is reason to believe that misrepresentation of one's expectations is not always in one's best interest. If one wishes an overoptimistic competitor to learn of his error, the best procedure is to provide him with good evidence that he is wrong, and a reputation for bluff is not conducive to this end. Indeed, if we were to attempt to devise a model of optimal bluffing, we would quickly be driven to a logical dilemma. Suppose that Arthur recognizes that through the learning mechanism, Bill's behavior is influenced by Arthur's own bargaining tactics because R_A is affected by r_A and r_A is in part a consequence of S_A. Arthur represents his estimate of the nature of this dependence with a function $R_B = f(S_A)$ where he may let the form of the function $f(\ )$ incorporate the uncertainty variables. Arthur's optimal bargaining strategy is now one which maximizes $U_A(S_A, f(S_A))$. By the symmetry of our model, however, Bill will devise a function which represents the dependence of R_A on Bill's own behavior, $R_A = g(S_B)$, and choose a strategy, S_B, which maximizes $U_B(g(S_B), S_B)$. This behavior, however, violates the premises on which the function $f(\ )$ was defined. In fact, the functions $f(\ )$ and $g(\ )$ are inconsistent at any level of analysis. Since the function $g(\ )$ depends on Arthur's choice of behavior, the function $f(\ )$ must incorporate this dependence. By symmetry, $g(\ )$ incorporates a similar dependence, and $f(\ )$, again, is misspecified. We are confronted by an infinite regress.

We could, of course, escape by abandoning the assumption of symmetry between the parties. If Arthur recognizes the dependence of Bill's expectations on his own strategy, but this insight is not shared by Bill, then Arthur has a distinct advantage. His bluffs work, and the settlement moves to his benefit. There is room here to distinguish a more skillful from a less skillful negotiator. The theory is not otherwise altered, however. The function $f(\ )$ is an estimate which may be too optimistic, for example, in that Arthur may expect his bluffs to work better than they do, and Arthur may have to learn to revise his expectations downward in the usual fashion. Moreover, as Bill becomes more experienced, Arthur's bluffs will become ineffective and the operation of the process will become symmetric again.

A FINAL NOTE

The theory which has been outlined here reflect this author's conviction that expectations and learning play a central role in bargaining. The introduction of expectations has often been criticized, however, on the grounds that it reduces the empirical usefulness of the theory by employing variables which are not directly observable by any third party. Of course, any theory may be better than none, and we might further argue that since virtually all bargaining models already extant rely heavily on utility functions, the empirical testability of the theory is compromised very little by the addition of an expectations function. Nevertheless, empirical usefulness is the objective of any theory, and it is worthwhile to extend our original list of six implications of the theory into a few practical areas.

We begin with the most obvious:

> (7) Parties with access to potent threats will do well (in terms of settlement payoff), as will those who are relatively unconcerned about the timing of an agreement.

Such implications as these are already widely accepted, apparently simply because they appeal strongly to the intuition. They explain such beliefs as: large strike funds will operate to a union's advantage in wage negotiations or that a large stockpile of finished products will benefit an employer.

Less obvious are conclusions which apply to the dynamics of the bargaining process.

> (8) Very large initial payoff demands may worsen a party's settlement payoff.

This implication is drawn from the observation that large initial demands will require, at some time or other, large apparent concessions which will slow the other party's learning.

> (9) Political negotiations will take more time than economic negotiations.

This may sometimes be the case simply because the passage of time is of less concern to the parties, but it may be expected also because political issues are less well defined than are economic issues, and the presence of easily quantifiable variables contributes to rapid learning.

> (10) Multidimensional negotiations may actually come to settlement earlier than unidimensional ones.

In this paper, we have not been able to examine the searching component of multidimensional negotiations. We would like to note, however, that if issues in a negotiation are settled in sequence, one exchange being initialled before the next is seriously considered, then the flow of information between the negotiators is greatly increased. It becomes possible for each party to gauge the expectations, values, and intransigence of the other with much more confidence than is possible if the only available information is to be found in early and undoubtedly exaggerated payoff demands. Adjustments in expectations are correspondingly accelerated and settlement may arrive sooner. Unfortunately, we cannot assert this conclusion unambiguously because a large number of issues naturally require more time just for their definition. On the other hand, it is possible that our case could be put even more strongly: the persistence of bluffing and distrust in a unidimensional negotiation may block information flows so completely that the learning process ceases to operate entirely thus forcing the parties to turn to outside assistance through mediation (which is designed to improve communication in a negotiation) or arbitration (which is designed to determine a settlement).

> (11) Even in the presence of an equilibrating tendency in the learning process, initial expectations will be reflected to some degree in the final settlement, and these initial expectations are themselves determined by observable variables.

If profits are high, union members are likely to look to forthcoming wage negotiations with optimism, and the settlement will reflect that optimism. For this reason, employers are often concerned not to appear too prosperous when the current contract expires. If the United States makes large trade concessions to the Common Market, the Soviet Union will be inclined to view upcoming grain deals with more optimism, and this will operate to their benefit in the final settlement, whether or not the United States intends to be generous. In short, the settlement of a negotiation will move to the benefit of party A if similar or parallel negotiations are commonly seen to have been favorably settled by parties in the same position.

Some empirical testing of these conclusions has already taken place. Siegel and Fouraker (1960) have provided experimental support for the conclusions that high time costs accelerate the bargaining process and that optimistic expectations (or aspirations) will delay a settlement, and they have also found the expected tendency for a party with the most reliable basis for learning to lose somewhat in terms of settlement payoff. These results have been reproduced by Contini (1968) in a similar set of experiments. Outside the arena of controlled experimentation, Ashenfelter and Johnson (1969) have investigated the expectations hypothesis in the form of a suggestion that factors which might generally increase labor union expectations will delay wage settlements. Their results conform to our prediction and Siegel and Fouraker's experimental conclusion on this point, but the study is weakened by the fact that no use is made of any formal bargaining theory beyond a naive adaptation of the Hicks (1932) model, so that one is unable to draw any inferences regarding the settlement point itself. Moreover, these authors use the occurrence of strikes as their measure of time delay without any acknowledgement that as manipulative actions, strikes may be determined by other forces as well. Nevertheless, this study is an encouraging indication that the use of expectations in the theory need not take it outside the realm of applicability, and it is to be hoped that some of the other implications of bargaining theory will soon be subjected to similar testing.

John G. Cross is Professor of Economics at the University of Michigan and an Associate Research Economist at the Mental Health Research Institute. He is the author of a book on The Economics of Bargaining *and of several articles which apply learning processes to the theory of economic behavior in a number of areas.*

3. Negotiation as a Psychological Process

BERTRAM I. SPECTOR
CACI, Inc.

> This paper develops a microlevel framework to analyze dyadic negotiation processes and outcomes. The Lewinian paradigm of behavior determination is used as a conceptual foundation to describe and synthesize the impacts of personality, perception, expectation, persuasion, and the interaction of these factors on negotiation dynamics. The findings of a bargaining experiment that employed this framework reveal that behavioral styles are activated by decidedly different sets of motivational elements and perceived psychological climates. The interaction of bargainer personalities also influences the choice of negotiating strategies. Moreover, the results indicate that outcomes are more strongly determined by personality and perceptual predictors than by the use of mutual persuasion.

There is one element common to all types of negotiation, no matter how diverse they may be in content or procedure. Persons, in the roles of negotiators, are required to communicate positions, make demands and concessions, respond to changing signals, and arrive at outcomes. At this microlevel of analysis, negotiation can be viewed as a set of personal and interpersonal dynamics that result in outcomes of varying acceptability to the participants.

From a microlevel perspective, the resolution of conflicting interests through negotiation is motivated by:

(1) the individual personality needs of negotiators;
(2) the personality compatibility among negotiators representing opposing parties;
(3) negotiator perceptions and expectations of the opponent—his strengths and weaknesses, his intentions and goals, and his commitments to positions; and

---

AUTHOR'S NOTE: The author extends his thanks to I. William Zartman, Morris I. Stein, and Joseph H. Moskowitz for their insightful comments on previous versions of this manuscript.

(4) persuasive mechanisms employed to modify the bargaining positions and values of the opponent to achieve a more favorable convergence of interests.

These microlevel phenomena help to determine the nature of the bargaining process and outcome, whether it deals with lover quarrels, parent-child relations, labor-management conflicts, or bilateral arms-limitation talks. If negotiation is defined as a process of value and behavior modification in which peaceful means are used to alter divergent positions toward a common convergence of values, microlevel analysis is especially appropriate to capture variation in the dependent variable—value change by the negotiators—as well as the impact of personal and group dynamics on affecting that change.

According to one count (Rubin and Brown, 1975), over 500 recent studies of bargaining have tested hypotheses linking psychological factors to behavioral process and outcome variables. Some researchers have discovered strong relationships; others have discovered either weak relationships or have totally disconfirmed the existence of psychological explanations (see reviews of the literature in Spector, 1975; Druckman, 1973; and Rubin and Brown, 1975).

The authority of most of these findings is questionable on two counts, one conceptual and the other procedural. First, most of these studies take a single-trait approach; that is, they examine the relevance of a single psychological determinant in isolation from other psychological and contextual variables. While this procedure may enhance experimental control in the analytical design, it eliminates a dimension of complexity in personal and interpersonal relations that motivates process and outcome variables in actual negotiation situations. Simplicity of design may serve to mask true relationships. Second, many studies have sacrificed substantively based bargaining scenarios in their experiments to observe and measure psychological variables more easily. Without content, these bargaining experiments— epitomized by the Prisoner's Dilemma game—tend to be more game-like than actual negotiations, elicit trivial and bored responses from participants, fail to track longitudinal process, and offer narrow behavioral options that constrict the full expression of personality (Maxwell and Schmitt, 1968; Vinacke, 1969; Shaw and Thorslund, 1975).

Several analyses (Terhune, 1970; McGrath, 1966; Vinacke, 1969) advocate the potential utility of a model that integrates psychological and contextual factors to describe the negotiation process and explain the evolution of outcomes. This article attempts to extend the work of these authors by postulating explicitly a psychological-process model of negotiation that synthesizes the impact of personal, interpersonal, and situational factors in bargaining. Lewinian field theory provides the conceptual underpinnings of the model.

RESEARCH QUESTIONS

Essentially, the negotiation model that is developed in this article attempts to determine the extent to which personality, perception, expectation, persuasion, and the interaction of these factors within negotiator dyads can adequately describe and explain the process and outcomes of bargaining. *Negotiator personality* identifies basic predispositions toward the opponent and motives for future actions and responses. Personality factors are likely to influence the toughness or softness of positions that are taken, the strength of commitment to these positions, strategy choice, opening tactics, the potential for compromise and concession, and the personal need for goal maximization. Although negotiators are often representatives of group interests, many historical accounts and treatises on negotiation (deFelice, 1976; deCallieres, 1963; Nicolson, 1964; Douglas, 1957; Cooper, 1975) indicate with much conviction that personal predispositions and motives are highly prevalent driving forces in the bargaining process nonetheless.

Perceptions and expectations of the opponent's strengths, weaknesses, intentions, commitments, and goals are likely to affect negotiator responses, the tone of interpersonal communication, and the learning process. Perceptions of threat, for instance, may cause some negotiators to retreat to more cautious positions, while others might become more aggressive and hard-nosed. Expectations of cooperation or conflict, softness or toughness, and caution or risk are likely to influence communications as negotiation interactions proceed. Moreover, learning and flexibility in position-taking may be impeded if a negotiator's perceptual framework is invariably closed to new conceptions of the opponent (Rokeach, 1960). This closed-mindedness and intense suspicion has been a major stumbling block in activating comprehensive negotiations between the Arabs and Israelis (CACI, 1977).

The use of *persuasive techniques* and their success in modifying negotiator values toward initially desired end-states should help to achieve acceptable outcomes (Schelling, 1960; Zartman, 1974). Mutual power and influence relationships, if employed effectively and credibly, should result in eventual concessions and convergence of formerly conflicting interests. If power attempts are unsuccessful, bargaining values and positions are not likely to change and negotiations may become stalemated.

Finally, the *interaction of psychological and contextual factors* is crucial in the development of the model. Interaction can be viewed from two perspectives. First, the mix of personality between opposing negotiators is likely to influence their behavioral rapport and the type of outcome they are likely to reach. Terhune (1970) has suggested that adversary bargainers in dyadic negotiation who have complementary personality characteristics are likely to reach jointly acceptable outcomes. Noncomplementary personalities, on the other hand, are likely to be highly defensive, rigid, and unyielding, resulting in deadlocked outcomes.

A second type of interaction that must be analyzed involves the intersection of the bargaining context and personal factors. It is very possible that certain personality characteristics, for instance, become instrumental in motivating the bargaining process only under particular negotiating conditions. This mediating influence of context has been noted by several researchers (Terhune and Firestone, 1966; Bartos, 1967b). Perhaps it is only when the bargaining process reaches a particularly riskful or stressful turning point that highly aggressive or highly power-oriented needs, if they are present in a negotiator's personality, become prominent in determining the nature and course of position-taking and choice of tactics.

The negotiation model that is developed provides an integrated framework to analyze the joint impact of these psychological factors. It can be applied in real or experimental-bargaining situations to examine the following conceptual propositions about process and outcome phenomena:

(1) Do negotiator personality traits determine bargaining behavior directly? Or does personality influence bargaining behavior indirectly through organizing the negotiator's perceptual set or belief system?

(2) Does personality become an important predictor of the bargaining process only under certain perceptual and objective circumstances?

(3) To what extent does personality compatibility or incompatibility within negotiator dyads influence the behavioral rapport?

(4) Is the bargaining reality, defined by current bargaining interactions, a major determinant of a negotiator's perceptual and expectational climate? Or is the general world perspective or belief system developed as a function of personality structure a better predictor of negotiator perceptions and expectations?

(5) Do negotiators act in terms of their perceptions and expectations of their opponent? Or do they act in relation to the objective stimuli of demands and concessions?

(6) To what degree do persuasive power strategies effectively modify negotiation values, reduce conflict, and make successful outcomes attainable?

A FIELD THEORETIC APPROACH

The foundation of the negotiation model is Lewin's deceptively simple paradigm, $B = f(P,E)$, where B = behavior, P = person, and E = environment. For Lewin, behavior is a result of the dynamic interaction of personality with its environment (Cartwright, 1959). A person's environment consists of *forces* and *valences*. Forces describe a relative tendency or resistance to change. Driving forces facilitate change, while restraining forces create barriers to behavior modification. They may be activated by the actions of others, by impersonal elements in the situation, or by one's own biological or psychological needs. A person assigns valence or value to different regions in the psychological environment depending on whether they contain objects that aid or hinder personal goal achievement. Forces are attracted and directed toward regions with positive valence, but repelled from regions with negative value (Lewin, 1968, 1935).

Social power can be described in this conceptual context of environmental forces and valences. A person employing power is imposing driving and/or restraining forces on the life space of another individual to induce change in the target's valence for various goal objects. Compliance with the power initiator's desires may be forthcoming if the forces imposed by the power exerciser are credible and the costs or benefits that are imposed are sufficient to alter the target's expectations about pursuing its present course of action (Zartman, 1976). The desired result of a power attempt is to modify the target's forces and valences by creating a choice shift for the target between proceeding as originally intended and modifying behavior in accordance with the desires of the power exerciser (Lewin, 1951; Deutsch, 1968).

According to Lewin, the element P in the equation represents an inner personal system comprised fundamentally of *needs* and *tensions*. Needs are motivational states which, when aroused, release energy and increase tension in the inner personal system, throwing it into a state of disequilibrium. The goal of the system is to return to equilibrium by satisfying aroused needs, achieving the desired end-state, and thereby reducing tension. Thus, needs and tension motivate behavior in the direction of change from the present state of the system. But Lewin's link between needs and behavior is not direct. Needs interact with the psychological environment to determine the behavioral outcome (Deutsch, 1968; Lewin, 1936).

Aroused needs confer valence on objects. In other words, regions of the environment are imparted values that are coordinated with the state of inner tensions. These valences organize the environment into regions of attraction and repulsion that become more prominent to the individual as tensions increase. Valences, in turn, steer and direct forces toward or away from objects. These forces help to facilitate the behavioral and attitudinal change that eventually satisfies the aroused need, lowers tension to an equilibrium point, and enables goals to be achieved. When appropriate change does not occur, tensions may continue causing further search for appropriate behaviors and attitudes or, in the extreme, causing neurotic episodes (Lewin, 1935).

As an example, when a state of tension (manifested by hunger, for instance) is aroused in a person because of the absence of availability of food (an impersonal, restraining force creating tension in the need for sustenance), certain objects in the environment, notably those associated with eating, may acquire positive valence, and new forces (own, driving forces) that attempt to facilitate acquisition of these goal objects will emerge. The satisfaction of the aroused need and an accompanying reduction of tension may result from successful behavioral performance in obtaining the desired goal. Even in the face of other negative environmental forces and barriers that frustrate reduction of the activated need and increase tension (such as exorbitant food prices for what is available), a person may attempt to overcome these impediments, if the need is sufficiently intense, by formulating alternative paths of behavior to achieve his goal. Forces acting on a person toward obtaining the goal of food will cause behavioral change (Lewin, 1951).

Lewin's paradigm describes the interaction of factors that determine *individual behavior.* However, *interpersonal transaction,* emphasizing the interdependence between actors, can be represented by an expanded equation to fit the dyadic bargaining context. Terhune (1970; 1974) suggests this adjustment by stressing what is implicit in Lewin's theory: if unitary behavior is a function of the interaction of personality and environment, analysis of interpersonal transaction must take into account the personality and environment interactions of the two or more individuals who are impinging on each other's life spaces, as well as the interrelationship among their personality characteristics and psychological environments. Empirically, Terhune found evidence for the proposition that over time, dyadic interaction becomes a system of interdependent reciprocal behavior rather than the outcome of two independent behavior patterns. Thus, the personality characteristics of each participant do not express themselves full-blown, but instead accommodate and adjust to the dyadic system of which they are a part. Terhune's equation describes dyadic interpersonal transaction as a function of (a) the individual personality characteristics of the two persons, plus (b) the history of prior relations and expectations between the two persons, plus (c) the interaction of personality traits within the dyad, plus (d) impersonal properties of the objective and psychological environment, plus (e) the interaction of dyad personalities under different environmental circumstances.

A DYADIC NEGOTIATION MODEL

Lewin's paradigm, $B = f(P,E)$, and Terhune's extension to include interpersonal transaction, can be employed to interpret the complex dynamics of the dyadic negotiation process and outcome. Negotiators come to the bargaining table with certain *personal predispositions* toward their own goals, how to achieve them and with what strength of commitment; toward their bargaining counterparts, how tough their responses should be; and toward the concepts of equity and justice in negotiation. These predispositions are reflected in the negotiator's personality needs and motives. The *psychological environment* and ambience of the negotiation process are represented by the negotiator's perceptions and expectations of his opponent's positions, goals, intentions, commitments, strategies, and actions.

Personality and environment interact within each negotiator's life space to yield manifest bargaining strategies and tactics that are intended to drive the situation toward goal achievement. Persuasion, in the form of power attempts, can be employed to change the opposing negotiator's valences toward certain goals by making them more compatible with one's own valence patterns (Spector, 1975; Zartman, 1976). The interdependence of opposing negotiators in a dyadic context is reflected in the *outcome* they can achieve jointly by their efforts at mutual persuasion. As valences toward goals become more compatible, conflicts of interest decrease, and a convergence of positions becomes possible. However, if valences toward goals are not modified sufficiently, deadlock is a likely negotiation outcome. Figure 1 depicts the structure of the dyadic negotiation model.

One important background factor, the negotiator's role, is absent from this model. Negotiators may come to the bargaining table with minimal role obligations, empowered to strike the best compromise possible, or with formal role functions as delegates of a group, committed to certain positions and bound by rigid instructions. The greater the degree of role obligation demanded of negotiators, the greater are the constraints on concession-making and the greater the prob-

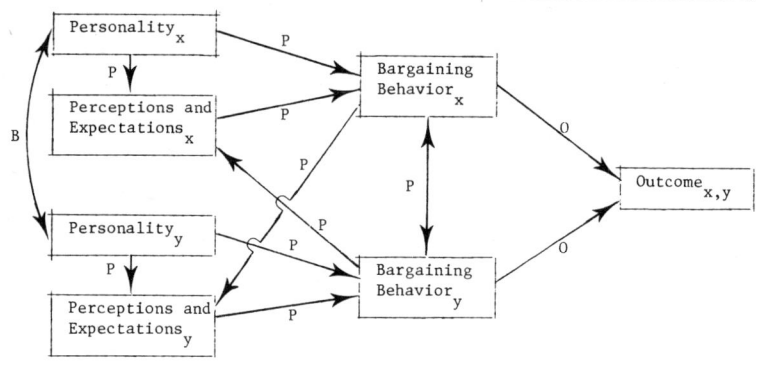

Key B = Background phase, P = Prcess phase, O = Outcome phase.

Figure 1. A Dyadic Model of Negotiation

ability of deadlocked outcomes (Druckman, 1973). Extensive role requirements may even tend to mask personality and bargaining style characteristics.

Whether personality or role is more important in explaining the dynamics of the bargaining process and outcome has not been specified empirically, but tends to vary from one bargaining setting to another. Douglas (1957) makes the point that the constraints of role responsibilities often succumb to more prominent personality motives once the negotiation process evolves. However, the model is limited when the negotiator's role becomes a conspicuous driving force in the bargaining process.

The model consists of three phases: the background, process, and outcome phases. Each is described below.

BACKGROUND PHASE

In the background phase, the personality mix of bargaining adversaries can be observed. Dyadic bargaining enables each negotiator to serve as a catalyst, facilitator, or impediment to the other. Complementary personalities are likely to communicate with each other in a cooperative and nondefensive way. Highly dissimilar personalities, on the other hand, may be more rigid and defensive in their dealings, with a higher probability of reaching deadlocked outcomes.

PROCESS PHASE

The process phase contains the most complex relationships. Perceptions and expectations are shaped not only by the manifest positions and actions taken by the opponent, but also by the personality structure of the negotiator. Behavioral attempts to persuade the other side usually entail efforts to alter the other's values toward his own goals. The effective use of power and persuasion should alert a negotiator's perceptions to the utility of changing current values and goal patterns.

Personality also shapes one's perspective and expectations of particular objects and goals. For instance, a bargainer who has a high need for harm avoidance may perceive a threatening communication as a danger signal and seek to escape. On the other hand, a bargainer in a similar situation who has a high need for achievement might view a threatening signal as an obstacle to be overcome and approach it in the spirit of lively competition.

Another element in the process phase is the behavior factor. Behavior—including demands, offers, concessions, and attempts to persuade—is influenced by personality, perceptions, expectations, and the behavior of the other negotiator. Lewin's behavior determination paradigm is most prevalent at this point in the model. Personality needs are aroused by perceptions of stressful and riskful forces in the bargaining environment (McGrath, 1966). Bargaining strategies are summoned in response to this arousal state to avoid excessive demands to reduce one's bargaining position. Such behavioral movement is also aimed at producing favorable changes in the opponent's position thereby reducing stressful force fields and improving the possibilities for goal achievement.

In the negotiation process, the mutual use of power to maximize one's own interests while achieving a common convergence of interests creates a complex mixed-motive ambience of trust and suspicion. Such an environment is generally charged with high emotional content and tension, sufficient to arouse prominent motives in a negotiator's personality. These aroused needs seek satisfaction and tension reduction through the development and use of effective bargaining strategies.

The objective and subjective environment also impacts on the negotiator directly. A negotiator's subjective interpretation and expectations of the opponent's position and behavior provides the basis for strategic planning, whether the image is true or biased. The objective consequences of an opponent's actions can also impart major physical or psychological constraints and opportunities on one's actions. For instance, naval blockades, verbal commitments, promises to reward, and time limits to respond are likely to place certain objective limits on a bargainer's choice of behavioral response.

Experienced and attentive negotiators can benefit from an implicit information-feedback loop in the bargaining situation. Interactive behavioral signalling transmits not only explicit power communications, but also tacit information about the motives of the bargainers. As the negotiation process proceeds and becomes more intense, negotiators may be able to infer the personality dynamics of their opponent from his manifest actions and reactions over time (Nierenberg, 1973). The more information negotiators can bring to bear on the past behavioral responses of their opponents, even if under different circumstances, the more reliable these personality inferences will be. With this type of insight, bargainers can estimate how opponents may perceive their actions and how they may respond in the future. The greater the understanding negotiators possess of their counterparts' motivation, the greater their ability to develop a maximizing strategy for themselves.

OUTCOME PHASE

Bargaining outcomes are conceived as the culmination of power plays between the participants. They are normally not the result of a single effort. Convergence of interests is a gradual process because persuasion is a gradual process. Mutual attempts to use power to influence the other side's positions and goals is not only a means of self-interest maximization, it is also a fundamental search process to identify likely areas for accommodation, sensitive issues best to be delayed, limits of acceptability, strengths of commitments, and optimal timing to ensure the stability of the bargaining parties and the agreement. Acceptable formulae and agreements in principle that maximize joint payoff can be achieved through this search process, which often begins in an informal sense prior to the onset of formal negotiations.

Of course, positive convergence is not always assured. Power may not be employed effectively or credibly by either party to persuade a sufficient change in positions. Then again, the distance between rival positions, commitment strength, time constraints, and enduring suspicions between negotiation participants may be so great as to irreparably eliminate the possibilities for convergence.

Even in agreement, however, the various participants may not perceive the final payoff to be just or equitable. Asymmetric power positions between the negotiating parties may put one at an advantage to demand high and concede little (tough bargaining), while the other may be forced to compromise many of its objectives and settle for a less than satisfactory agreement (Spector, 1976). Using this model, the power-balance between negotiators can be observed in the process phase and its implications for fair outcomes can be evaluated.

SOME EXPERIMENTAL FINDINGS

This model has been applied as the conceptual framework for a set of dyadic-negotiation laboratory experiments (Spector, 1977). The objective of this model-validation exercise was to determine the degree to which the negotiation process and outcome could be explained by reference to the psychological dynamics postulated in the model. Unlike several single-trait experiments (see Rubin and Brown, 1975; Spector, 1975), the findings of this analysis confirm the potency of psychological explanations.

Using a hypothetical business-like redistributive-bargaining scenario developed by the author, Stein's Self-Description Questionnaire as the personality measure (Stein, 1963), and volunteer college-student participants, the results indicate that negotiators with significantly different personality profiles and situational expectations are likely to employ very different behavioral bargaining strategies. Each distinct bargaining style is activated by a decidedly different set of motivational elements. Furthermore, the empirical findings show that these motivations are not always obvious or self-evident. Needs for achievement, dominance, aggression, defense, and counteraction against harsh demands were not significant predictors of strategy choice. Instead, several nonobvious motivational structures were found to activate the use of four basic behavioral patterns:

(1) Highly cooperative bargainers who agreed to *share their payoff* with the other side were motivated by self-oriented needs for social approval and emotional support rather than outgoing needs for cooperation and friendship.

(2) Altruistic bargainers who *transferred payoff* that could have been theirs to the opposing side were motivated by defeatist and harm-approaching needs.

(3) Bargainers who *bluffed and deceived* were motivated by needs for play, seduction, cleverness, and exhibitionism.

(4) Hostile bargainers who employed elements of *coercion* were motivated by the mirror-image hostility of their opponents.

Moreover, controlling for variation in the negotiators' psychological climate altered the motivational structures that activate the bargaining process and outcome. Given high threat perception, bargainers tend to be more defensive and fearful of their opponents. Under low threat conditions, few personality needs are aroused and the choice of bargaining strategies is largely a matter of responsiveness to the opponent's actions.

The degree of similarity between adversary personalities also has an important impact on the choice of strategies. Bargaining dyads composed of complementary personalities were able to let their defenses down and employ risky, fait accompli strategies. Nonsimilar bargaining pairs tended to be more cautious and defensive in their transaction.

Contrary to the assumptions of the model, outcomes are found to rest more heavily on personality and perceptual predictors than on the use of mutual persuasion. Bargainers obtained higher payoffs if they were *not* motivated by aggressive needs, were perceived to have friendly intentions, and had adversaries who were excessively impulsive, escapist, and ineffective. There are several possible explanations for this inconsistent finding. First, the college volunteers were unsophisticated in their use of persuasion and may have employed it ineffectively and without credibility. Second, several experimental sessions were ended prematurely before achieving a mutually agreed stable outcome. These cases may have confounded the empirical results. Given more time, these negotiators may have been able to use persuasive mechanisms effectively toward achieving an acceptable accommodation.

CONCLUSIONS

These empirical results tend to validate the utility of the model and an integrated psychological approach toward explaining negotiation dynamics and outcomes. The model's conceptualizations deserve further attention. Whereas the single-trait approach to a psychological explanation of bargaining has borne limited and somewhat obvious results, this model provides a structured framework that case analysts as well as experimenters can apply to examine various complex interactions.

Moreover, the model offers the analyst a flexible and nondeterministic tool. Each negotiation case is conceived to be a distinct and unique mixture of personality, perception, expectation, and persuasion. Different negotiators will bring their different styles to the bargaining table. Even the same negotiator may behave differently if confronted with a changed environment. Attempts at persuasion are likely to evoke different responses if the actors, timing, and threat environment are altered. The model can help to uncover and pattern these complex and highly variable relationships and shed light on the psychological dimension of negotiation.

Bertram I. Spector is a Senior Research Associate in the Policy Sciences Division of CACI, Inc., a research firm located in Arlington, Virginia. His research has focused on the psychological dimension of political behavior, and in particular, on negotiation dynamics. Currently, he is analyzing the long-term consequences of alternative Middle East peace plans that may be negotiated in the near term.

4. Negotiation as a Joint Decision-Making Process

I. WILLIAM ZARTMAN
Department of Politics
New York University

Negotiation is one of a limited number of decision-making modes whose characteristics, taken as assumptions, are not compatible with most of the theoretical work on negotiation to date. The concession/convergence approach has problems of symmetry, determinism, and power, but above all fails to reflect the nature of negotiation as practiced. Negotiators begin by groping for a jointly agreeable formula that will serve as a referent, provide a notion of justice, and define a common perception on which implementing details can be based. Power makes the values fit together in the package and timing is important to making the formula stick. The article provides examples from cases and experiments are discussed, including the results of a new survey of UN ambassadors using miniscenarios. Finally, the strengths and weaknesses of the formula/detail approach are assessed.

In attempting to develop scientific comprehension of a subject, it is as important to understand the nature of the subject itself as it is to develop theories to explain how it works. Different theoretical approaches developed independently of the subject can generate counterintuitive insights and original explanations, but such explanations are not applicable unless they relate to its true nature. Such an observation may seem so obvious as to be puzzling, and over time it is self-enforcing. In the long run, theories that misapprehend reality show themselves to be incapable of explanation and prediction and are abandoned (Kuhn, 1962). But in the short run they may prove tenacious, as students debate whether the theory is inapplicable or merely in need of further refinement. The theory takes on its own life and attractiveness and its proponents develop an investment in the given approach. It is therefore important to continue to pose the question of correspondence between theory and reality, while still pursuing the debate over the internal development and consistency of current theory. Even an "as if" approach only assumes—but does not establish—that particular correspondence and may in fact be very misleading; "as if" needs to be related to "as is."

There are two sides to this effort. One is an independent examination of the subject to discover its nature, properties, and processes, to serve as the basis of a reality test for theory. The other is a formulation of theory in terms which can be identified, applied, and tested in observation and experiment, to provide for the operationalization of the theory. Much has been written about the relationship of reality and operationalization to theory; it need not be repeated here. The present discussion will proceed to a review of these two criteria in regard to a particular area of theory.

The argument in this essay is that negotiation is one of a limited number of decision-making modes. As such, it has a set of characteristics which identify and distinguish it from the other modes, and which, taken as assumptions, are not compatible with much of the theoretical work on negotiation to date. Instead, there are distinct patterns which appear in the actual practice of negotiation and which can be used as a basis for new directions in theoretical analysis.

Political science can be reduced to a study of structural modes of decision-making. The study of politics as choice or decision has advanced a good deal in recent years but unevenly, and few authors have looked specifically at negotiation in this context. Twenty years ago, Robert Dahl embarked in an interesting direction by identifying four types of decision-making processes based on leader-nonleader relations and meeting two conceptual requirements: "categories should actually fit governmental behavior [and] should not be incompatible with one another" (Dahl, 1955: 47). The four types were democratic (upward control), hierarchial (downward control), bargaining (reciprocal control), and price (self-control). Unfortunately, the typology was not pursued in his later work and is unmentioned in *Modern Political Analysis* (Dahl, 1976). Kenneth Arrow also identifies a number of decision-making systems based on the degree of centralization and the coincidence (identity) of both information and interests. (Arrow, 1974: 69) His typology is threefold—authority, bargaining, and consensus—but the implications of the categories are not developed. Anatol Rapoport more fully explores three modes of conflict—fights, games, and debates—which can also be regarded as decision-making modes, the decision being made by eliminating, outwitting, or convincing the opponent, respectively (Rapoport, 1960). In international relations, E. H. Carr (1949: 218) found three processes of peaceful change, two presupposing a political order and one not. They are the judicial process among parties of equal status and no power, the legislative process among parties with power but subordinate to legislative authority, and the bargaining process in which the parties have both equality and power and when all decisions are unanimous. All of these typologies have common elements which, added to others, can provide the essential characteristics for analyzing the basic processes of decision-making.

There are at least three identifiable modes of social decision-making. The first may be called *coalition,* the process of making a choice by numerical aggregation, involving voting majorities, rules of collective choice, and legislation. Decision by coalition is a 0-sum process in that one side wins and the other loses.[1] The winners win by being more numerous than the losers; there are many parties, fixed values, and a twofold choice (yes or no) on any given proposal. Neither side has any power over the other outside of the process of choice itself, if only because each side only exists through the act of constituting itself to make the choice. Thus, any side can make the decision alone, if it is big (powerful) enough, with power being associated with size and its ramifications (position in building up a majority winning coalition, for example).

Obviously, coalition is the basic component of real events such as voting and legislating, although the real events are much less pure and neat than their abstract core. This complexity, however, does not prevent their analysis in terms of the concept. In fact, even though coalition and legislating are two different orders of things, it is not only the power and logic of the former but also the correspondence between coalition theory and the essential nature of legislation that allows the former to be so useful in explaining much of the latter. Each one of these elements could be elaborated on (see Riker 1962; Brams, 1975); together they form the assumptions which identify coalition as a decision-making process and the categories in which other assumptions must be made to distinguish other modes of decision-making.

Judication differs from the others in that it is a hierarchical process, during which parties plead before a single judge or executive who aggregates conflicting values and interests into a single decision that

---

1. Coalition is used here in a narrower ("total conflict of interest") sense than in Axelrod, referring to a decision-making process and not simply a matter of forming a government (1970: ch. 8).

may or may not favor one of the parties more than the other(s).[2] It is hard to conceive of decision-making by a single judging individual in terms of sums; there is one deciding party, variable values which are combined into a decision, and a one-fold choice on any given subject (i.e., the judicator picks his decision, which is made decisive by his choice). He does not even cast his vote for the position of one party or another, thus creating a majority, since he is free to invent his own position which his vote alone turns into a decision. Since the process is hierarchical, one side has all the power to make the decision and the parties before him can only avail themselves of the means of persuasion, to reason, plead, and promise (and their correlates) in order to affect the decision. It should be emphasized that, like the other processes discussed here, judication refers to social or collective decision-making. As an individual, noncollective process, it is the only form of decision-making, since, whether a part of coalition, judication or negotiation, the individual person must make up his mind alone. Here, however, the social unit included a number of parties not just the judge-executive but also the contending parties before him.

The third mode of social decision-making, *negotiation,* differs from the other two on most counts. Negotiation is a process of two (or more) parties combining their conflicting points of view into a single decision (for similar attempts to identify characteristics, see Young, 1975; Tracy, 1975; Zartman, 1974; Kelley, 1970). It is a *positive-sum* exercise, since by definition both parties prefer the agreed outcome to the status quo (i.e., to no agreement) or to any other mutually agreeable outcome. Both sides come off better in the agreement than in the absence of the agreement, or else they would not agree (a point that is theoretically true but may have some exceptions in reality and even some complications in theory in regard to threats). There are *fixed parties* and *flexible values;* a decision is made by *changing the parties' evaluation* of their values in such a way as to be able to combine them into a single package, by persuasion, coercion or force (on the first two, see Zartman, 1971 and Zartman, 1976; and George et al., 1971). In the process, the parties exercise a *threefold choice* (yes, no, maybe or keep on talking). Choice is neither numerical (the size of the parties does not matter to the outcome) nor hierarchical (parties are formally or precedurally equal and fixed). Both sides have *power over each other.* This latter characteristic is evident in two important

---

2. I know of no theoretical work that probes the nature of this process, (this includes the works on judicial decision-making cited in Zartman, 1974: 385).

ways: negotiation takes place when stalemate occurs or, otherwise stated, when a decision is impossible by other means, and hence when—in some sense—the parties have equal stalemating power; and negotiation is a joint decision-making process in which both parties are necessary to the decision or, otherwise stated, in which each party has veto power. In addition, the parties have mixed motives, so that it is impossible to speak of a winner and a loser as in coalition, or of a pleader and a decider as in judication; both parties have reasons to agree and to disagree, to cooperate and to conflict, to concede and to compel.

Within these characteristics, then, the important theoretical questions to explain become: how are decisions made by negotiation; i.e., how are values combined in order to produce a single, joint, agreeable outcome?; and, are there unique outcomes which are the foreseeable (predictable, determinant) result of the process defined in some particular terms? (For similar attempts to pose key questions, see Coddington, 1968.) It should be noted that the questions require two answers relating to the way things are done (reality) and their conceptual explanation (theory).

From these summary characteristics it is easy to see that the three modes lend themselves differently to theorization. It does not minimize the work of the imaginative scholars who have worked on the problem to note that coalition is clearly the process most susceptible of theoretical treatment. It deals with numerical aggregation, twofold choice and 0-sums. Judication is much more difficult, as the work on judicial decision-making shows. Although it may be possible to forecast the decisions of given individuals on the basis of their past actions, there is no theoretical approach that has proven capable of handling the judication process itself, for its characteristics do not easily lend themselves to theory. The process of negotiation lies in between. A growing amount of theory has been developed, capitalizing on the aspects of the process which appear to be most amenable to theorization. Although eight different approaches to the study of negotiation have been identified (Zartman, 1976; and Tracy, 1975), four deserve brief mention here because of their theoretical development. The following paragraphs are not meant to contain a full critique but merely to present a few summary ideas as background to the subsequent discussion.

First mention should be made of the personality or psychological approach which looks at the decision makers themselves more than at the process. It seeks to explain bargaining effectiveness at conflict resolution in terms of such variables as the behavioral characteristics of the negotiators and their perceived and actual use of interpersonal strategies.[3] Admittedly, in one sense this approach is the most appropriate to the analysis of negotiation and is certainly more applicable than it would be to coalition, for example. It focuses on the fixed element of the process—the parties—and their ability or propensity to modify the variable element—the values at stake. In terms of the criteria mentioned earlier, the psychological approach does well. It deals with realistic aspects of negotiation using concepts that are possible—even if not always easy—to operationalize.

However, by the same token, to analyze the agent rather than the process is to focus on the secondary rather than the primary element of decision-making, whether the process be negotiation or judication. In a crude simile, the driver, marksman, and cook are important ingredients in their respective processes, but they are secondary or ancillary to matters of mechanics, ballistics, and recipes. In any case, it is not yet possible to give a full evaluation of the psychological approach since its findings have not yet been combined into a general theory of negotiation or even reduced to the identification of a few key variables (see Rubin and Brown, 1975: 299f.).

Second is the economic approach with characteristics that are quite the opposite of the psychological. The economic approach does not lack putative theories, but their determinancy above all depends on artificial constructs and unoperationalizable concepts, such as indifference curves, negotiating fronts, and Pareto-optimality.[4] Theories of bilateral monopoly seek to explain a jointly determined outcome in terms of the rational tendencies of the parties to reach an optimal point of intersection on their lists of interchangeable preferences. The problem is not one of identifying the wrong processes, but rather of assuming away all the interesting elements that make the process work and would make it understandable. Component assumptions—interchangeable preferences, a specific type of rationality, power-free determinancy—are neither real nor operationalizable, and attempts to add new aspects of preference—such as ophelimity (Pen, 1952) or reciprocal demand intensities (Wade and Curry, 1971)—bring the approach closer neither to reality nor to operationalization.

The economic theories' determinant outcomes have little or no predictive power (Hamermesh, 1973; Young, 1975: 143, 287), for

---

3. Good recent examples are Deutsch, 1973, and Spector, 1975. Among recent synthesizing work such as Swingle, 1970 and Druckman, 1973, Rubin and Brown, 1975 is the best.

4. A good selection of such work is presented and evaluated in Young, 1975. See also Coddington, 1968 and Coddington, 1973.

their very determinancy makes them count as irrationality any element of power, persuasion, or coercion that could cause deviation from the predicted result. These criticisms are not directed against the internal consistency of the theories, which has already been the subject of a good deal of debate, but rather against their usefulness in understanding reality. Not surprisingly, economic theories of negotiation have mainly been confined to citing labor bargaining as an example, but they have been no better in explaining such outcomes than they have in improving understanding of other types of negotiations.

A third approach, the strategic, involves similar problems. Game theory seeks to explain negotiated outcomes in terms of rational-choice behavior toward a given array of values. The approach is an important part of coalition theory and can also provide important insights into the process, and it is particularly well-suited to analyze the decision whether to negotiate or not (see Rapoport, 1966, 1974; Brams, 1975), notably in Prisoners'-Dilemma and Chicken-type situations. It is, however, unsuited for analysis of the negotiation process. Reference to the characteristics of the decision-making modes exhibit the reasons. Negotiation is the process of varying values, and game theory deals with fixed values in which outcome is inherent in their structure. Therefore, it can show the array of values and the outcomes of choice at any given moment, but it cannot show the essential characteristic of negotiation, the process of their changing. Game theory mistakes repetitive strategy for interactive strategy in which parties use various means of persuasion to modify the others' values. Even its determinism proves its own undoing in predicting results for there are a number of persuasive theories establishing different determinant outcomes, each a function of its particular assumptions.

The approach that has come closest to grasping the nature of negotiation is process analysis, most developed in the study of concession/convergence (three excellent works are Siegel and Fouraker, 1960; Cross, 1969; Bartos, 1974; see also Cross, 1977; Bartos, 1977; Hopmann and Smith, 1977, this volume). This approach views negotiation as a learning process in which the parties react to each other's concession behavior. The approach responds to an intuitive understanding of many examples of negotiations, such as wage bargaining, rug buying, and territorial concessions, and is particularly attractive because it is amenable to addressing the age-old concerns of writers on negotiations: how to bargain best? (see de Callieres, 1963; Pecquet, 1738; de Felice, 1976; Nicolson, 1964). The approach has provided some of the most imaginative, rigorous, and useful work both in theory and in experimentation on the subjects of negotiations.

But there are problems. First, the approach cannot overcome the problem of symmetry on several levels. Because the findings of the convergence/concession approach are available to both parties, there is no advice on how to bargain best that is not equally accessible to the other side, leading the parties back to the stalemate that characterizes the situation ripe for negotiation! The very nature of the approach keeps it from answering the question which it addresses. There have been attempts to overcome this problem by recognizing the possibilities of short-term or tactical assymetries. "In other words, one should be soft against an opponent likely to be tough, tough against one likely to be soft" (Bartos, 1967a). But this conclusion, supported by logic and experimental evidence, is based on one crucial assumption: that agreement is preferred to nonagreement. Thus, against a "softie" one may be tough and win more, but against a "toughie" one can only be soft if any agreement is to be reached at all. Such advice follows directly from the assumptions of the convergence/concession approach but is only mildly helpful in understanding negotiations and scarcely helpful at all as a form of advice.

Second, the approach cannot—or has not—overcome the problems of determinancy (see Coddington, 1973; Tracy, 1975). Convergence concession has been developed as a determinant theory which eliminates certain problems of advice. But again the learning process, as a key to the analysis of negotiation, raises other problems of applicability, although their solution can be found within the general approach. To begin with, concession rates are as difficult as indifference curves to locate in the real world. If understanding an outcome depends on pre- or post-diction from a known behavior expressed with mathematical precision as a concession rate, it hangs on the dubious assumptions that such a rate can in fact be calculated from the past and that it will hold in the future. Thereafter, the theory runs afoul of the basic characteristics of the negotiations process, for, like any determinant theory, it leaves no room for skill, tactics, and power. Once set in motion, running like a machine to a given conclusion, the approach has appropriately been termed "cataclysmic" (Rapoport, 1965).

There is a way out of this problem within the approach itself, and that is to turn the learning theory into a teaching theory, that is, to recognize that behavior not only responds to behavior—an error-activated case of infinite regress in extreme, as has been pointed out—but, because of that fact, behavior can be used to evoke responsive behavior. In this way, learning theory could be used to incorporate the necessary element of power in negotiation, since the role of the parties is to change the values of the other in order to bring about a mutually agreeable result. But in the process, the insights of the determinant theory are exploited but the determinancy is lost. The challenge remains, for learning theorists to meet.

But there is a further problem about convergence/concession analysis. It has been mentioned that, intuitively and experimentally, it corresponds to identifiable cases of negotiation. But does it capture the essence of the process? Does it reflect the nature of negotiation as found in the majority of real cases? In a word, is negotiation, as it is practiced in many forms, a matter of two parties arriving at their joint decision by inching incrementally toward each other from specific initial positions. Or if certain unreal assumptions have to be made to handle the problem theoretically, do these assumptions respect the nature of the process or do they depart from that very nature?

The problem has already been recognized (see Raiffa, 1953; Braithwaite, 1955; Landsberger, 1955; Douglas, 1957; Coddington, 1966; Zartman, 1971; Bartos, 1974). Writers have identified a phenomenon of mixed rates, or endgame, in which the parties both act tough in order to test each other and then jump to a proposed agreement, moving in such a way as to present an outcome that is favorable to the proposer but agreeable to the other party as well. The party which jumps first is able to formulate the terms of an agreement and therefore seize the edge of advantage between favorable and agreeable. Such behavior is especially characteristic of deadline bargaining but is also found in cases where no formal deadline exists. Such behavior has been analyzed within the context both of concession/convergence and of strategic models, but there is some real question as to whether it represents incremental inching toward an agreement or rather a different behavior more appropriately described as jumping.

DISCUSSION

On the other hand, as already noted, concession/convergence analysis depends on the identification of specific positions. It is therefore limited in its application to quantifiable cases of the types suggested —wages, rugs, boundaries—and perhaps even in those cases there are other topographical elements which affect the inching process in a way that is not revealed in the theories and experiments.

The problem with any of the existent schools of analysis which deal with the structure of process and making decisions out of values—

i.e., all but the psychological school among the ones discussed above—is that they have to assume a fixed array of items with precise and intrinsic values under discussion, like Bill's and Jack's treasures in Nash's (1950) example. This assumption contains two digressions from reality. It first ignores the fact that the very list of items under negotiation is a matter of negotiation; it may often be possible to come to an agreement about specific items under discussion only by packaging some of them together and ignoring others. The second error is to consider changes affected in the evaluation of these items to be purely a tactical matter, accomplished without reference to any other underlying values which give the original items their worth. In other words, it considers the stakes in negotiation to be "inchable" values composed of discrete increments in such a way that a little more or a little less can be independently determined and does not affect the nature of the item itself.

If these two aspects of the finite value assumption were incidental to a basic process of making decisions by negotiation, deviance from reality would be unimportant, at least for the initial formulation of the theory. But they are matters which are crucial to the nature of the process itself. Because of this fact, negotiations in the real world are generally not matters of incremental convergence—despite all the images of the parties "coming closer together" in common parlance —but of something else. In other words, the trouble with concession/convergence theory, its inability to explain real events, lies not in its internal development as theory, but in its lack of corespondence with the way things take place.

Since this assertion is the major thrust of the rest of this paper, it needs a good deal of support. This will be developed in three different ways: by an identification of the types of negotiation processes, by examples from actual cases, and by reference to data generated in current research. Rather than a matter of convergence through incremental concessions from specific initial positions, negotiation is a matter of finding the proper *formula* and implementing *detail*. Above all, negotiators seek a general definition of the items under discussion, conceived and grouped in such a way as to be susceptible of joint agreement under a common notion of justice.[5] Once agreement on a formula is achieved, it is possible to turn to the specifics of items and to exchange proposals, concessions, and agreements. Even then, details are resolved most frequently in terms of the referents which

---

5. One such notion of justice among many is the formula for "fairness" used by Bartos, 1977.

justify them and give them value rather than in their own intrinsic values. This means that convergence does not take place by inching from fixed positions toward a middle, but rather by establishing a referent principle from which the value of the detailed item will be derived.

It is still not clear whether formula/detail is the only pattern of negotiation, or merely the dominant one. Admittedly, there are cases when the items under negotiation are well enough established through prior agreement to enable convergence/concession bargaining to take place. Moreover, a third type of negotiation, which can be called progressive construction, can also take place when parties are not ready to handle items as a group but would rather deal with them seriatim, or when negotiations on a broad subject are viewed over a long time span as in disarmament (Wall, 1975). But since the convergence/concession types that do exist usually only take place when a formula has already been adopted, and since progressive construction negotiation frequently either operates within a formula or, over a long time period, contains a succession of formulae, this paper will concentrate on formula and detail as being the most typical and most important type of negotiations.

This is no place to indulge in lengthy diplomatic histories. But a brief discussion and a few references will help point out that major negotiations of recent years—Cuba, Vietnam, Middle East—are best analyzed from the formula/detail approach.

Cuba has been subject to a number of different analyses from two angles: one involves competing models purporting to provide the best explanation of events (Allison, 1971; Holsti, 1972; Holsti et al., 1964; Forward, 1971); the other involves competing definitions of the proper range of items to be covered by an agreement in the 1962 missile crisis (Bernstein, 1976; Marshall, 1965). The two analyses do not speak to each other or to common concerns. The first assumes that what happened was uniquely reasonable and successful, and therefore provides a nearly perfect case study for inductively derived models; the revisionists (of both right and left) discuss, or more frequently contest, whether the appropriate items were exchanged.

None of the studies of the confrontation has sought to make use of one of the theoretical approaches described above, presumably because none was found to be helpful in explaining outcomes. Interestingly enough, a concession/convergence model could have been applied, complementing Holsti's and Forward's communications models, to show how alternatives were narrowed to a final outcome that, predictively, may well have been a good bet but was certainly not necessarily a sure thing. However, it is stretching the concession/convergence approach from a precise model to a literary allusion to try to make it fit such an uneven series of events as a strategic choice of ends and means, a quarantine announcement, retraction of a naval perimeter, and acceptance of a specific exchange of contingent actions, to mention only the concessions on the American side.

It is more appropriate to consider the Cuban crisis within the framework of formula and detail. In this approach, the two types of analyses can be brought together; the problem to be solved was the discovery of a formula that could include items of sufficient importance to both sides to be accepted by them. The various revisionist formulae were considered at the time and can be considered in the analysis, but they did not fit the requirements of the definition. The idea of including missiles only and not Castro, and of accepting no counterpart such as Turkey or Berlin, on the American side, and the idea of extracting a counterpart promise on the invasion of Cuba, on the Soviet side, were parts of the definition of an acceptable formula, which finally appeared in the exchange of letters of 26-27 October. The subsequent Ilyushin incident was part of the detail phase. At the same time, analysis of the Cuban missile crisis as an attempt to find a mutually agreeable formula also leaves an important place for the study of power, the ability of the parties to modify the other's evaluation of the items at stake. To be sure, this process is akin to the one described by Zeuthen (Zeuthen, 1930: 106; cf. Young, 1975: 80, 134, 147, 184), involving a continual comparison between the expected values of settlement and the expected values of conflict, but it leads to a search for an appropriate formula and then for accurately implementing details, not to successive exchanges of concessions.

The Paris negotiations to end the Vietnam war have already been analyzed in terms of alternative models, showing that the concession/convergence model is neither useful in analysis nor accurate in reflecting the actual course of events (Zartman, 1976). Again, the model could be stretched to fit: if the stalemate occurred because both sides insisted on negotiated victory on their terms, concessions on both sides provided an intermediate position finally agreeable to both sides. If this accurately represents the outcome, it does not reflect the process. The Paris negotiations involved a two-year period of American attempts to propose various formulae (October 1970-October 1972), followed by a period of joint search for details, during which proposals were accepted or rejected rather than incrementally modified. If concessions were made, they were for the most part whole concessions exchanged rather than partial concessions to a midpoint, as is usually meant. Again, power was an important and controversial aspect of the process. If a concession/convergence approach could be modified to take the various forms of power employed into account, it would not, however, show any direct relation between the use of power and the making of concessions—even in the case of the Christmas 1972 bombing. But in the search for a formula, and in the maintenance of that formula during the search for details, force, coercion, and persuasion did contribute to the process by modifying or supporting such elements as territorial referents, credibility, deadlines, and the weights given to the component elements of the agreement.

The final example to be cited in passing is the case of the Kissinger rounds in the Middle East (see Quandt, 1975; Sheehan, 1976). At first glance, it might appear that such territorial negotiations in which two incompatible concepts on a new withdrawal line were brought gradually into coincidence would be prime instances of concession/convergence. Yet even here, the appearance of inching is misleading. Instead of making successive changes in the location of a withdrawal line in response to specific means of persuasion, the parties cast about for a formula for an agreement which would contain a particular location for the line and also the principles that justified that location. Here formula and detail were closely related in time as well as in concept, and at some point specific spots—such as Quneitra or the three hills in the Golan sector—became details to be settled within the formula already adopted rather than elements of the formula itself. A full analysis of the three Mideast negotiations awaits further data on the events, but a study of these rounds in terms of competing models would be an enlightening exercise.

A further confirmation of the usefulness of the formula/detail approach comes from a high official commenting recently on the way to get negotiations moving again on the Palestine problem.[6] He said that decisions were first needed on the "negotiability" and the "terms of reference" of the issue, and when asked to elaborate on the latter notion he indicated a need to "spell out a formula under which Palestinians and Israelis could negotiate together comparable to Resolution 242," indicating the "purpose of the negotiations, e.g., the purpose of both sides is to restore peace . . . The recognition could follow." Such a description clearly indicates negotiation by formula and detail, not by concession and convergence.

6. Off-the-record Middle East study-group session, 1976.

In sum, even a cursory reference to the three major negotiations of recent times shows that they were conducted through a search for a single formula satisfactory to both sides, followed by a further search for the implementation of this formula through specification of the details necessary to affect the agreement. In no case was the process one of exchanging small concessions that modify opposing positions until they come into coincidence. The reasons are clear. Concession/convergence would be most likely to yield an incoherent agreement, a mosaic made up of little pieces chipped down to size in order to fit but providing no overall pattern. Concession/convergence implies that the variable value in question is the concession rate rather than the items at stake, that the item itself has no intrinsic value, and that a little more or a little less does not affect the nature of the item. While this assumption may not be totally inaccurate in regard to used-car haggling or rug buying, it is not even accurate in regard to other apparently similar negotiations such as wage bargaining or aid determination (see Hammermesh, 1973; Zartman, 1971: 67-74), and even less so when it comes to less simple, quantitative stakes.

The substantive incoherence of the concession/convergence approach is also visible in the experiments that are designed to test it (cf. Bartos, 1974: 377-389; Winham, 1977a: 15-17). When players are called on to bargain an agreement in which it is a simple aggregate payoff and not the substance of the agreement that matters, their actions reflect these conditions: the results lend themselves to a concession/convergence interpretation because there is no substance to the negotiations to impose a more realistic pattern; the reports of caucus and negotiating sessions show an absence of coherence and reasons for action. When experimental subjects are given a chance to define their own stakes and control their value rather than accept fixed, externally determined values, however, they tend (1) to invent a formula first to cover their own positions and then to provide the basis for a mutually satisfactory agreement, and (2) increase their satisfaction with the results to the extent that they do develop such a formula. This is evident in preliminary results from team runs of Spector's Camp Game (adapted from Spector, 1975), where two teams negotiate the allocation of seven facilities in a game-grounds which they have jointly purchased. A final example of an experimental situation of bargaining which throws some light on competing interpretive approaches is the Fermeda Workshop. In this simulated attempt that was ultimately unsuccessful, it is clear from accounts (Walton, 1970) that there was no inching, concession or convergence, but rather a number of attempts to find a formula—which failed.

The importance of formula/detail to the negotiation process is currently the subject of investigation of a survey-research project designed to test the theoretical findings of students of negotiation against the experience of seasoned diplomats, and at the same time to tap the instincts of the diplomats in such a way as to make their experience available to others in assimilable form.[7] More generally, the project seeks to bridge the gap between theory and reality.

One set of surveys in the research project involves the use of mini-scenarios, short, two-person narrative games in which the interviewer reveals preprogrammed moves successively in response to the answers of the interviewee. The scenarios are constructed to contain a number of theoretical propositions or questions, translated into narrative terms. The first question is whether negotiators follow a concession/convergence or formula/detail approach. The second is whether concessions they might make follow a regular and intrinsic pattern, or whether they are determined by other referents. The third concerns the relation between the two negotiating parties' concession rates: one set of theories suggests that the relation is *reciprocal* and that concessions from one side will be met by concessions of equal magnitude on the other (Deutsch, 1973). Another set of theories suggests that the relation is *exploitive,* and that concessions on one side will engender concessions of opposite magnitude on the other (Siegel and Fouraker, 1960; Bartos, 1974). A third set suggests that the relation is *unresponsive* and that negotiators will hold tight until they get close to a deadline and then seek to force the other party into a favorable final concession (Douglas, 1957; Coddington, 1966). A fourth set suggests that the relation is projective and that both parties naturally aim at a target point between their two initial positions and concede in such a way as to arrive at that point at the same time (Nash, 1950; Shapley, 1953; Rapoport, 1966; Young, 1975).

Two scenarios, among others, are used to test these notions. They differ in the degree to which specific increments are indentifiable in the stakes. One scenario casts the negotiator as a representative of a school board negotiating with the union for a teachers' pay raise; stakes here are precise monetary values with concessions expressed either as regular increments in money or in percentages. The other scenario concerns a piece of territory left in disputed ownership between two countries by a shifting river boundary; stakes here are discrete

---

7. The Project for the Stimulation of International Negotiating Skills (SINS) of the Academy for Educational Development, Inc., New York, funded by the Rockefeller Foundation.) In this work, I am most grateful for the skillful assistance of Maureen Berman, who conducted the interviews. The scenarios can be obtained by writing to the author.

components of the disputed territory (city, suburbs, rice field, oil fields, amenable to sectoring by the shape of the riverbeds), but the sense of absolute or relative increments is not as immediately apparent. Interviewees are first asked how they would approach the problem. They are then given an opening bid from the other side and asked for a response, an estimated reaction, and an expected outcome. Following these steps, they are given a new bid (reflecting one or more of the above theories) and the game proceeds. Mini-scenarios were run with UN diplomats at the ambassadorial level. Complete results are reported elsewhere (Berman and Zartman, forthcoming), but summary answers can be given to the three research questions.

The 50 interviews show first that most of the respondents look at negotiations as a matter of finding an appropriate formula and its implementing details, rather than of converging on a point through incremental concessions. Support of the proposition is relative rather than absolute, however. In the territorial negotiations where the increments are less apparent and the nature of the conflict already defined, there is hardly any concession/convergence behavior, but in the wage dispute it is much more frequent. However, concession/ convergence behavior in the latter case is generally associated with passive negotiation in which the party merely reacts from frame to frame, whereas formula/detail behavior is associated with an active search for a solution. Hence, as seen in the Camp Game cited above, formula/detail is associated with greater satisfaction with the solution. This is not surprising since the approach pays greater attention to substance and content and seeks an outcome which respects the concerns of both sides as much as possible.

Second, even the concession/convergence behavior is governed to a large extent by external referents rather than simply responses to the other party's concession rate. Thus, most of the diplomats who responded incrementally to the other party's wage concessions still did so with reference to a cost-of-living figure, and the much smaller number who responded incrementally to territorial concessions were trying to find a stable equilibrium point in terms of referents that would hold an agreement into place—a behavior closer to a successive submission of formulae than to pure concession behavior.

Third, whatever the approach to the negotiation scenarios, the respondents generally reacted similarly toward the other party's opening level and concession behavior. One common pattern was to return toughness for toughness and softness for softness: when the programmed party conceded regularly, the interviewee also made concessions, although at a slower rate. Another pattern saw a higher opener to produce a higher result, although not proportionally so. The "outlandishly high" openers in the territorial and wage disputes produced both a higher expected outcome in the eyes of the respondent and a higher negotiated outcome in his behavior, but in addition yielded a higher incidence of breakdown.

Finally, many respondents made a concession—often only a symbolic move—at the end when they felt agreement was in sight and they believed that the other side would accept their package. This behavior occurred whether the interviewee had been making regular concessions or whether, as was more frequently the case, he had been holding firm on his opening bid up to the final point. Yet this final concession also had another nature. It was part of a move to jump to an agreement, as already noted in the theoretical literature, but was usually not simply an isolated figure but part of a package that tied down all the items at stake within a comprehensive justification. In other words, the final concession generally appeared as a detail within a winning—or presumably winning—formula. Thus, even what seemed to be concession/convergence behavior is better understood as formula/detail.

CONCLUSIONS

The argument presented here is summarized as follows: current theoretical approaches to the study of negotiations do not correspond to the conceptual characteristics or assumptions of the subjects as a mode of decision-making and do not deal with the process as it is actually practiced. In the hands of the more experienced and more successful negotiators, negotiation tends to be a matter of finding a formula encompassing the optimum combination of interests of both parties and then of working out the details that implement these principles. Both a practical understanding and a theoretical explanation of the negotiatory mode of decision-making must therefore deal with the process as a matter of formula and detail.

This conclusion masks one major problem and a large number of advantages. The problem is important: unlike the concession/convergence approach to negotiation or the strategic approach to coalition, formula/detail does not lend itself readily to theorization.

Although a few stabs have been made at developing new approaches to handle such types of problems, none has gone very far (e.g., Boulding, 1956). The difficulties are formidable. A theory of negotiation must encompass an infinite number of possible combinations of items with variable evaluation attached to them, and include as well the impact of the exercise of power. It must also deal with multiple optima, timing, and strategic advantage and reasons for rational choice of nonoptima. A theory which indicates the best possible combinations of values would be useful, even though it did not predict which would be chosen. However, such a theory is difficult to envisage at this point (cf. Druckman, 1977; Tracy, 1978).

Indeed, the area for developing theories that is closest to the context of formula/detail might be small group theory as related to two fixed groups with established identities but flexible interests, (including an interest in agreement on a joint decision). But this area of theory has not yet addressed itself to the stated problem nor provided any rigorous basis for its solution. Another way to analyze formulae, playing on the terms of a different theoretical tradition, employs a "minimax winning coalition" of issues; a principle that covers the maximum of the proposer's interests and the minimum of the other party's necessary for an agreement. Cognitive maps might help locate this combination (see Axelrod, 1977).

If social science were replete with effective theories explicating most of its processes, such a problem would be a major drawback. However, considering the state of theory in social science in general, such difficulties are not unusual. And despite their presence, there is a good deal to be gained, beyond simple fidelity, by recognizing the real nature of the negotiatory process.

The first advantage is that the approach shows that, for conceptual reasons, and in any useful terms, negotiation is not a determinant process. The latter qualification is important since theoretical formulations could be made in unoperationalizable or artificial terms. But negotiation involves not merely a reaction to past moves from the the other side but also the initiation of forward-oriented moves to guide the other party toward the preferred target. It also involves subjective responsiveness to both parties' exercise of power. For these reasons, a determinant outcome is conceptually impossible, both in the concession/convergence and the formula/detail approach. At best, either can indicate ways of calculating optimal points or tactical insights showing how to play better, even if not the best (as in Nash, 1950; Cross, 1969; Schelling, 1960; Rapoport,1974a). Since they could be of practical use to negotiators and could enable both practitioners and analysts to judge outcomes and seek reasons for deviation from the ideal such findings would be extremely useful.

Second, the formula/detail approach guides further study. Among all the possible formulae one could find in a particular encounter, the question always arises, "why this one at this time?" leading to the practitioner's form of the question, "how to find the best formula and make it stick?"[8] Although others have alluded to a notion of a formula before without specifically identifying its nature or importance (e.g., Schelling, 1960: 104; Burton, 1969: 83-87) no one has yet worked out conceptual means of handling the aggregation of different quantities of divergent elements into various packages, and then of relating these calculations to the right moment. Clearly, in the process of jumping or proposing the winning formula, there is some importance to doing it at the right time and there is also importance in being able to hold out or force out further proposals. The second element has been touched on in some concession/convergence studies but as assumptions rather than as calculations and as an aspect of concession, not of formula (cf. Young, 1975: 145-163, 183-190, 253-266).

Third, in addition to providing a more accurate portrayal of reality, formula/detail also forms a general approach in which both psychological and concession/convergence findings have their place. The former, in dealing with the characteristics of the agent, can provide useful information on the relation between agent behavior and the process of finding a formula and its implementing details (Spector, 1977b). Since it is at the point—once the terms of reference of the agreements have been decided—that convergence through incremental concessions is possible in some types of subjects, concessions/convergence findings are compatible with the detailed phase of formula/detail. Some negotiations do proceed in this fashion in particular areas, under a governing formula or as part of a larger process, and the negotiators' behavior can be analyzed somewhat by the model.

Fourth, the formula/detail approach also has room for the analysis of power as added value. As yet, no theory of negotiation has included power, thus making it difficult for theories to explain negotiation as a political process. It is only by conceptualizing power as a modifier (negative and positive addition) to the original value of the items at stake that one can explain how formerly incompatible elements can be combined to fit into a formula acceptable to both sides (Zartman, 1974: 397f.). The process of finding an acceptable formula in-

---

8. These questions are the subject of a book by Zartman and Berman, 1979.

volves two types of actions: a selection of values for inclusion in the proposal and a modification of these values through persuasion, coercion, and force. If no modification were necessary, negotiation would be merely a matter of discovery and no conflict would be present.

Fifth, the formula/detail approach is able to meet the ancient problem of prescription as no other approach has been able to do. The presumed determinism and symmetry of the concession/convergence approach has been its prescriptive undoing. If the outcome were determinate, no advice would be given to the parties as to how best negotiate. If any advice were available to both parties in the game against each other, then no one could be told how to upgrade their tactics. But if the nature of negotiations is understood as formula and detail, then it becomes possible to advise both parties to devise an optimum formula in such a way as to benefit both parties, thus stimulating the development of tactical means of improving the package for one or both parties.

Finally, the formula/detail approach permits a more healthy and constructive public attitude toward negotiation. At present the public tends to look at negotiation as a matter of concessions, rather like an athletic match, in which our concessions are losses and theirs are gains. ("We conceded the point but rallied in the next round.") As a result, negotiation loses its positive-sum character and negotiators are under pressure to hold out and to devise bargaining chips. Negotiation as a search for a formula and its details permits a more positive and creative attitude to the resolution of conflict and the making of decisions.

I. William Zartman is Professor of Politics at New York University. He is coauthor and editor of The 50% Solution *and is currently preparing a book, under a Rockefeller foundation grant through the Academy for Educational Development's project for the Stimulation of International Negotiating Skills (SINS), on how to negotiate.*

5. Boundary Role Conflict

NEGOTIATION AS DUAL RESPONSIVENESS

DANIEL DRUCKMAN
Mathematica, Inc.

The boundary role conflict suggests two types of functions in negotiations: monitoring the other side for evidence of movement and monitoring one's own side for evidence of preferences. These functions differ in terms of focus and information-processing. This paper addresses these functions in terms of two general models, referred to as the negotiator as bargainer and the negotiator as representative. The negotiator-as-bargainer model assumes responsiveness between opposite-number negotiators. Two versions of this model showed that responsiveness can be based on both one's own previous concessions and the other's concessions or it can be a more complex function of expectations and evaluations. Each of the versions was supported in part by the data which suggested that these may be early and late processes in negotiation. The negotiator-as-representative model assumes responsiveness between the negotiator and his constituents. Such responsiveness is depicted in the form of a utility model where the negotiator attempts to balance n-components of value in the process of building a package. He is concerned with maximizing the value of the package in terms of both his own and his constituents' priorities. Experimental results suggest that the model accounts for a significant portion of variance in actual decisions. Finally, implications are drawn toward a reconceptualization of the boundary role conflict.

The modern-day international negotiator takes part in a process that has become the primary forum for articulating relationships among nations. He is a participant in an exercise that is designed to manage

AUTHOR'S NOTE: *An earlier version of this paper was presented at the annual meeting of the International Studies Association, St. Louis, March, 1977. Views expressed in this paper are those of the author and should not be interpreted as necessarily representing the official views of the U.S. Government or of Mathematica, Inc.*

complexity in the international system, and he functions primarily as a problem solver. His contributions consist of synthesizing, or mediating among, the diverse claims made by other actors in the ongoing process of international relations. These functions and contributions are construed as role obligations.

In the bilateral case, the negotiator is obligated to be responsive to the competing claims of his own and the other side. This dual responsiveness may be regarded as the defining feature of negotiation, referred to in the literature as a *boundary-role conflict* (BRC; see Walton and McKersie, 1965: 283 ff.). The BRC can be represented as psychological complexity—as a juxtaposition of images that the negotiator has of the interface between the opposite-number representatives, of the own-nation/other-nation relationship, and of the relationships among the various factions within his own party, and his own posture (Perry, 1957). Some commentators have described this problem as two-track negotiating—i.e., negotiating simultaneously with the bureaucracy and with the other side. The SALT process is perhaps the most illustrious example of such negotiations (see, e.g., Newhouse, 1973; Wolfe, 1975).

The bidirectional responsiveness, reflected in the juxtaposition of images is the monitoring function in international negotiation: where should *we* be? where are *they*? Negotiators monitor their opposite numbers; they also monitor their constituents (Winham, 1977a). The extent to which they are responsive to one *or* the other affects the course of a negotiation. The direction of responsiveness emphasized by a negotiator has implications for the way in which information is processed and presented in international conferences. These implications are developed here in terms of two general models of negotiation in the bilateral case: bargaining and representation.

THE NEGOTIATOR AS BARGAINER

The bargaining model assumes responsiveness between opposite-number negotiators. In its simplest form, the model assumes that each bargainer's concession is a direct and calculated response to the other's previous concession in an action-reaction cycle. The only information needed to make a concession calculation is the size of the other's concession (see Druckman, forthcoming). This model can be subsumed under a more general model which assumes that a bargainer is responsive to both his own and the other's previous concessions. According to this model, a bargainer's response is a function of his own previous pattern of concession-making as well as the other's concession rate. This two-parameter model is presented here as one version of the negotiator as bargainer. A second variant is a more complex version. It is based on Coddington's conceptualization of an expectation/evaluation/adjustment process; it assumes, inter alia, indirect responsiveness. Each is discussed here in turn.

VERSION 1

Whether it pays for one to be tough or soft may depend both on the other's response and on his (the other's) own pattern of concession-making. This variant claims that the other responds both to one's previous demand—direct responsiveness—and to his own previous demand—internal responsiveness. Put another way, a change in offers, a concession, is linear with the bargainer's own last offer, $A_{n_{i-1}}$, and his opponent's last offer $B_{n_{i-1}}$. This can be expressed as

$$A_{n_i} - A_{n_{i-1}} = aA_{n_{i-1}} + bB_{n_{i-1}} + c \quad a, b > 0, \tag{1}$$

where n is the round number, i is the offer number, a and b are concession-rate parameters, and c is a constant. If terms are transposed, this equation can be written in simpler form:

$$A_{n_i} = aA_{n_{i-2}} + bB_{n_{i-1}} + c \tag{2}$$

Expression 2 has the advantage of being stated in a form that can be evaluated by multiple-regression procedures.

It should be noted that these expressions are similar to Bartos' (1974) adaptation to negotiation of the Richardson arms-race model. (The main difference between his expressions and ours is that we refer to changes in *offers* while he focuses on changes in *demands*.) Instead of depicting the defense budgets of two enemy nations, Bartos refers to the negotiating demands made by two bargaining opponents. However, following Bartos, it is important to note two assumptions that are made when the model is applied to bargaining:

(1) that a>0—i.e., a concession will be made if the bargainer's last offer $A_{n_{i-2}}$ is *high*, and

(2) that $b > 0$—i.e., a concession will be made if the other's last offer $B_{n_{i-1}}$ is *low*.

Bartos goes on to say that: "Of the two, assumption (2) is more fundamental for two reasons: First, . . . it amounts to assuming that the process of negotiation is reciprocative. Second, it is obvious that once (2) is made, (1) must be made also if there is to be any negotiation at all" (1974: 77). He then presents a formal justification for the assumption that bargainers reciprocate concessions. For our purposes, the justification provides an hypothesis to be evaluated experimentally and in situ. We turn now to a consideration of this evidence.

Bartos' data only partially support the adapted Richardson model. The tendency to reciprocate concessions was weak and occurred only under certain conditions. Bargainers were just as likely to exploit each other's concessions as they were to reciprocate: the tougher was a negotiator's opponent, the softer did he tend to become. Yet neither the tendency to reciprocate nor the tendency to exploit accounted for a substantial portion of the variance in the bargainer's concession-making behavior. The size of his concessions was as much a function of his own previous behavior ($aA_{n_{i-2}}$), taking both own and other parameters into account. This two-parameter model improves predictability over the single parameter of a simple action-reaction model (Druckman, forthcoming).

The importance of a bargainer's own previous behavior is highlighted by the series of within-bargainer correlations obtained in two other laboratory studies. Recent analyses of data collected for the Druckman et al. (1972) and Druckman and Bonoma (1976) bilateral monopoly experiments indicates that: (a) the sequential-phase correlations between early and late concessions ranged from .23 to .55; (b) earlier concessions accounted for a large portion of the variance in total concessions, with about 40% accounted for by phase 1 concessions ($r = .63$), and 64% accounted for by concessions in phases 2, 3, and 4 ($r = .81, .82,$ and $.80$, respectively); and (c) a bargainer's concession on the first trial, before the other's programmed concession rate began, predicted concession-making in later phases as well as total amount of concessions, with r's of $-.62$ between trial 1 and total, $-.35$ between trial 1 and phase 3, and $-.42$ between trial 1 and phase 4. (The more the concesson in trial 1, the less the total concession as well as concessions in later phases.) The third finding is especially interesting since trial 1 concessions were *independent* of the other's bargaining behavior.

Taken together, these results support the contention that bargainers establish their own concession-making pattern apart from the pattern established by their opposite number.

The above evidence calls attention to the importance of an internal dynamic in bargaining. It does not, however, argue against the notion of mutual responsiveness in negotiation. Responsiveness is likely to occur in both directions. An interesting implication drawn from Bartos' analysis is that eventually bargainers arrive at an equilibrium in concessions. It consists of a gradual discovery of the appropriate ratio of concessions, expressed by Bartos as

$$\frac{C^*}{\underline{C}^*} = \frac{a\underline{d} + b\underline{d}}{a\underline{d} + \underline{b}d} \qquad (3)$$

where the C*s are the changes in demand for bargainer (C^*) and other ($\underline{C}^*$), b is the concession-rate parameter from 2 above, and d is a new parameter added to the model in order to take *time* into account (referred to by Bartos as a *modified* Richardson model). While it may take some time before this ratio is established, once it is determined it remains unchanged throughout the remainder of the bargaining process. The determination of such a ratio is perhaps the strongest evidence in support of the notion of mutual responsiveness in negotiation.

Some support for mutual responsiveness was obtained in the Bartos (1974) and Druckman et al. (1972) experiments. Sequential demand and concession correlations suggest that bargainers did respond to the immediately previous demand (concession) of their opponent. However, such responsiveness was weak: low correlations and limiting conditions (smaller bargaining groups in Bartos, 1974; early bargaining behavior in Druckman et al., 1972) indicate that factors different from the other's demands and concessions affected concession-making. Stronger evidence was obtained in a recent dissertation study by Stech (1977). He found a tit-for-tat process such that the other's competitive (intermediate, cooperative) bid at n − 1 was followed significantly more often by S's competitive (intermediate, cooperative) bid at n. Moreover, a number of PDG studies reported that subjects are responsive to *shifts* in the other's strategy (see the review by Druckman et al., 1972). However, none of these studies was an attempt to determine the *relative* amount of variance accounted for by own versus other responsiveness. A first attempt to do this is represented by the study recently completed by Love et al. (1977).

Love et al. (1977) designed a scenario in which subjects represented groups with different preferences for the outcome of a negotiation over the allocation of resources to diverse programs. The size of the conflict of interest *between* the groups and the extent of division over positions *within* the groups were manipulated. The effects of these variables on amount of concession-making, time to resolution, and type of settlement were assessed. The results were clear. The conflict of interest variable accounted for a significant portion of the variance on each measure of conflict resolution; the within-group division variable accounted for a negligible amount of variance. Subjects were more responsive to the differences *between* them then to the extent of polarization *within* the groups they represented. Moreover, perceptions of the amount of conflict, willingness to compromise, and so forth were influenced significantly by the extent of differences *between* them. This study is only a first step. The scenario will be used further to examine the conditions that affect the *extent* of external versus internal responsiveness.

But, what of negotiations conducted in situ, or simulations of such situations? Here, there is evidence from several studies that bears on the question of responsiveness. The evidence is provided by analyses of negotiations as diverse as early superpower arms control deliberations toward a ban on testing nuclear weapons and efforts between Egypt and the West to cooperate in achieving a project that could aid economic development along the Nile, inter alia. Most interesting perhaps is the recent study by Hopmann and Smith (1977). These investigators attempted to determine the extent to which the Richardson model depicted the process of the Partial Nuclear Test Ban Treaty of 1963. The results generally support the interactive process depicted by the model. Both sides were responsive primarily to their opponents—the effects were strong and significant. However, responsiveness was not symmetrical—i.e., the two sides (the United States and the Soviet Union) were not equally responsive. Specifically, the U.S. negotiators were more responsive to their opposite-number (Soviet) delegation than were the Soviets to them. The Soviet negotiators, on the other hand, were somewhat responsive to their own prior behavior, while for the United States this effect was negligible. Other differences between the two delegations included the effects of external events and perceptions: the U.S. negotiators were affected more than the Soviets both by events outside the conference and by their perceptions of Soviet actions inside the conference. The latter finding has implications for the second variant of our bargaining model and will be discussed below.

Analyses of other international negotiations suggest, however, that the tit-for-tat exchange observed by Hopmann and Smith may not be a general pattern. Spector's (1976a) analysis of the Aswan Dam negotiations indicates that both sides (the West and Egypt) were responsive primarily to their own objectives rather than to the other's moves. High intraparty correlations indicated little change in Western or Egyptian positions or behavior (i.e., cooperative versus hostile postures) through the course of the negotiation. Bargaining strategies were strongly related to bargaining positions: the greater the tendency to stop negotiating without agreement, the greater the use of a hostile strategy. Correlations between Egypt's behavior and the West's subsequent behavior (and vice versa) were weak. Neither side responded to the other's influence attempts. Egypt's perceptions were independent of the West's strategy, and the West's subsequent behavior was unrelated to previous Egyptian strategy. This strong internal dynamic, namely, each side's own bargaining position influenced its perceptions which influenced its objectives, led the author to claim that the problem of the negotiation was communication or a "total lack of comprehension of the other side's position and behavior" (Spector, 1976a: 370).

However, evidence for an internal dynamic may also take the form of *changes* in strategy. The changes may be a function of altered objectives or external events rather than the other's behavior, as noted in the author's parallel (simulate/in situ) studies. In one study, negligible or inverse intraparty correlations between early and late behavior by each side (construed as toughness/softness) indicated changed strategies ($r_1 = -.34$, NS; $r_2 = -.07$, NS). The fluctuations in strategy were different for each party to the negotiation: changes were not synchronized between the parties; when one side was tough, the other was conciliatory, as indicated by a high negative correlation between percent tough for one team and the other. Moreover, the activities of the two sides were unsynchronized: when one side attempted to bargain, the other was seeking instructions or debating the merits of general principles. Each side's strategy was shown to reflect a cultural style or to result from responsiveness to particular types of influences. The eventual agreement did not emerge from a process of mutually-converging concessions. Rather, it occurred as a result of time pressures and external events. Yet, there was also some evidence for a pattern of reciprocation. The pattern was asymmetrical: lagged correlations between one side's posture at n-1 and the others' at n indicated that one side reciprocated the other's moves to a large extent but not vice versa ($r_{1-2} = -.20$, NS; $r_{2-1} = .86$, 14 df, $p < .01$). This pattern may be referred to as lead-lag: one team followed the other *as if* in a leader-lagger relationship. While these results argue against *mutual* reciprocation, they do not refute the more general notion of responsiveness in negotiation. This study lends support to the two-parameter model proposed above. Both an internal negotiating dynamic and a lead-lag reciprocal pattern were obtained.

The evidence reviewed above makes plausible a model that takes the form of version 1. However, the extent to which negotiators were responsive to their own or other's moves varied from study to study. The second version is a more sophisticated model of responsiveness. It entails more complex information-processing requirements. We turn now to a description of this model.

VERSION 2

The second version also assumes mutual reponsiveness between opposing bargainers; however, unlike the previous model, responsiveness in this case is indirect. It is a complex, nonlinear function of perceptions or expectations and evaluations, and can be represented schematically as follows:

This type of model, stated originally by Coddington (1968) as a general conceptualization of two-person bargaining, reflects well the dynamic of international negotiating in the bilateral case. It is also similar to Iklé's (1964) characterization of international negotiations in terms of "shifting evaluations." He noted that agreement often comes about because changing evaluations lead to changing expectations of the other's willingness to compromise, which in turn softens (or hardens) a negotiator's position and produces a self-fulfilling prophesy. But he also cautions that this cycle can lead to undesirable consequences, as when the West came to expect the Sovietization of Czechoslovakia (which came about) but remained firm on Soviet control of northern Iran (which the Soviets relinquished). Recent analyses of laboratory data and selected cases provide documentation for the process depicted by this model. It would be instructive to present the evidence before elaborating the process further.

This pattern was obtained in the Druckman and Bonoma (1976) bilateral-monopoly experiment. The bargainer's decisions were influenced by his expectations regarding the other's behavior. Pre-bargaining information about the other and the other's concession-making behavior created expectations for the size of his future concessions. These expectations then were evaluated against his behavior which presumably led the bargainer to adjust his own concessions and behavior. The results of such evaluation and adjustment were reflected in the bargainer's concession-making trends through time (e.g., bargainers made larger concessions when they expected larger concessions from the other) and in his reaction at the end of bargaining when the other's pattern became apparent (e.g., disappointed expectations caused by a nonreciprocating opponent led soft bargainers to overreact by decreasing the size of their concessions). That non-laboratory bargainers display a similar pattern is suggested by the results of three other studies conducted in various settings, including early arms control efforts, reactions to scenarios by a sample of diplomats whose combined experience included a wide range of types of domestic and international negotiations, and interactions within the United Nations context of multilateral negotiations, construed as parallel (simulate/in situ) analyses.

The Hopmann-Smith (1977); Berman and Zartman (forthcoming); and the author's studies provide additional evidence suggesting an *indirect* form of responsiveness between negotiators. In the first study the U.S. negotiators responded to their *perceptions* of the opponent's actions toward them. When the United States perceived the Soviets in more positive terms, they tended to toughen their negotiating stands; when they perceived the Soviets in relatively negative terms, they softened their posture. As defined in that study, perceptions could be construed as attributions of intent—attributions condition expectations which, according to our model, determine the decisions made with regard to posturing. (For an elaboration of the relationship between attributions and expectations in gaming situations, see Druckman [1971b] pp. 535-536.)

The effect of expectations on behavior is illustrated by the Berman-Zartman (forthcoming) study on how diplomats negotiate. Diplomats responded to scenarios that varied in terms of the other's bargaining strategy. The other's opening offer created expectations which led the diplomats to adjust their response accordingly. Confronted with high opening bids, the diplomats expected high settlements and drawn-out negotiations. These expectations were confirmed as a self-fulfilling prophesy: the high opponent offers were reciprocated by low diplomat offers, resulting in stalemates. Even more interesting perhaps was the pattern observed when a diplomat, faced with intransigence, made a concession in order to indicate his willingness to negotiate. When the gesture was met by *continued* intransigence, the diplomat responded negatively by retracting his initial offer and standing firm. Thus, like the laboratory bargainers in the Druckman-Bonoma (1976) study, the Berman-Zartman diplomats were intransigent when they expected an unyielding position from the other, *and* disappointed expectations caused by a nonreciprocating opponent led generous negotiators to overreact by retracting their offers.

A third study is notable for similar results obtained in a simulation and in situ. Both situations permit multiple measurements as the conference unfolds. Negotiators adjusted their behavior in response to their perceptions of the extent to which both sides' behavior was synchronized. A large difference between the teams in percent tough led the softer team to increase its level of toughness, matching the level displayed by the harder team. The high level of *mutual* toughness led to an impasse. This pattern is suggested by the set of correlations obtained among indices of tough/conciliatory negotiating behavior (Total tough), differences between the teams in tough/conciliatory negotiating (Diff tough), and an index of the occurrence of deadlocks or impasses during the negotiations (Impasse). The contemporaneous correlations among these indices indicated that the difference between the teams, during impasses, in percent tough was small ($r_{\text{Diff tough/Impasse}} = -.35$, NS), and both teams were tough ($r_{\text{Total/Impasse}} = .63$, 13 df, $p < .01$). This is in contrast to the lagged correlations, indicating a strong positive relationship between Diff tough and Impasse ($r = .56$, 13 df, $p < .025$) and a negative relationship between Total tough and Impasse ($r = -.48$, $p < .05$). The two sets of correlations suggest that the large difference in percent tough prior to an impasse decreased during the impasse and both sides were hard. The softer side became harder. The adjustment made by the softer team followed an evaluation of the perceived difference in negotiating behavior of the two teams. It appears as if the adjustment was made when the size of the difference between the teams approached a threshold value. Threshold recognition requires a monitoring of the unfolding process as it moves through time. It is contended that such monitoring actually occurred, though at a general level.

The results of these studies support the assumpton that responses in negotiation are mediated by expectations, which are adjusted through the course of the conference. The process can be viewed as a sequence of steps:

(1) Initial expectations are *formed* on the basis of information about the other's attitudes, beliefs, negotiating goals, and so forth.

(2) The initial expectations are *evaluated* against the other's early bargaining behavior.

(3) Expectations are *adjusted*, if necessary, on the basis of the early evaluations.

(4) The adjusted expectations are *evaluated* again, later in the sequence, when the other's strategy becomes apparent.

(5) Expectations are *readjusted*, if necessary, on the basis of the later evaluation.

(6) The readjusted expectations are *compared* to one's own negotiating pattern to ascertain where *he* is at and where *I* am at.

Important changes in one's own strategy (response, decision) may occur after step 4 and then again after step 6. The negotiator's response to his perceptions of the other's strategy (step 4) may be exploitative, as when he toughens his response to the other's increasing softness (Hopmann and Smith, 1977), or reciprocative, as when the other's unyielding insistence met with intransigence (Berman and Zartman, forthcoming). His response to the comparison of own and other's pattern (step 6) may lead to an impasse, as when he toughens his posture to match the other's tough strategy (e.g., Druckman and Bonoma, 1976). Of special interest are the parallel results obtained in the laboratory and in situ. Some elaboration on this similarity seems appropriate.

In both settings an adjustment occurred as a result of the *comparison* between own and other's negotiating pattern (step 6). The adjustment took the form of reduced concessions in the laboratory or hardened rhetoric in situ. The resulting mutual toughness produced an impasse, defined as deadlock in the laboratory and as a breakoff of deliberations in situ. In both settings the impasse occurred when the size of the difference became apparent: in the laboratory, this occurred late in the session, at which point the other's concession rate strategy could be discerned; in situ this occurred at that juncture where the difference between the negotiating teams was large enough to be noticeable. In both settings, the lagger—subjects in laboratory or team 2 in situ—adjusted to the leader—programmed concession rate in laboratory or team 1 in situ (see discussion above).

The results of both types of studies illustrate the consequences of a comparison that leads to a judgment of unfair advantage. Other comparisons may suggest that neither side has benefited at the other's expense, in which case agreements should be concluded. Indeed agreements were negotiated in other conditions of the laboratory experiment (namely, increasing concessions by the programmed other) and at other junctures (to wit, turning points) in situ. Favorable comparisons took the form of judgments of equitable concessions or synchronized negotiating behavior. Some strategies or behavior that followed from the results of these comparisons (and other response combinations) are elucidated and demonstrated in Druckman and Bonoma (1976). In particular, a preliminary attempt is made to distinguish response combinations that may lead to impasses from those that are more likely to lead to agreements.

More generally, the studies provide support for the sequence of steps outlined above. Corroboration of findings obtained in the two settings lends confidence to the contention that version 2 describes the way in which information about/from the other is processed, and the implications of this processing for *responsiveness* to the other in negotiation.

The preceding analyses concentrate on the basic process of responsiveness. These analyses can be extended to a consideration of the way in which a negotiator may use responsiveness. If, as both versions of the model assume, a negotiator is responsive to the positions and concessions of his opponent, the opponent can manipulate his own positions and concessions in order to influence the negotiator. Responsiveness renders a bargainer capable of shaping the other's behavior, of causing the other to choose as he does. Such tactical maneuvering may take several forms, including concession-making strategies and such modes of communication as threats (negative consequences for noncompliance), promises (positive consequences of compliance), warnings, and commitment devices (e.g., linking one's position to a more general principle). If effectively executed, the former strategies should enable the bargainer to effect a change in the opponent's expectations for further concessions and evaluations concerning the likelihood of an agreement (see Druckman and Mahoney, 1977) while the latter tactics should enable him to place the burden of concession-making on the opponent (see Schelling's, 1960, discussion of the art of casuistry, and Druckman, 1976). Further development of the negotiator-as-bargainer model entails taking into account his arsenal of influence strategies.

CONCLUSION

The versions presented in this section are considered as alternative construals on the negotiator-as-bargainer model. The primary dimension of difference between them is complexity, with the second version taking account of more variables and processes than the first. The increased elaboration of the versions also highlights a complementarity among them. Direct responsiveness between bargainers is likely to characterize early bargaining while own/other responsiveness occurs as they develop a concession-making history. The expectation/ evaluation/adjustment sequence of version 2 affects bargaining behavior at the point where the other's strategy becomes apparent. Viewed this way, these are early, middle, and late processes. Viewed another way, version 2 could be regarded as the penultimate process, following from the earlier monitoring of the other and preceding the dramatic gestures that lead to impasses or agreements. In either case, the conjunction of the alternative processes and different phases could be regarded as hypotheses to be evaluated experimentally. We turn now to the second general model of responsiveness: the negotiator as representative.

THE NEGOTIATOR AS REPRESENTATIVE

If the negotiator-as-bargainer model is of the genre referred to as *unitary-rational actor models*, then the negotiator-as-representative model is cut from the class of models referred to as *bureaucratic (governmental) politics*. Whereas the former emphasizes internation interactions, the latter focuses on intranational interactions. Together these two types of activities constitute international negotiation.

Or, more broadly: "Applied to relations between nations, [the latter] model directs attention to intra-national games, the overlap of which constitutes international relations" (Allison, 1971: 149). The importance of internal bureaucratic politics in international negotiations has been well documented (e.g., Allison, 1971; Newhouse, 1973; Wolfe, 1975). These treatments concentrate on the interagency bargaining that occurs during (and influences the conduct of) an international negotiation. In most nations, different departments or ministries are involved in the process of making decisions about the substance and tactics of negotiation, and they often have competing preferences. Particularly notable are the conflicts between defense and foreign ministries over arms-control issues: these conflicts have been characterized as classic domestic struggles that hinder attempts to develop an overall policy toward the negotiation. Other conflicts are likely to occur among different role occupants within the same agency as when those who negotiate with alliances place a higher emphasis on military factors than their counterparts who negotiate primarily with the other side or with the bureaucracy (Hopmann, 1977). These examples highlight the differing emphases of diverse agencies and roles. From the standpoint of the negotiator, these emphases take the form of competing claims made regard to positions or postures that he ought to adopt. The following treatment depicts the way in which a negotiator attempts to reconcile these claims.

The negotiating representative must *arbitrate among diverse* agency positions. He must also decide on the extent to which he will *defend the "best"* position at the conference. These decisions correspond to the two components of representation described in the literature as position commitment and group loyalty (see, e.g., Zechmeister and Druckman, 1973). Both can be construed in terms of a weighting (or balancing) process: The former is the weight assigned to each position in terms of its relative importance; the latter is the weight assigned to the positions in terms of "degree of agency." The model is developed in two steps. First, alternative positions are construed as n-components of value. Second, the relative importance assigned to the n-components is weighted according to the negotiator's "sense of agency."

BUILDING A PACKAGE

As a negotiator, the representative attempts to build a package that will be acceptable both to the other side and to his bureaucracy. The process of building a package involves "monitoring certain feedback variables, such as domestic support for the negotiation, which indicate a willingness of the (negotiator's) government and others to cooperate in a negotiated settlement" (Winham, 1977a: 353). The importance of a package is emphasized by the diplomats interviewed by Berman and Zartman (forthcoming). These respondents noted that concessions and redefinitions of bargaining norms were determined in reference to an overall package. Resources for trade were often evaluated in terms of impact on the larger package within which these items were contained.

The package is a combination of offers made on a variety of items, e.g., numbers of ground forces to be redeployed, number and category of weapons systems to be removed from an area, ceilings to be placed on reinforcements. The offers can be construed as components of value, $w_1, w_2, w_3, \ldots w_n$. The negotiating representative establishes priorities among the set of components by considering them in terms of *relative importance or subjective worth*. The subjective worth of the package to negotiator i can be regarded as the sum of the worths of each component of value associated with a particular package. Thus, in the two-component case, if u_m is the manpower component, and u_n is the nuclear-weapons component, the value of the package (U'_i) to negotiator i is

$$U'_i = u_m + u_n, \qquad (4)$$

It is assumed that the subjective worth of each component is a linear function of its objective worth (w_m and w_n respectively). Thus,

$$u_m = aw_m + b, \text{ and} \qquad (5)$$

$$u_n = a'w_n + b', \qquad (6)$$

where a and a' reflect the relative importance of w_m and w_n, and b and b' reflect arbitrary differences in zero-point between objective and subjective worth—e.g., the point at which satisfaction turns into dissatisfaction. By substituting 5 and 6 for 4, we have,

$$U'_i = aw_m + b + a'w_n + b', \text{ or} \qquad (7)$$

$$U'_i = aw_m + a'w_n + b + b'. \qquad (8)$$

By setting $b'' = b + b'$, we have

$$U'_i = aw_m + a'w_n + b''. \tag{9}$$

However, since we are concerned with maximization—i.e., building the best package—it is not the actual size of a and a' that is important, but their relative sizes. To reflect relative importance, expression 9 is transformed into a new expression by a series of steps that involve multiplying and adding by a constant, substitution, and simplification. For our purposes here these steps are omitted. The result of the transformation is the expression:

$$U_i = \theta_i w_m + (1 - \theta_i) w_n, \tag{10}$$

where θ_i is the extent to which negotiator i considers the manpower component (w_m) to be relatively more important than the nuclear weapons component (w_n). As θ_i varies from zero to one, U_i will increasingly reflect w_m more and w_n less. (When $\theta_i = 1$, U_i will vary directly with w_m and independently of w_n.) According to this model, then, negotiators are assumed to seek that package which maximizes the value assigned to its components as:

$$\max_j \theta_i w_m + (1 - \theta) w_n. \tag{11}$$

The two-component version, presented above, provides the basis for a model that represents the process of weighting or balancing n-components. The latter is a generalized version of the former. It takes the form:

$$U'_i = \sum_k u_k, \tag{12}$$

where $u_k = a_k w_k + b_k$, so that

$$U'_i = \sum_k (a_k w_k + b_k). \tag{13}$$

Then a series of steps that parallel the development of the two-component version lead to the expression,

$$U_i = \sum_k \theta_k w_k, \tag{14}$$

which can also be expressed as a maximization function similar to 11 above.

The essential notion of the generalized version is that each component of value is considered *relative* to all other components, such as $\theta_1/\theta_1 + \theta_2 + 1 - (\theta_1 + \theta_2)$ in the three-component case. If in the three-component version any two of the three weights equal .33, then the remaining weight will also equal .33, and U'_i will be the simple sum of the three components, and so on.

As stated above, the model depicts a negotiator's *preferences* for the components of a package. It does not describe his *behavior*. To assume that the one follows directly from the other is no more justified than to assume an isomorphism between attitudes (or values) and behavior. Both remain empirical issues. Some clarification on the nature of the relationship between preferences and actual decisions is provided by work in progress. An experiment designed to evaluate the predictive accuracy of the two-component version of the model can be summarized briefly. (Further procedural details and results are presented in Druckman, forthcoming).

The experiment was a simulation of committee decision-making. Four committee members were to make decisions concerning the funding of alternative packages construed as programs. Members (subjects) represented different agencies, each with a stake in the outcome. Agency preferences for the programs were based on values assigned to the components w_m and w_n. Subjects represented their agency's values. Estimates of θ were provided by responses to a questionnaire item which asked subjects to indicate (on a seven-step scale) their own perception of the relative importance of the components, w_m and w_n. Following a role-induction session, committee members exchanged messages intended to influence other members to support or block the proposed programs. The outcome consisted of a winning coalition of members whose pooled resources enabled them to support or reject the program package. For each committee member an outcome index was constructed. The four values of this index included being *in* a successful blocking coalition (1), being *out* of a successful funding coalition (2), being *out* of a successful blocking coalition (3), and being *in* a successful funding coalition (4).

The data provided by this experiment was used to evaluate the model. Each member's final decision was predicted on the basis of the values of the components, w_m, w_n, and θ. Multiple correlations between these components and the outcome index were computed for each of the three program-packages to be decided by the committee. The correlations for the three programs were .61, .67, and .57, each accounting for a significant portion of the variance in the outcome index. Another set of multiple Rs were computed excluding the subjective component, θ, from the prediction equation. These correlations were .49, .58, and .51, respectively. A comparison of the two sets indicated that, in each case, adding θ to the equation resulted in a significant *increment* in variance explained ($F_{1/93}$ = 19.5, 18.6, and 8.1, respectively). These results suggest two general conclusions: (a) final decisions did reflect preferences, and (b) predictability is enhanced when the subjective component, θ, is included in the equation. Both conclusions support the contention that preferences, represented by the values of the model components, are indicators of actual decisions made with regard to the nature of the agreed package. However, while the model seems to capture the way a negotiator processes information toward building a package, it does not take account of *the extent* to which he is responsive to his agency's preferences. We now turn to a further extension of the model that takes account of degree of agency.

DEGREE OF AGENCY

Representation is defined in terms of the extent to which the negotiator represents his agency's priorities. If these correspond to his own priorities, there is no problem. More often, however, individual priorities differ to some extent from agency preferences. When this occurs, the negotiator must decide which way to go. His sense of obligation is reflected in his willingness to forfeit his own subjective rankings in favor of the group positions, when these conflict. It is this conflict that can be reflected in our components of value model. This is done by letting α_i represent the degree of agency for negotiator i, such that when α_i is 1, the negotiator is a pure agent for the group; when α_i is 0, he acts strictly according to his own priorities; and as α_i varies from zero to one, he increasingly represents the group and decreasingly takes his own views into account. To begin, θ_k can be divided into two parts: $\theta_{g,k}$—the group's weight for component k—and $\theta_{i,k}$—the negotiator's weight for component k. Each is assigned a weight of α, which represents the extent to which one or the other is taken into account. Thus,

$$\theta'_k = \alpha_i \theta_{g,k} + (1 - \alpha_i) \theta_{i,k}. \tag{15}$$

The generalized version, reflecting all k components of the package (U_r), is

$$U_r = \sum_k \theta'_k w_k. \tag{16}$$

By substituting expression 16 for θ'_k and shifting terms, we have

$$U_r = \sum_k (\alpha_i \theta_{g,k}) w_k + [(1 - \alpha_i) \theta_{i,k}] w_k, \tag{17}$$

which can be simplified by setting

$$U_g = \sum_k \theta_{g,k} w_k \tag{18}$$

and

$$U_i = \sum_k \theta_{i,k} w_k \tag{19}$$

so that the negotiator attempts to achieve the package that maximizes the expression

$$\max_j \alpha_i U_g + (1 - \alpha_i) U_i, \tag{20}$$

which reflects the value of the package U to the representative r in terms of his sense of agency in representing group g, and compares with expression 11, a maximization function for the nonrepresentative dealing with only two components of value.

Expression 20 is a preference function that can be evaluated by an experiment similar to the one performed above for evaluating expression 10. Such an experiment would require estimates for α similar to those obtained for θ. It would evaluate the extent to which the expanded version of the model predicts actual decisions. Or, put another way: does α add a significant increment to the variance explained, over and above that explained by the n-components of value version represented by expression 14? While this particular experiment has not been designed, another implication of α has been explored.

Degree of agency influences both relative emphasis on the components of a package and extent of commitment to those positions.

The former affects decisions concerning the type of proposal to make to the other side. The latter affects the willingness to compromise positions in order to attain an agreement with the other side. The former can be evaluated by the type of experiment described above. The latter has been evaluated by a recent experiment on the effects of accountability on negotiating behavior (Mittelmark et al., 1977; see also Druckman, forthcoming for further details on procedures and results). This is summarized here briefly.

In the recent experiment accountability was defined as the extent to which the representative was responsible and responsive to his group: highly accountable representatives were appointed and required to report regularly concerning their deliberations; low accountable representatives were elected as relatively free agents. This manipulation was embedded in a simulation of a policy-making council whose members represented different groups with particular interests in the outcome and ideological (value) stances. The extent of conflict of interests and values among the groups were also manipulated: conflict of interest was defined as vested interest in the final decision (namely, extent to which the decision would have implications for the *control* of resources); conflicting values were defined as extreme or moderate orientations underlying the positions taken on the issues in dispute. The effects of these factors on dyadic-negotiating behavior were assessed.

A particularly intriguing finding from this experiment is that the accountability variable served to mediate the effects obtained for the conflicting interests and ideologies variables. The conflict-of-interest variable was significant when accountability pressures were high: high conlict-of-interest dyads had more trouble resolving their differences than low-conflict dyads. The differences between the conditions under low-accountability pressures were nonsignificant. Interestingly, however, the ideological-conflict variable was significant when accountability pressures were low: high conflict-of-ideology dyads were less satisfied with the outcome, perceived compromise to be more like defeat, and perceived negotiations to be more futile than low-conflict dyads. Opposing decision makers were more responsive to their differences in ideology when they were not accountable directly to their group. Conversely, they were more responsive to their vested interests when they were accountable.

Construed in somewhat different terms, the finding can be shown to have implications for our model. Accountability (degree of agency) can be regarded as a weight that determines the relative emphasis (responsiveness) placed on the components, interests, and ideologies. When it was high, vested interests were emphasized; when it was low, conflicting ideologies were salient. An emphasis on interests resulted in resistance to compromise due, presumably, to a heightened sense of commitment to the group positions. The emphasis on ideologies under low accountability did not result in resistance to compromise, due, presumably, to a lessened sense of group commitment. (Rather, the effects produced concerned perceptions of the conflict and of the negotiations.) As noted above, this is one type of effect of the variable, degree of agency. Another effect is on the *choice* of the components of the package or the positions per se. This effect remains to be explored.

Choice of components suggests another aspect of packaging not considered in this treatment. This is the notion of repackaging issues and programs as captured in Zartman's (1977) analysis of formula and in Tracy's (forthcoming) concept of structure. Their discussions highlight the fact that the issues or programs per se may be a variable. The practice of creating new packages involves reconceptualization, redefinition, disaggregation, and reintegration. These processes also contribute to the formulation of negotiating positions. For this reason, inter alia, it would seem appropriate to include them in a model. Such a model would be a more complex rendition of the concept of packaging. Attempts to add these processes to those construed above will be a forthcoming development.

BOUNDARY ROLE CONFLICT: TOWARD A RECONCEPTUALIZATION

As different cuts on negotiation, the models extend the concept of boundary role conflict. As co-occurring processes in negotiation, the models retain a defining feature of the concept. The extension renders the concept more complex than previously construed. The defining feature suggests an interplay between the processes such that a negotiating dilemma is created. Each of these notions is an elaboration toward a reconceptualization of the boundary role conflict.

As originally defined, the boundary role conflict is the conflicting aspects of a negotiator's role obligations: the expectations of his own side that emerge from an internal consensus on the positions he is to take and the expectations of the opponent that must be taken into account if an agreement is to be reached. The dilemma inherent in this definition has been captured in at least two experiments where effects on bargaining behavior were observed (Frey and Adams, 1972; Wall, 1975b). However, the models developed and the evidence reported above suggest that the components of the BRC are not simply competing demands but, perhaps, fundamentally different processes.

Responsiveness to the other takes the form of a sequence of comparisons and adjustments leading to impasses or agreements. Responsiveness to one's own side consists of ascertaining the relative emphasis to be placed on components of a package prepared as negotiating positions. The differences between these two monitoring functions are in terms of dynamics and influences: the former is in the tradition of dynamic-equilibrium models, the latter is a component of a variance model; the former emphasizes perceptions and concessions while the latter emphasizes group commitment and priorities. Preliminary relationships among these variables are demonstrated above. More important, however, is the heuristic value of the methodological strategy: observations made in situ served to elucidate the processes; the laboratory experiments served to confirm (or refute) the hypothesized relationships.

The competing demands of the BRC are also *interacting* pressures on a negotiator. This aspect of the original definition is preserved in the conceptualization developed here. The differences between the models notwithstanding, the processes are not regarded as being mutually exclusive during the course of a negotiation. They are complementary and intertwined, the one influencing the other in a reciprocal manner. Whereas the negotiator-as-bargainer model (version 2) highlights the juncture where a change in posture is likely to occur, the negotiator-as-representative model suggests the probable nature of the modification. According to the former model, changes in posture occur when the other's strategy is discerned and after a comparison between own and other's pattern is made. *Which* concessions are made and the *extent* of the concessions depend on the relative importance of the various parts of the package and on the degree of agency. Both variables are estimated as components of the latter model.

Together, the two models provide a framework for evaluating changes in postures or negotiating behavior. Adjustments result from dual responsiveness: cues from one's own side are balanced against those from the other as the negotiator attempts to decide which way to go. And, it is this *bidirectional* monitoring function that defines the BRC. The interaction between the processes involved in this function remains a topic for investigation. Further elucidation awaits the results of these studies.

CONCLUSIONS

The boundary-role conflict suggests two types of monitoring functions in negotiation: monitoring the other side for evidence of *movement* and monitoring one's own side for evidence of *preferences*. Each of these functions was represented by a simple model. Differences between the functions made difficult the development of a more general model incorporating both functions. The differences are in terms of focus and information-processing.

The negotiator-as-bargainer model assumes responsiveness between opposite-number negotiators. Such responsiveness can take several forms. It can be a direct calculated response to the other's concessions (see Druckman, forthcoming), it can be based on both one's own previous concessions and the other's concessions, or it can be a more complex function of expectations and evaluations. It was contended that the latter version—complex function—reflects well the dynamic of international negotiation. According to that model, negotiators monitor the other's concessions as a trend. A negotiator's reponses are mediated by expectations which are adjusted through the course of the conference. Information-processing can be represented by a sequence of steps involving the *formation* of, *evaluation* of, and *adjustment* of expectations based on a comparison of where is *he* at now? and where am I at now? Evidence from the Hopmann-Smith, Berman-Zartman, and the author's studies support this characterization.

The negotiator-as-representative model assumes reponsiveness between the negotiator and his agency (agencies). Such responsiveness was depicted in the form of a utility model where the negotiator attempts to balance n-components of value in the process of building a package. He is concerned with maximizing the value of the package in terms of both his own and his agency's priorities. This is essentially a weighting process. The cognitive processes involved consist of defining and ordering the various components of the package and ascertaining his agency's preferences for this ordering. Both of these functions were reflected in the model. However, as the number of components increase and as his agency's positions diverge from his own, the information-processing requirements become rather complex. The former can benefit from technological aids. The latter requires reconciliation mechanisms that are part of the bureaucratic political process.

Finally, it should be reemphasized that the two types of models are not presented as alternative conceptualizations of international negotiations. Both processes occur simultaneously in negotiations (see, for example, Wolfe's 1975 treatment of SALT as a two-track negotiation). The models should be viewed as complementary, notwithstanding the differences between them noted above. However, complementarity would be enhanced if a more general model, incorporating both processes, could be developed. Such a challenge will be a forthcoming consideration.

Daniel Druckman is Senior Research Analyst at Mathematica, Inc. in Bethesda, Maryland. His major interests are in the areas of interparty conflict resolution, policy decision-making, negotiations, and simulation. He has published numerous articles and monographs on these topics. He is the editor of Negotiations: Social-Psychological Perspectives, *published in 1977 by Sage.*

Part II: Applications

6. A Game-Theoretic Analysis of the Vietnam Negotiations

PREFERENCES AND STRATEGIES 1968-1973

FRANK C. ZAGARE
Departments of Politics and Economics
New York University

This article employs game theory to analyze two games played at the Paris Peace Talks of 1968-1973 by the United States, the Republic of Vietnam, and a coalition of the Democratic Republic of Vietnam and the National Liberation Front. The stalemate of the first game, which lasted from the inception of the Talks in 1968 to the winter of 1971-1972, is shown to have resulted from the coincidence of the preferences of the players and from their game-theoretically defined best strategies. The article offers two interpretations of the outcome of the second game. Under the first interpretation, the two-track solution, the most-preferred alternative of the United States, is shown to have resulted from a shift in the Communists' preference order. Under the second, this game is shown to be vulnerable to a deceptive strategy by the United States. Under either interpretation, the optimal strategy of the United States entailed announcing that it would prefer to prolong the war rather than capitulate to the Communists.

The Paris Peace Talks of 1968 to 1973 remain an enigma to historians and political scientists alike. As one analyst has noted, "little is... known about what brought them about, what went on, what came out, and even who won. The 'why' behind any of these simple descriptive questions is even further from a clear answer" (Zartman, 1976: 372).

Part of the reason for this limited understanding is manifest: the recency of the negotiations and the lack of pertinent documents and

AUTHOR'S NOTE: *I would like to thank Steven J. Brams, Gerald Demaio, the late Oskar Morgenstern, Bertram Spector and Richard N. Swift for reading an earlier version of this manuscript and making many helpful suggestions.*

memoirs. The difficulties of making a complete analysis are compounded because the negotiations were protracted, spanning over four years. In addition, the players in this game, especially the United States, were generally secretive about their actions and, as Szulc has pointed out, were able "to develop completely distinct public and private negotiating positions" (1974: 23-24).

These problems make acute the need to evolve a theoretical framework for interpreting the Paris negotiations. In this article, I shall attempt to illustrate how to use the theory of games to explain some of the persistent questions surrounding the events leading to the end of the war in Vietnam. Specifically, I shall attempt to explain why the Talks were resolved as they were; why the negotiations were so protracted; why particular strategies were employed; and why the players were seemingly inflexible in their choices of strategies.

For analytical purposes, the Paris negotiations will be conceptualized as comprising two distinct games: the first, which can be characterized as a stalemate, lasted from the start of the Talks in 1968 to the winter of 1971-1972; and the second, from the spring of 1972 to the signing of the Paris Agreement in January 1973.

In the first section, the first Paris game will be examined and the reasons for the stalemate explored. In the next section, the second game will be studied and, because of inconclusive evidence, two interpretations of American actions will be given. Finally, in the concluding section, this analysis will be summarized and its implications for future analysis delineated.

THE PARIS PEACE TALKS: 1968-1972

The first Paris game was precipitated by the Tet offensive of 1968. Before then, the war in Vietnam was a two-person game. The important players were the United States and the Republic of Vietnam (RVN) on one side, and a coalition of the communist state in the north (the Democratic Republic of Vietnam or DRV) and its military arm in the south (the National Liberation Front or NLF), on the other.

In this game, although both sides had different military goals, each sought a military solution to the conflict. After Tet, however, the Americans had to abandon their strategy of military victory. As Kissinger (1969: 216) noted, "Henceforth, no matter how effective our actions, the prevalent strategy could no longer achieve its objectives within a period or with force levels politically acceptable to the American people."

By making a military decision impossible, Tet set the stage for a negotiated settlement of the war. On March 31, 1968, along with his decision not to seek reelection, President Johnson announced a bombing cutback in North Vietnam in the "hope that this action will lead to early talks" (Pentagon Papers, 1971: 4:272). By May 13, private contacts between the United States and the DRV were made and on January 25, 1969, public talks began.

THE POSSIBLE OUTCOMES OF THE GAME

The decision to commit the United States to a negotiated settlement subtly changed the way participants viewed the possible outcomes to the conflict. Whereas before Tet, the players viewed the outcomes dichotomously as either a military victory or defeat, after Tet, the range of alternatives expanded to three.

The Americans suggested the first alternative to the conflict: a military settlement first, followed by a political solution. As the United States viewed the situation, negotiations would take place on two tracks, with the Americans negotiating with the DRV about military matters, and the South Vietnamese with the NLF over political issues.

The communists proposed the second alternative. The DRV-NLF wanted to deal with both military and political issues simultaneously. As a final alternative, the Paris Talks might reach a stalemate. A failure to reach an agreement would result in a continuation of the war, the status quo.

It is important to note that the first two alternatives lack substantive content. As will be seen, the major difference between these two alternatives is the form of the negotiations because the form would dramatically affect the final outcome. As Kissinger (1969: 218) astutely observed, "'the way' negotiations are carried out is almost as important as 'what' is negotiated."

By conducting the negotiations on two tracks, the United States hoped to obtain the return of its POWs in exchange for withdrawing from Vietnam. Such a settlement would allow the United States to remove the Vietnamese albatross from around its neck without appearing to suffer a defeat. The United States also hoped to extract a promise from the communists to withdraw North Vietnamese troops from the south. However, even if the communists would not give this promise, the return of the American POWs would leave the DRV-NLF without substantial bargaining leverage against the Americans. For this reason, the United States refused to tie the return of the POWs to any other issue.

Without the leverage the prisoners provided, the communists would have to renegotiate a political settlement with South Vietnamese President Nguyen Van Thieu, whose government the United States hoped would be both politically and militarily strong as a result of a program of increased aid that President Johnson also announced on March 31. Johnson believed that if this scenario were followed, Thieu would, at worst, have to concede some areas of control to the communists. At best, he would be able to maintain a tight hold on the political situation in the south and perhaps continue a more limited war with American support.

By contrast, the communist proposal for conducting the negotiations implied a different solution. By using whatever military leverage they had over the United States, the communists hoped to extract political concessions from the Americans, including, conceivably, the resignation of the Thieu-Ky-Khiem clique. Because the communists gauged the costs that a continuing conflict would have on the Johnson (and later the Nixon) administration to be high, they saw simultaneous political and military discussions as an avenue for negotiating a coalition government (Porter, 1975: 70, 95-96). Such a government would endow the NLF with legitimacy and give it a substantive role in the political process in the south. The communists were confident that a legitimate coalition government would eventually result in their control of the south. Because the dictatorial methods of President Thieu rendered his right-wing military group unpopular, this confidence seemed well-founded.

In light of the preceding analysis, let us adopt the following notation for the set of alternatives, $A = \{a_1, a_2, a_3\}$, where

- (a_1) two-track negotiations, probably resulting in a pro-American regime in South Vietnam;
- (a_2) one-track negotiations, probably resulting in a coalition government and eventually a communist South Vietnam;
- (a_3) the status quo, a continuation of the conflict.

THE PLAYERS AND THEIR PREFERENCES

Besides setting the stage for negotiations, Tet also had the dramatic effect of increasing the number of players in the game. Before Tet, the goals of the US-RVN coalition coincided: to achieve military supremacy throughout the south. After Tet, however, the objectives of the members of this coalition began to diverge. The South Vietnamese clung to their goal of defeating the communists militarily; for them, Tet was a victory and tended to reinforce their desire to gain military ascendancy. In contrast, since the U.S. leaders now believed that a military victory would take longer than they had expected and would cost more than was politically acceptable, their primary concern was to remove the United States from the war. Their goal now clearly conflicted with their ally's.

From the time that the United States began to withdraw from the conflict, the game in Vietnam started to evolve into a game among three players: the United States, the RVN, and the communist coalition. With the breakup of the US-RVN coalition and the resultant introduction of a third player, the structure of the game in Vietnam was drastically altered.

For the first Paris game, the rankings of the alternatives are relatively straightforward. After the psychological blow of Tet, the United States began to prefer a negotiated settlement that would enable them to block North Vietnamese (and Soviet) expansion into South Vietnam and the rest of Southeast Asia. Hence, they ranked a_1 first. However, during this game, the United States preferred to continue fighting, a_3, rather than to negotiate on communist terms. Thus, the preference order of the United States is indicated as (a_1, a_3, a_2).

The RVN, in contrast, was committed to a military solution to the conflict, a_3. President Thieu did not want to concede any political power to the NLF. However, he preferred the American proposal, a_1, to that of the DRV, a_2, because it offered him an increased probability of retaining control in the south. Thus, the South Vietnamese preference order was (a_3, a_1, a_2).

Like the United States, the DRV/NLF was also committed to ending the war by negotiating. Before Tet, the communists had declared that they would not negotiate until the United States unconditionally stopped bombing the north. However, after Tet, they came to feel that "the balance of forces was most favorable both within Vietnam and internationally to move for peace negotiations" (Porter, 1975: 72-73). Despite their willingness to negotiate, however, the communists, like the Americans, were unwilling to negotiate on their opponent's terms. After all, they had fought both the French and the Americans to a standstill, and they believed that the settlement should reflect both their political and military position in the south. Thus, they preferred to continue fighting, a_3, to the two-track solution proposed by the United States, a_1, and they ranked that alternative which, in their eyes, would give them what they deserved, a_2, higher than both of the other alternatives. Hence, the preference order of the DRV/NLF was (a_2, a_3, a_1).

In summary, we have the following configuration of players and preferences:

(1) United States: (a_1, a_3, a_2)
(2) RVN: (a_3, a_1, a_2)
(3) DRV/NLF: (a_2, a_3, a_1)

THE POWER OF THE PLAYERS

In this game, four two- and three-member coalitions were possible:

(1) the grand coalition of all three players,
(2) a US-DRV/NLF coalition,
(3) a DRV/NLF-RVN coalition,
(4) a US-RVN coalition.

Let us examine all but the first of these coalitions and try to determine the extent to which its formation could affect the way in which the game is resolved. The grand coalition will not be examined since it obviously could bring about any outcome if it formed.

If the United States and the DRV/NLF coalesced, they could impose each of the three possible alternatives on the RVN. With each possible coalition, of course, the actual outcome would depend on the agreements its members reached. Similarly, an all-Vietnamese coalition would also be a winning combination. If the DRV/NLF and the RVN joined together, the United States would not be able to prevent that coalition from dictating the outcome without altering the nature of the game. In contrast, the final coalition between the United States and the RVN was limited in its ability to impose a solution on the communists. The weakness of this third coalition is easily seen by examining the three possible outcomes of the game.

If the United States and the RVN wished to negotiate either a two-track solution (a_1) or a one-track solution (a_2), the acquiescence of the DRV/NLF was necessary because the communists had the power to continue fighting unilaterally (a_3) and, in addition, could prevent a total American withdrawal by refusing to release American POWs even if the United States removed its troops and discontinued bombing the north (Kalb and Kalb, 1974: 400).

The ability of the United States or the RVN to prolong the war unilaterally was also severely limited. One of the pretexts for American involvement in Vietnam was that the RVN had requested its aid. If the RVN and the DRV/NLF coalesced and requested American troops to withdraw, the United States would lose whatever justification it had for participating in the war. Given the general unpopularity of U.S. involvement, both domestically and internationally, an all-Vietnamese coalition would have made it virtually impossible for the United States to continue fighting.

The RVN was likewise unable to continue the war alone. At the time the Talks began, Saigon was almost without an ally abroad. Its heavy dependence on American aid precluded it from fighting for more than a few months if American support was cut off as a result of a U.S.-DRV/NLF coalition.

Thus, if a player's power is judged by the extent to which he is able to control the outcome of the game, the DRV/NLF possessed more power in this game than either the United States or the RVN. Because only the communists were able to wage war unilaterally, they were able, if they wished, to veto each of the other two outcomes. In addition, they could bring about either of the two other alternatives if they coalesced with at least one other player.

Hence, the decision rule operating in this game is as follows: decisions could be made only when at least two of the three players agreed on a single alternative *and* that alternative was not vetoed by the DRV/NLF. Otherwise, the status quo prevailed.

A GAME-THEORETIC EXPLANATION OF THE STALEMATE

Given the set of alternatives and this decision rule, the outcome matrix given in Figure 1 results. The reader will notice that there are three dimensions to this figure. Each dimension represents the outcomes associated with the strategy choices available to the players. For convenience, call the dimensions *plane*, *row*, and *column*, and assume that they are controlled by the DRV/NLF, the United States, and the RVN respectively.

Because the players must choose from three alternatives, each may choose to pursue one of three strategies: a_1, a_2, or a_3. This essay assumes that the choice of the plane, row, and column players associated with

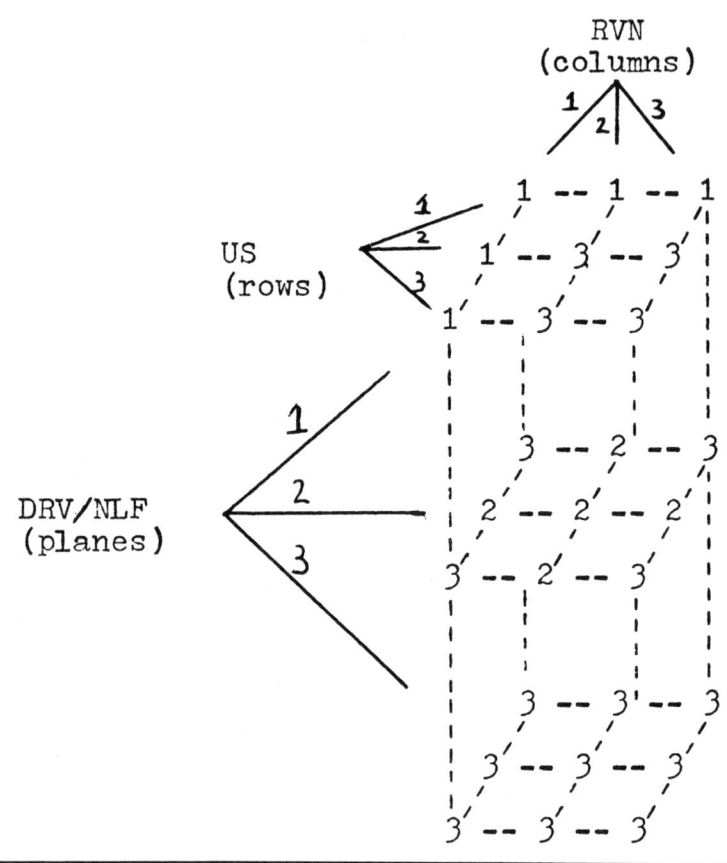

Figure 1: Outcome Matrix for the Paris Peace Talks

the strategy "pursue a_1" is the first plane, the first row, and the first column, respectively, and similarly for the other strategy choices.

The possible outcomes of this game, a_1, a_2, and a_3 are represented in Figure 1 by the numbers 1, 2, and 3 respectively. They are assigned to the outcome matrix by a function defined by the decision rule. For example, if the DRV/NLF chooses its strategy "pursue a_1" (the first plane), the United States chooses its strategy "pursue a_2" (the second row), and the RVN chooses its strategy "pursue a_3" (the third column), there is a three-way split of strategy choices and, as specified by the decision rule, the outcome is a_3, the status quo. Hence, at the intersection of these three strategy choices (the first plane, the second row, and the third column), the outcome a_3 is found. Since each of the three players has three strategy choices, there are 3 x 3 x 3 = 27 possible combinations of choices, and thus 27 different ways in which the final outcome can be reached.

The fact that the only entry in the third plane is a_3 reflects the veto power the DRV/NLF possessed. By playing its strategy "pursue a_3," the communists could, unilaterally, ensure the status quo. By comparison the third strategy choice of the row player (the United States) or the column player (the RVN) contains entries other than a_3. All three outcomes are possible if either the United States or the RVN chooses its third strategy—depending, of course, on the actions of the other players.

What strategy should each player select to ensure the best possible outcome for himself? The answer to this question depends on his knowledge of the rules of the game and of the other players' preferences. Let us say that a player possesses *complete information* if he is fully informed about both the rules of the game and the preferences of the other players; otherwise, he possesses *incomplete information*.

If information is complete, a *sophisticated* strategy is a player's rational strategy, given that all the players choose sophisticatedly (Farquharson, 1969). A sophisticated strategy is arrived at by the successive elimination of dominated strategies by each of the players.[1] A strategy is *dominated* when there is another strategy available to a player which produces at least as good a result in every contingency and a better result in one or more contingencies. If one strategy dominates all the other strategies of a player, we say that it is *straightforward.*

It is not difficult to show why the configuration of preferences indicated above and the use of sophisticated strategies by the players would lead to the adoption of a_3, the status quo, as the outcome of this game. If we refer to the Figure 1 outcome matrix, it can be seen that the first strategy of the United States, the second strategy of the DRV/NLF, and the third strategy of the RVN are straightforward, that is, no matter what combination of strategy choices are chosen by the other two players, each player could do no worse, and could possibly do better, by selecting these strategies.

Since straightforward strategies are unconditionally best, it can be assumed safely that a player possessing one will use it. And because the use of these straightforward strategies produces a three-way split of

[1]. For a detailed discussion of sophisticated strategies and outcomes, see Farquharson (1969) and Brams (1975; ch. 2).

strategy choices, the sophisticated outcome of this game,[2] found at the intersection of the first row, the second plane, and the third column, is a_3.

THE DYNAMICS OF PLAY

The first game of the Paris Talks lasted from the inception of the private talks in 1968 to the winter of 1971-1972. For three-and-a-half years the Talks remained stalemated, few compromises were made, and the fighting continued. For three-and-a-half years, each of the players played the sophisticated strategies indicated above. The United States sought a two-track solution while continuously signaling that it would prolong the war rather than accept a simultaneous military and political settlement. The DRV/NLF pressed for a one-track solution and resisted the American offers by fighting while negotiating. Finally, the RVN did everything it could to ensure that the political process in the south remained closed. By frustrating the operation of an open- political system, the RVN helped to perpetuate the war.

A few days after Richard Nixon was inaugurated in 1969, his administration proposed the two-track approach to the communists. Nixon was optimistic about a favorable reaction to this proposal which he felt offered the communists an important concession. Previously, President Johnson had pledged to withdraw American troops six months after "the other side withdraws its forces to the North, ceases infiltration and the level of violence subsides" (New York *Times*, Oct. 26, 1966: 20). Now, Nixon proposed a simultaneous withdrawal.

To make Hanoi more amenable to his proposal, Nixon decided to urge the Soviet Union to pressure the DRV/NLF to accept the new American offer. By refusing to cooperate with the Soviets at the SALT Talks and by threatening to escalate the conflict unless the DRV/NLF cooperated in Paris, Nixon felt that he could induce the DRV/NLF to accept peace on his terms. The threat of escalation, coupled with the new peace initiative, could hardly have made the message received

2. Technically, the assumption of complete information is not needed to arrive at the sophisticated outcome of this particular game since players with a straightforward strategy need to be aware of only their own preferences in order to calculate their sophisticated strategy. However, since this assumption, and an important modification of it discussed below, is necessary to the analysis of the second Paris game, I have made it throughout this essay. Because of the numerous contacts the players had with each other and the extensive world-wide media coverage of the negotiations, the assumption of complete information is not unrealistic in this game.

by the DRV/NLF clearer: although the United States would prefer a two-track settlement, a_1, it was willing and able to continue fighting, a_3, rather than negotiate on Hanoi's terms, a_2.

While the United States was indicating its preference order to be (a_1, a_3, a_2), the RVN assiduously resisted efforts to open up the political process. The Americans were eager to assuage congressional and domestic criticism and for Thieu to present a plan for elections. In addition, Nixon believed that the communists would only accept the two-track proposal if they felt that they would not be denied access to national-political power. Thieu's plan for elections, however, was designed to ensure that he would retain control of the political process. He proposed an electoral committee to observe the counting of ballots and an international organization to observe the elections. However, "the committee envisioned by Thieu clearly would have no power, and the election would still be carried out by the Thieu regime" (Porter, 1975: 84-85). Thus, by closing the door to any meaningful communist participation, the RVN was able to frustrate a settlement. Its strategy was consistent with its preference order (a_3, a_1, a_2).

The communist announcement of (a_2, a_3, a_1) was just as clear as the announcements of the United States and the RVN. While agreeing to negotiate in Paris, they launched a large-scale offensive in February, and in May the NLF issued a ten-point program calling for a coalition government.

By the fall of 1969, then, each of the players had succeeded in communicating its preferences to the others. It is hardly surprising that Nixon's national-security advisor, Henry Kissinger, was "suddenly pessimistic about the prospect of ending the war on 'honorable' terms" (Kalb and Kalb, 1974: 164). To break this deadlock, Kissinger and Le Duc Tho, a member of the DRV politburo, met secretly on four occasions early in 1970. However, the talks were fruitless because "the two sides were totally opposed to one another on the basic issues of war and peace" (Kalb and Kalb, 1974: 176).

After the invasion of Cambodia in April 1970, the next important peace initiative came in September when the United States indicated that it would accept a cease-fire in place as a prior condition for a settlement. The implications of the so-called leopard-spots solution was that the United States would recognize communist power in local communities while the DRV would allow Saigon to retain formal sovereignty over all of the south. The communists rejected the American offer even though the new proposal included a concrete offer to withdraw all American troops. They still insisted on a simultaneous political and military solution. As a result, 1970 ended as had 1969, with the war stalemated and hopes of a settlement dim.

The spring of 1971 saw renewed American optimism. At the end of May, Kissinger presented another proposal to Le Duc Tho. Although Tho rejected it and insisted "that any proposal that did not include political elements could not be negotiated" (Kalb and Kalb, 1974: 209), he countered with a nine-point proposal in which Kissinger saw the outlines of a settlement that he could accept as a basis for negotiations.

In August, Kissinger proposed an eight-point plan mirroring Hanoi's plan and pledging American neutrality in the elections scheduled in the south in October. However, while Hanoi was digesting the proposal, the two main-opposition candidates in the race were eliminated, making the American pledge academic. Thus, the eight-point program was summarily turned down by Hanoi and 1971 ended, as had the three previous years, in a stalemate.

A careful analysis of all these proposals indicates that all three players were again playing sophisticatedly. Porter (1975: 91) has noted that the American plan "was carefully conceived, like its predecessors, to yield nothing of substance." He argued that the proposal left the United States free to put a date on withdrawals after a cease-fire had been negotiated, thus in effect proposing a military solution followed by a political settlement.

In turn, the DRV/NLF rejected these proposals because the important political issues would no longer be negotiable once an agreement was signed, especially since a cease-fire was not "so much a step toward a final settlement as a form of it" (Kissinger, 1969: 227). Also, by frustrating the participation of even the non-communist or neutralist element in the national elections, Thieu demonstrated his desire to maintain the status quo rather than bring about a settlement, even one advantageous to him.

It is not surprising, then, that the outcome of this game was a continuation of the war. As long as each participant ranked the alternatives as it did and selected its sophisticated strategies, the outcome was bound to be a_3. However, in early 1972, a rapid-fire series of events occurred that precipitated a structural alteration in the game. As will be shown in the next section, these events allowed the game to be settled—at least temporarily—in a nonviolent way.

PARIS: 1972-1973

Like the previous game, the second game of the Paris Peace Talks was ushered in by a major communist offensive. On March 31, 1972, four full communist divisions crossed the Demilitarized Zone and a day later communist troops in Cambodia made a concerted move toward the city of An Loc. Within a month, the provincial capital of Quangtri fell. An American offer on May 2 to withdraw in four months in return for a cease-fire was rejected by the DRV/NLF, who hoped to force the United States to help overthrow Thieu. Hence, on May 8, in a final effort to halt an impending attack against Saigon, Nixon ordered the mining of Haiphong Harbor and round-the-clock B52 sorties against both Hanoi and Haiphong. As a result, the supply lines of the DRV/NLF were cut, the expected attack on Saigon was averted, and the communist offensive fizzled out. As will be seen, however, the importance of the spring offensive was not military; rather, its importance lies in the fact that it altered the preference order of the DRV/NLF.

When Nixon ordered the mining of Haiphong, he was aware that his actions could hurt his chances for reelection later that year. Within two weeks of the day he made this decision, he was scheduled to go to Moscow for a summit meeting with the top Soviet officials. If the American escalation was to force the Soviets to cancel the summit, Nixon's record in foreign affairs might suddenly be vulnerable. Coupled with the expected domestic protest to the escalation of the war, the probability of his reelection might be lowered considerably. Surprisingly, however, the expected domestic uproar never materialized and the Soviets did not call off the summit meeting. For the time being, Nixon's gamble appeared to be paying off.

Because they were now committed to a policy of détente with the United States, the Soviet leaders were eager to cooperate with Nixon on Vietnam. When Nixon was in Moscow in May, Soviet party boss Leonid Brezhnev indicated to Nixon that it would be in the interests of both nations to terminate the war in Vietnam (Kalb and Kalb, 1974: 376-377). A few weeks later, Soviet President Nikolai Podgorny traveled to Hanoi for talks with the North Vietnamese. Podgorny told them to be more flexible in their negotiations. His message to Hanoi was clear: Moscow wants to see a settlement in Paris soon (Kalb and Kalb, 1974: 382-383). While Podgorny was in Hanoi, Kissinger journeyed to Peking where he was greeted by the Chinese Premier Chou

En-lai. It has been reported that Chou told Kissinger that the Chinese fear of a Soviet military buildup along their border caused them to place good relations with the United States ahead of their commitment to Hanoi (Kalb and Kalb, 1974: 383).

As a result of eroding Soviet and Chinese support and because of Nixon's new found ability to continue fighting and even to escalate the conflict, the communists now came to feel that it would be to their advantage to end the war. Because they now preferred to reach a settlement, even one which included recognizing the legitimacy of the RVN and the power of its president, Nguyen Van Thieu, to a continuation of the war, the new communist-preference order was (a_2, a_1, a_3). Whereas previously they had ranked the alternatives (a_2, a_3, a_1), they now reversed the ranking of the latter two alternatives preferring a_1 to a_3.

THE IMPLICATIONS OF THE NEW COMMUNIST-PREFERENCE ORDER

The new communist-preference order, which would soon be reflected in a series of new proposals at Paris, completely altered the nature of the game. If the other two players ranked the alternatives as before, the sophisticated outcome of the new game would be a_1. (The outcome under the previous configuration was a_3.) This change is easily seen by referring to the outcome matrix (Figure 1). As before, both the United States and the RVN have straightforward strategies. The unconditionally best strategy for the United States is "pursue a_1," while "pursue a_3" is best for the RVN. But now, in contrast to the first game, the DRV/NLF does not have an unconditionally best-strategy choice.

If complete information is assumed, then each player is able to determine which players in the game have a straightforward strategy. Since a player with a straightforward strategy will always do best by playing it, one can assume that both the United States and the RVN would not play either of their two dominated strategies. Therefore, these strategies can be eliminated from further consideration.[3]

After eliminating these strategies, one can reduce Figure 1 to the outcome matrix shown in Figure 2. Since both the United States and the RVN have straightforward strategies, only the DRV/NLF has more

---

3. In this analysis, it is assumed that a player with a straightforward strategy adopts that strategy immediately. This simplification in Farquharson's (1969) reduction method is suggested by Brams (1975: 67-78).

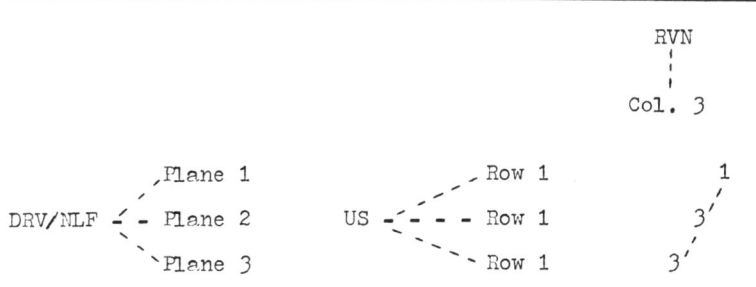

Figure 2: Reduced Outcome Matrix for the Paris Peace Talks Game of 1972-1973 Given Stable US Preferences

than one strategy choice left. The outcome associated with its first strategy choice, a_1, is clearly preferred to the outcome associated with either its second or third strategy, a_3. Thus, the communists' rational choice is to "pursue a_1," and the outcome of this game is a_1.

AMERICAN PREFERENCES: TWO INTERPRETATIONS

One might ask at this point whether or not the preferences of the United States and the RVN remained unchanged during this period. Later, it will be shown that the RVN's preferences remained the same until the final days of the negotiations and that this preference shift did not have an effect on the final outcome of the game. The American case, however, is more complex, and because of the lack of conclusive evidence, two interpretations of American actions during the closing months of the Paris Talks will be offered.

There is no good reason to believe that the American preference for the two-track alternative, a_1, changed after the spring offensive of 1972. The question seems to be whether the United States now preferred to leave Vietnam after concluding an agreement on communist terms, a_2, to the status quo, a_3, or continued to prefer a_3 to a_2. Throughout the final year of negotiations, Nixon seemed willing to withdraw from Vietnam, even on communist terms, before the presidential election in November. As has been noted, after the fall of Quangtri in May, the United States offered the communists very generous terms for ending the war. Of this proposal, the Kalb brothers (1974: 340) concluded that "Nixon wanted to get out of Vietnam so badly that all he was asking of Hanoi was an exit visa."

When Kissinger met Brezhnev in Moscow in May, the Soviet leader speculated that Hanoi would probably emerge victorious from the political struggle that was certain to follow a settlement. It has been reported that Kissinger did not try to change Brezhnev's expectations (Kalb and Kalb, 1974: 377), a possible sin of ommission by Kissinger, but also possibly an indicator of a true American-preference shift. If this shift were real, and if it were known to the other players, it would have important repercussions on the outcome of the game. If this possible shift in American preferences is accepted for a moment, the following configuration of players and preferences arises:

(1) DRV/NLF: (a_2, a_1, a_3)
(2) United States: (a_1, a_2, a_3)
(3) RVN: (a_3, a_1, a_2).

Given these rankings, only one player, the RVN, has a straightforward strategy. Assuming that the RVN adopts its straighforward stategy, "pursue a_3," the reduced outcome matrix is as shown in Figure 3.

From Figure 3, one can see that the third strategy of both the United States and the DRV/NLF ("pursue a_3") is dominated. If these strategies are eliminated from consideration, Figure 3 can be further reduced to Figure 4. (Both figures assume the new set of American preferences.) It should be noted that Figure 4 cannot be reduced any further. Neither of the two remaining strategies of the DRV/NLF or of the United States dominates each other. Thus, unlike previous examples in which the successive elimination of dominated strategies results in one outcome, this game admits more than one sophisticated outcome. Hence, the outcome of this game is *indeterminate.*

In summary, then, given the shift in DRV/NLF preferences discussed above, the outcome of the second Paris game was shown to be a_1, the two-track solution, the alternative most preferred by the United States. However, if American preferences shifted along with the communists', with a_2 second and a_3 third, the second Paris game was shown to be indeterminate.

If one assumes a player would prefer his first choice with certainty to taking a chance on a less-preferred outcome resulting, it is obvious that the United States would prefer the determinate outcome, a_1, to an indeterminate solution. Assuming the shift in American preferences, is there anything the United States could do to rectify its strategically unfavorable position? If information is complete, the answer is no. Sophisticated strategies are optimal given complete information: they

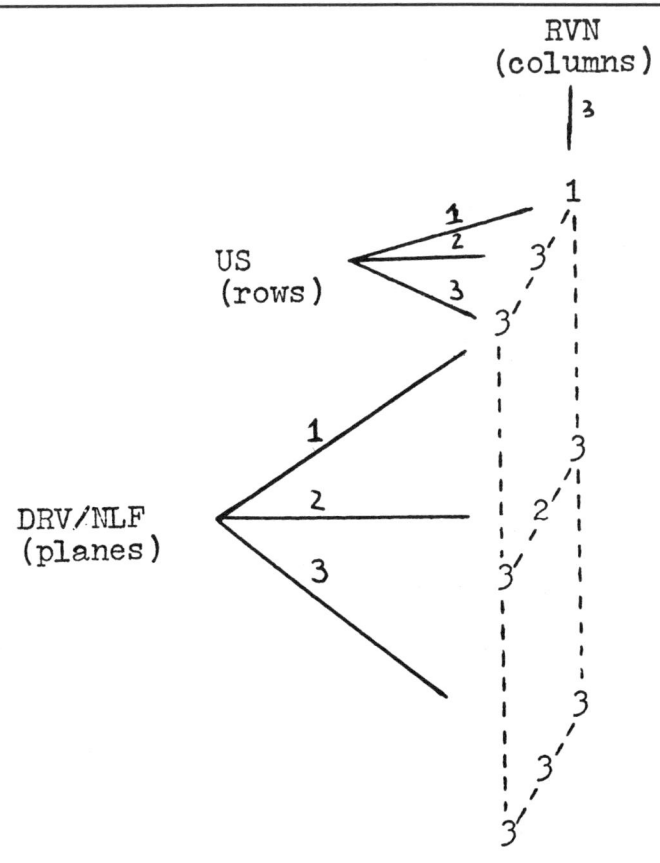

Figure 3: First Reduction of the Paris Game of 1972-1973 Given a Shift in US Preferences

cannot be improved upon if the other players are sophisticated. However, if the United States could conceal its new preference order from the other players, announce its preferences to be (a_1, a_3, a_2), and act *consistently* with this announcement, it could deceive the other players. Since this type of deception is not detectable unless the other players know the true preference order of the deceiver, it is called *tacit deception* (Brams and Zagare, 1977).

By announcing (a_1, a_3, a_2) as its preference order and by tacitly deceiving the other players, the United States could map the indeterminate game into the determinate game. Because the United States prefers the outcome in the determinate game, it would be rational for

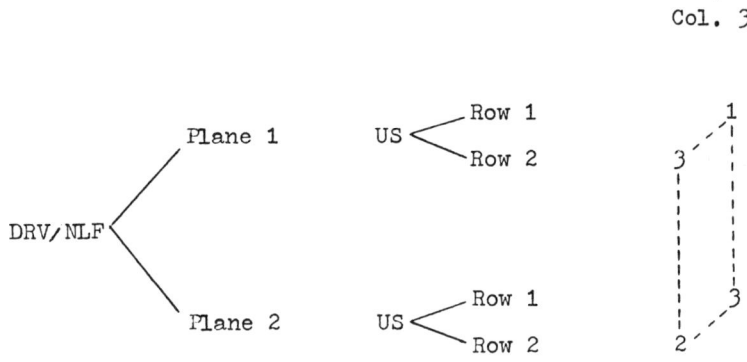

Figure 4: Second Reduction of the Paris Game of 1972-1973 Given a Shift in US Preferences

the United States to announce this false preference order and tacitly deceive the DRV/NLF and the RVN.

Without resolving the question of which set of preferences best reflected the (true) U.S. preferences, we are left with two alternate scenarios:

(1) The true American preference order was (a_1, a_3, a_2). In this case, the outcome of the game is the first choice of the United States, a_1.

(2) The true American preference order was (a_1, a_2, a_3). Given this ranking, the outcome of the game is indeterminate. However, this game is vulnerable to tacit deception. A false announcement of (a_1, a_3, a_2) by the United States would map this game into the one described above and induce the first choice of the United States as the outcome of the game.

In either case, it can be seen that it would be rational for the United States to announce (a_1, a_3, a_2) as its preference order.

After briefly discussing the implications of a shift in the RVN's preferences at the end of the negotiations, it will be shown that after the shift in the DRV/NLF's preference order, the announcements of the communists correspond to the new rankings assigned to them and that RVN behavior also reflected their assigned preference orders. In addition, because the United States announced (a_1, a_3, a_2) as its preference order, its most-preferred alternative, a_1, was the outcome of the game.

THE CONSEQUENCES OF A SHIFT
IN THE RVN PREFERENCE ORDER

Earlier it was noted that the RVN's preferences remained stable until the final days of the negotiations when they changed from (a_3, a_1, a_2) to (a_1, a_3, a_2). As will be seen below, this shift was induced by large United States shipments of military supplies to the RVN and massive bombings of the north by the Americans in December 1972. Although this shift changed the RVN's optimal strategy from "pursue a_3" to "pursue a_1," it had no effect on the outcome of the game since the sophisticated outcome of the second game, a_1, is an equilibrium outcome and not vulnerable to strategic calculations (see Brams, 1975: 63-67). What changes, though, is the point of agreement. Without the shift in the RVN preference order, the sophisticated outcome is found at the intersection of the first plane, the first row, and the third column. With the shift, a_1 is obtained at the intersection of the first plane, the first row, and the first column (see Figure 1).

THE DYNAMICS OF PLAY

Soon after the Moscow summit meetings, a change in the DRV/NLF's attitude became apparent. As early as August, Kissinger is reported to have sensed a softening of their position, and by September, the DRV/NLF had proposed a new peace plan which, for the first time, did not include a specific demand for Thieu's removal and which implicitly recognized the legitimacy of the regime in the south. Meanwhile, Kissinger met with Thieu and reassured him "of the firmness of Nixon's resolve on Vietnam" (Kalb and Kalb, 1974: 389). A month later, he told Le Duc Tho that the United States would not sign any agreement that would result in Thieu's removal.

The big breakthough came on October 8 when Le Duc Tho proposed a plan in which the two-track solution was accepted for the first time by the communists. This proposal called for a cease-fire, the release of all captured and detained personnel, the creation of a "National Council of Reconciliation and Concord." More significantly, it did not call for either Thieu to resign or for the parties to form a coalition government. Almost immediately, Kissinger acccepted the DRV/NLF's draft as a basis for negotiations, and within three days both sides had reached an agreement and had even devised a timetable to implement their pact. All that remained was to get Thieu to acquiesce and

America's long involvement in Vietnam would be over and the bitter civil was there terminated.

For the United States, getting Thieu's cooperation was important although, strictly speaking, unnecessary. Thieu could threaten to continue fighting without American aid. He would thereby hinder the ability of the United States both to withdraw with some semblance of dignity and also to obtain the release of its POWs. In addition, if the agreement were forced on Thieu, other allies might begin to question the sincerity of American commitments elsewhere.

Thieu's agreement proved more difficult to obtain than the United States had anticipated. Thieu felt that he had not been informed about the imminence of a settlement and that he was now being presented with a fait accompli. He not only refused to sign the agreement but also presented Kissinger with a list of 26 changes he wanted made in the draft. Because of Thieu's demands, the timetable for implementing the agreements was altered. Kissinger cabled Hanoi and indicated that another negotiating session was necessary.

The communists thought Nixon was stalling until after the election, at which time he would, theoretically, have more leverage to impose a less favorable solution on them. In an obvious attempt to force Nixon's hand before the election, the communists revealed the terms of their latest proposal and the details of the secret meetings preceding it. Kissinger moved quickly to reassure the American public that "peace is at hand," but the Paris Talks did not resume again until November 20, well after the election.

One of the reasons why the October agreement was not consummated was that both the communists and the RVN were uncertain about American preferences. Thieu felt that he was being betrayed and that once the American troops were withdrawn, Nixon would forget him. The DRV's interpretation of Nixon's intentions only served to reinforce Thieu's paranoia. While Kissinger was in Saigon conferring with Thieu, *Newsweek* (Oct. 30, 1972) published an interview with DRV Prime Minister Pham Van Dong in which Dong suggested that after a cease-fire had been arranged, a coalition government would be established.

After the October agreement fell through, Nixon and Kissinger spent most of their time trying to convince both the communists and the RVN that their preference order was (a_1, a_3, a_2). In November, Thieu was given a year's supply of military hardware while Nixon privately assured him that the United States would intervene if the communists launched a full-scale offensive. And when the Talks were stalled again in early December, Nixon resumed massive air attacks against the north. The bombing was meant as a signal to both Vietnamese actors. As Zartman (1976: 391) has noted, "Washington decided to bomb Hanoi until Hanoi and Saigon gave in."

The on again, off again Talks began again on January 8, 1973, and progressed rather swiftly after that. Nixon had succeeded in making his intentions clear to both sides: he had threatened to cut off aid if the RVN did not acquiesce, and Thieu capitulated;[4] he had threatened to continue bombing if Hanoi did not agree to the two-track solution, and Hanoi capitulated.

By January 13 the players had reached an agreement. The accord was signed on January 23 and implemented four days later. The important provisions of the agreement called for:

(1) A cease-fire in place.
(2) The release of all military POWs. (The release of political prisoners in the south was left to future negotiations between Saigon and the NLF.)
(3) The creation of a National Council of Reconciliation and Concord which, as *Time* (Feb. 5, 1973: 13) noted, would leave "the entire political future of South Viet Nam up to negotiations between the Saigon government and its Communist rivals."

In short, the agreement corresponded pretty closely to the original American proposal of January 1969. The tragedy of Vietnam is that it took over four years to work it out.

SUMMARY AND CONCLUSION

This article has analyzed two games played at the Paris Peace Talks of 1968-1973. In both games, the principal players were the United States, the Republic of Vietnam, and a coalition of the Democratic Republic of Vietnam and its military arm in the south, the National Liberation Front.

The first game, which lasted from the start of the Talks until the winter of 1971-1972, was shown to have lasted so long because the structural coincidence of the preferences of the players and their game-theoretically defined best (sophisticated) strategies locked the players into a hopeless stalemate that was not resolved until the structure was changed and a new game started. An American rapprochement with the

4. It was at this point that the RVN preference order shifted.

Soviets and Chinese early in 1972 provided the needed change. As a result, the preference order of the communist Vietnamese was altered, and the second Paris game precipitated.

Because information about American preferences is inconclusive, two interpretations of the second game were made. Under the first interpretation, the two-track solution, the most preferred alternative of the United States, was shown to have resulted from a shift in the communists' preference order. Under the second, this game was shown to be vulnerable to a deceptive strategy by the United States. Only by falsely communicating its willingness to continue fighting could the United States ensure its most-preferred outcome. Under either interpretation, the optimal strategy by the United States entailed announcing that it would prefer to prolong the war rather than capitulate to the communists. This was shown to have occurred.

In addition to providing a framework for analyzing these two games, I believe that this chapter illustrates some of the advantages of a game-theoretic approach for the study of negotiations. For one thing, this approach allows us to specify *precisely* the configuration of preferences that lead to a stalemate or to a negotiated settlement. For another, it allows us to identify those circumstances that provide an actor with an incentive to take actions that contradict his true or announced preference order. (For a complete listing of games vulnerable to a deceptive strategy, see Zagare, 1977.)

It should also be noted that this chapter serves an additional function. By assigning empirical content to some key game-theoretic concepts, Farquharson's (1969) model of strategic voting, as extended by Brams and Zagare (1977), is operationalized and tested. To the extent that the findings of this study mirror the real world, the theoretical results contained in those works are supported.

In conclusion, I hope that I have illustrated the usefulness of game theory as an explanatory tool and as an instrument for retrodicting historical events. It has not often been used for this purpose,[5] but the Paris Peace Talks seem to demonstrate that the study of international relations and diplomatic history can benefit from the insights it offers.

Frank C. Zagare is Adjunct Assistant Professor of Political Science, The Cooper Union, and Research Associate in the Department of Economics, New York University. An article by the author has appeared in Social Science Research. *He is currently doing research on the relationship of power to game theory.*

5. For one example, see Brams and Muzzio (1977).

7. Tactical Advantages of Opening Positioning Strategies

LESSONS FROM THE SEABED ARMS CONTROL TALKS 1967-1970

BENNETT RAMBERG
Center for Arms Control and International Security
University of California, Los Angeles

This study assesses Soviet and American positioning strategy during the negotiation of the 1971 treaty banning nuclear weapons and other weapons of mass destruction from the seabed. It finds the superpowers employed both maximalist and equitable postures in the initial draft treaties they submitted. Evidence suggests that the negotiation would have been concluded more expeditiously, the outcome being the same, had the United States and the Soviet Union at the outset adopted equitable positioning strategies on the three focal points of the negotiation—the comprehensiveness of the prohibition, its geography, and verification—rather than opting for preferences commonly recognized as anathema to the other.

Among the first problems states entering negotiation resolve is their respective stands on the issues before them. Taking a stand is not simply

---

AUTHOR'S NOTE: The author is grateful to Dr. Seyom Brown and Professor Robert Osgood for critical comments of an early version of this manuscript. Thanks also goes to *Journal of Conflict Resolution* referees. The paper was researched at facilities provided by The Johns Hopkins University School of Advanced International Studies, the Stanford University Arms Control Program and Princeton University's Center of International Studies.

an expression of interests. Rather, tactical considerations come into play as well. This study explains and assesses Soviet and American positioning strategy during the negotiation of the 1971 Treaty on the Prohibition of the Emplacement of Nuclear Weapons and Other Weapons of Mass Destruction on the Sea-Bed and the Ocean Floor and in the Subsoil Thereof with a view toward advancing some general hypotheses about positioning strategy within the obvious limits of a case study.

POSITIONING STRATEGY:
A REVIEW OF THE LITERATURE

Literature bearing on negotiation suggests that a conferee has the option to avail itself of one of three positioning strategies: maximalist, equitable, or integrative.[1] The *maximalist* strategy entails a party asking from its adversary more than it feels it is likely to attain. *Equitable*-positioning involves the participant taking a stand it feels is fair to all concerned. The conferee that takes an *integrative* approach presents its colleagues with multiple alternatives from which they may choose one to negotiate. Characteristically, all three strategies will contain some degree of flexibility for bargaining purposes. Whether positions are expressed formally or informally may have tactical import. *Formal*-positioning involves a conferee's explicit association with a particular draft treaty or a working paper. *Informal*-positioning is an oral statement of preference not associated with any particular formal declaration.

The literature on negotiation contains a number of assessments of the utility of the three major types of positioning strategy. A review of the treatment of each will assist in our explanation and assessment of what took place in the seabed negotiation.

MAXIMALIST-POSITIONING

Students of negotiation who tend to look favorably upon maximalist-positioning present a number of rationales in support of their

1. The term integrative is derived from Richard Walton's and Robert McKersie's (1965: 5, 144-183) reference "to the system of activities which is instrumental to the attainment of objectives which are not in fundamental conflict with those of the other party and which therefore can be integrated to some degree," i.e., what game theorists call a non-zero-sum game.

preference. They often start from the assumption that the initial stands taken by most are not immutable. Rather than viewed as final statements of expectations, they should be regarded principally as information-seeking devices. In the words of one study,

> Our estimate of the opponent's minimum disposition is often very uncertain. We cannot find out whether we were wrong to our disadvantage unless we put forward what we think is a Sham Bargaining Position. In other words, if we try, we might discover that our opponent accepts more than we thought he would [Iklé and Leites, 1962: 26].

Beyond attaining information, sham bargaining may modify an opponent's minimum preferences in a desirable direction by making "him believe or feel that he would prefer an agreement to no agreement on terms more favorable to me than he originally thought" (Iklé and Leites, 1962: 26). It also provides something to give up or swap; it acts as a bargaining chip. Iklé and Leites (1962: 26-27) have observed:

> Given the fact we are to some extent constrained by Negotiation Mores according to which it is bad to stand pat and concessions ought to be met by concessions, Sham Bargaining Positions permit us to show "flexibility" or to make "concessesions" without seriously jeopardizing our Minimum Disposition.

Lastly, asking for more than one expects to attain makes it difficult for an opponent to estimate one's minimum preferences. In the words of an American labor conciliator,

> In skillful hands the bargaining position performs a double function. It conceals and it reveals. The bargaining position is used to indicate—to unfold gradually step by step—the maximum expectation of the negotiator while at the same time concealing for as long as necessary his minimum expectation (Edward Peters quoted in Stevens, 1963: 62).

Does sham bargaining give a party license to take positions that even the party would not find acceptable if implemented? Certainly it would seem to, if the objective for entering the talks is primarily for purposes of propaganda. But what if the intention is primarily to achieve agreement? At least some political scientists would assert that the advocacy of unacceptable demands is appropriate in this circumstance. Henry Kissinger, (1961: 205) while an academic, argued:

> If agreement is usually found between two starting points, there is no point in making moderate offers. Good bargaining technique would suggest a point of

departure far more extreme than what one is willing to accept. The more outrageous the initial proposition the better is the prospect that what one "really" wants will be considered a compromise.

Kissinger's observations appear to have some empirical foundation. Sawyer and Guetzkow (1965: 482), in their broad study of negotiation, suggest this point in their summary of a small-group experiment conducted by two psychologists:

> Psychological experimentation has explored the related concept of "level of aspiration," which may be a factor in determining initial minimum disposition and rate of concession from the initial position. Siegel and Fouraker operationalized this concept by telling one member of a bargaining pair that if he achieved $6.10 he could participate in the second part, in which he would have a chance to double his winnings; the other subject was told the same, but the amount specified was $2.10. In an otherwise symmetrical situation, the former group averaged $6.25, the latter $3.25. On the basis of the empirical and rational analysis Siegel and Fouraker suggest that ". . . .the bargainer who (1) opens negotiation with a high request, (2) has a small rate of concession, (3) has a high minimum level of expectation and (4) is very perceptive and quite unyielding, will fare better than his opponent who provides the base upon which these relative evaluations were made."

Other evidence supporting this proposition can be found in some treatises of arms control negotiation. A member of the American Strategic Arms Limitation Talks (SALT) delegation, William Van Cleave, has argued (U.S. Congress, 1972: 202) that the Soviets successfully employed "nonnegotiable" positions in modifying American preferences during the first round of those talks.

> The Soviet approach included positions that the Soviets must have expected to be nonnegotiable. These extreme positions could then be used to cause change in the United States position or they could be removed at any time as major concessions. The Soviets may have been surprised at the way some of these "non-negotiable" positions (for example FBS [forward base systems] and NCA [National Command Authority] defense) eventually became negotiable but quite possibly they thoroughly anticipated it.

Ikle'(1970: 9) has been so impressed by the Soviet employment of the maximalist-positioning that he has recommended that it become a part of standard American posturing tactics:

> All too frequently the positions of the communist powers are viewed as immutable. During the formulation of the United States' negotiating position within the State

Department and in interagency discussion in Washington, it happens often that a possible American proposal or a Western demand is voted down as being "unacceptable" to the opponent. Our negotiators and policy planners in fact make them so. Since the positions of Communist governments, much as our own tend to change only gradually under the influence of negotiation our abstaining from "unacceptable demands" denies us a possibility of modifying a communist position.

EQUITABLE-POSITIONING

The equitable school of thought contends that the negotiator ought to take a stand at the outset that he feels reasonably confident is fair to all sides (Bartos, 1977). The approach need not exclude bargaining room, i.e., allowance for concession or reformulation. Leeway can be provided through ambiguity. Undertaking a negotiation in this manner is the most judicious as well as expeditious mode of conflict resolution.

This contention challenges the utility of maximalist bargaining by arguing that the potential gain the strategy offers will tend to be overshadowed by likely costs. The most serious is deadlock. Ikle'(1964: 207) observed this danger:

> Of course if both sides use this [maximalist] tactic its effect may well cancel out. Your opponent will not accept your proposal as long as he thinks that it is only a "bargaining position:" in fact, he may not even make concession from his "bargaining position" until you have lowered yours.

Concomitant with deadlock is time loss. John Cross (1969: 47) argues,

> Whenever a party increases his demand, he increases the payoff which he expects to receive at the time of settlement but he also delays the date of that settlement by the amount of time determined by his opponent's rate of concession.

Maximalists argue that demanding sham positions have merit, notwithstanding the time spent, "when the utility increase is exactly offset by the time delay which results from "a marginal increase in demand" (Cross, 1969: 47). From the equitable perspective, this equation is not likely to be satisfied, particularly when a party is reasonably certain that it will be unable to induce its opponent to modify its position. In this circumstance the time loss associated with maximalist-positioning will not be compensated. When the maximalist position a conferee adopts reflects a difference of interest between himself and his opponent, this cost is unavoidable. However, when an alternative posture that is likely to move a target party or satisfy its objective is available, proponents of equitable positioning contend that their positioning outlook should govern a state's initial-bargaining strategy rather than that of the maximalist's. Dean Rusk (U.S. Arms Control, 1962: 107) for example, has asserted that it should not be American policy to put forward proposals solely for their propaganda value or to propose settlements in expectation of refusal from the other side. He contends that doing so would not be consistent with American interests. In arms control, the time costs of sham bargaining translate into lost opportunites to restrain new forms of technology and strategic competition which complicate the diplomatic effort.

INTEGRATIVE POSITIONING

A third school of thought on the question of positioning is the integrative. It perceives conflict resolution most easily achieved through the presentation of alternatives designed to quickly uncover interests that can form the basis for the resolution of a problem. According to Walton and McKersie (1965: 138) the strategy

> assumes that alternative courses of action (potential solutions) are not immediately apparent but rather have to be discovered or invented. It also assumes that the full consequences of a course of action are ... not obvious; instead they have to be inferred from an analysis of the facts available....[The undertaking] involves thorough and accurate gathering of information about alternatives and their consequences. The parties attempt to be imaginative in perceiving alternatives and persistent in exploring the fullest range of alternative solutions. Invention and creativity are essential in order for appropriate arrangements to be developed for coping with the problems.

Accounts of SALT prove instructive in evaluating this approach.

During the American preparation for SALT, Kissinger and his staff put together a series of position papers that the United States ultimately presented to the Soviets in tandem in an effort to find common interests that could be resolved. In a review of this process which appears to have applicability to integrative-positioning generally, Alton Frye (1974: 82-84) assesses both its pluses and minuses. He argues that SALT suggests that the greatest recommendation of the strategy lay in the fact that it focused "upon identifiable areas of mutual concern that would seem to maximize the probability of agreement" (1974: 84). On the other hand, he criticizes the process for leaving the choice of issues to be resolved to the discretion of the adversary. During SALT, the United States placed itself in a position of leaving the determination of the agenda largely up to the Soviets. The consequence of this, Frye concludes (1974: 84) was to produce a negotiation and agreement on issues that represented the lowest common denominator of mutual interests which in turn precluded the talks from seriously tackling more difficult and more significant questions such as the control or prohibition of multiple independently targeted reentry vehicles (MIRV). The ultimate consequence of this failure was to allow MIRV development in both countries to proceed unabated, and perhaps to lose the opportunity to assert control over it. Frye's remarks thus imply that integrative strategy is not always propitious for attaining the resolution of difficult questions nor for maximizing a party's interests.

POSITIONING DURING THE SEABED NEGOTIATION

The driving force behind seabed arms control was Arvid Pardo, Malta's Ambassador to the United Nations. On November 1, 1967, Pardo delivered an address to the UN First Committee in which he expressed his fears that orderly development of the ocean floor would not be achieved unless military exploitation was stemmed (U.S. Arms Control Agency, 1968: 548). Reports circulating at the time, that the superpowers were contemplating emplacement of strategic nuclear-weapons systems on the seabed underscored Pardo's apprehensions (Panel on Oceanography, 1966: 33; Martin, 1967: 33-34; Pardo, 1974).

Seabed arms control required the resolution of three central issues: scope of the prohibition, its geographic breadth, and verification. Resolution of these problems in turn required the reconciliation of a number of diverse interests.

The scope of the prohibition was in one respect the least difficult to resolve: the interests of only two states, the United States and the Soviet Union, required reconciliation. Only they maintained a direct strategic stake in the extensiveness of seabed militarization. (Presumably, military allies of both had an indirect interest in the resolution of the problem as it bore on the military capability of their alliance leaders.) The United States, reflecting a deep concern over Soviet submarine capabilities, was the principal user of the seabed for military purposes, maintaining an elaborate series of sonar arrays in both the Pacific and Atlantic oceans at an estimated cost of $400 million[2] The Soviet Union did not maintain a comparable commitment to track American submarines; its interest lay in diminishing American capability in order to enhance its own freedom of movement underseas. Neither superpower had placed weapons of mass destruction on the ocean floor, although both had considered the idea of placing ICBM's on or under the seabed in the mid 1960s (Panel on Oceanography, 1966: 33; Pardo, 1974). As late as February 1969, the American Joint Chiefs of Staff were interested in keeping the option open (Wenk, 1972: 288-293).

Resolution of the geographic breadth of the prohibition and means to insure compliance were more difficult issues to resolve than was the comprehensiveness of the prohibition. All conferees wanted to insure that an arms-control treaty not establish precedents that would adversely affect their claims to the ocean (United States Department of State, 1974; United Nations, 1958; United Nations, 1960). These ranged from 3 miles to 200 miles reflecting different economic interests in fisheries and continental-shelf mineral resources; defense and navigational considerations; and on the part of some states, a certain amount of jingoism. For example, the United States claimed a three mile territorial sea. The American claim reflected its strategic interest in assuring its fleets maximum area to operate. (Dean, 1958: 610-612; Foss, 1964; 32-36). The Soviets considered a twelve mile territorial limit necessary for coastal defense. (Butler, 1971: 41).

The principal forum of the seabed-arms control negotiation was the Conference of the Committee on Disarmament (CCD). The Committee, convened in 1962 following bilateral Soviet-American discussions in 1961 establishing the multilateral arms-control forum outside the UN framework, was comprised of the superpowers themselves, their military allies, and nonaligned parties. Originally numbering 17 conferees, the Committee was enlarged in 1969 to 25 of which 6 were non-communist allies, seven were communist military allies, and the

---

2. In 1969, the Soviet submarine fleet was comprised of an estimated 320 submarines, 53 carrying approximately three ballistic missiles each and 47 carrying approximately eight antishipping-cruise missiles each. For elaboration of military employment of the seabed, see Institute of Strategic Studies, 1970: 809; Pardo, 1968: 129-130; Stockholm International Peace Research Institute (SIPRI), 1970: 117, 144-145.

remaining were nonaligned.[3] The United States and the Soviet Union acted as cochairmen of the committee. In this capacity, they were responsible for establishing the committee's agenda and the date it would convene its annual sessions.

In August 1968, the United States and the Soviet Union placed on the disarmament committee's agenda an item calling for "prevention of the arms race on the seabed" (Sachs, 1971: 57). In December 1968, the General Assembly passed a resolution calling for the pursuit of efforts to assure the "reservation exclusively for peaceful purposes of the seabed" (United States Arms Control Agency, 1969: 802). The agenda item and the resolution were the culmination of an undertaking which followed Pardo's 1967 remarks in the UN Ad Hoc Committee to Study the Peaceful Uses of the Seabed and the Ocean Floor Beyond the Limits of National Jurisdiction to arrive at a United Nations draft resolution defining the comprehensiveness of seabed-arms control to be codified by the Committee on Disarmament. Its failure to specify the scope of arms control to be sought resulted from the superpowers' inability to reconcile conflicting draft resolutions notwithstanding intensive efforts to do so. The American proposal called for an agreement that "would prevent the use of this environment [the seabed] for the emplacement of *weapons of mass destruction;"* the Soviet draft advocated that the Committee prohibit "the use *for military purposes* of the seabed and the ocean floor beyond the limits of the territorial waters of coastal states" [emphasis added] (Sachs, 1970: 318, 320).

The CCD's 1969 session convened on March 18 at which time the Soviet Union submitted a draft treaty. It declared,

> The use for military purposes of the seabed and the ocean floor and the subsoil thereof beyond the twelve-mile maritime zone of coastal States is prohibited. It is prohibited to place on the sea-bed and the ocean floor and the subsoil thereof objects with nuclear weapons or any other types of weapons of mass destruction and to set up military bases, structures, and other objects of a military nature [United States Arms Control Agency, 1970: 112].

3. Before it was enlarged in 1969 the CCD was named the Conference of the Eighteen Nation Committee on Disarmament (ENDC). The composition of the CCD included the following states: Western bloc—United States, Great Britain, Italy, Canada, Japan, Netherlands (and France, which has never taken its seat); Eastern bloc—Soviet Union, Romania, Czechoslovakia, Poland, Bulgaria, Outer Mongolia, and Hungary; nonaligned bloc—Brazil, Mexico, Burma, India, Ethiopia, Nigeria, United Arab Republic, Sweden, Argentina, Pakistan, Morocco, and Yugoslavia. For a history of the CCD see Burns, 1970.

Verification of the prohibition would be achieved by opening "all installations and structures . . . on the basis of reciprocity to the representatives of Other States Parties to the Treaty" (U.S. Arms Control Agency, 1970: 112).

At the time the Soviets tendered their draft, the United States had yet to achieve an internal consensus as to how it formally intended to position itself on all the central issues. Beyond maintaining a commitment to denuclearization, its response to the Soviet challenge on the issues of breadth and verification was only suggestive. The United States proposed, for example, that several alternative means to resolve the geographic breadth clause could be reviewed. These included a specified horizontal distance from the coastline, a depth limit, or a reference to outer limits of national jurisdiction. The American delegation failed to indicate its preference. As for verification, it called for some appropriate provision to be included in the agreement. It tentatively suggested that procedures "might" be drawn from the precedent of reciprocity, excluding the veto clause, of the outer-space treaty (U.S. Arms Control Agency, 1970: 134-138).

On May 22, 1969, the United States formally set forth its counterpoise to the Soviet submission. It called on signatories "not to emplant or emplace fixed nuclear weapons or other weapons of mass destruction or associated fixed launching platforms on, within or beneath the seabed" beyond a three mile coastal zone (United States Arms Control Agency, 1970: 211-212). To insure observance of the Treaty, the draft declared,

> The Parties to the Treaty shall remain free to observe activities of other States on the seabed and ocean floor, without interfering with such activities or otherwise infringing rights recognized under international law including the freedom of the high seas. In the event that such observation does not in any particular case suffice to eliminate questions regarding fulfillment of the provisions of this Treaty, Parties undertake to consult and to cooperate in endeavoring to resolve the questions [U.S. Arms Control Agency, 1970: 212].

EXPLANATION OF POSITIONING

A summary chart of superpower positions and the theoretic tactical advantages of which they availed themselves is presented herein (Table 1). A comparison uncovers the following: on the issue of the compre-

TABLE 1
Seabed Positioning Strategies

Positions and Advantages	Comprehensiveness		Geography		Verification	
	U.S.	USSR	U.S.	USSR	U.S.	USSR
Maximalist information gathering device may modify opponent's preferences provides something to swap makes difficult for adversary to determine proponent's position		demilitarization	beyond 3 mile limit			installations open on basis of reciprocity
Equitable means of instant conflict resolution minimizes possibility of deadlock reduces time expenditure minimizes opportunity costs minimizes propaganda contest	weapons of mass destruction			beyond 12 mile limit		observation and consultation
Integrative focuses on identifiable areas of mutual concern reduces possibility of deadlock attempts to minimize time expenditure minimizes propaganda contest			informal options: horizontal distance from coast; depth limit; outer limits of national jurisdiction		informal options: some appropriate provision; right of reciprocal access and inspection	

hensiveness of the prohibition, the Soviet Union adopted a maximalist strategy, the United States an equitable. The same was true on the issue of verification, although the Americans initially adopted an informal integrative strategy. On the geography matter, however, it was the Soviets who embraced an equitable strategy. The Americans, after opting for an informal integrative effort formally positioned themselves maximally.

It was a common assumption among American policy makers at the time of the negotiation that the Soviet call for demilitarization was propaganda oriented in order to enhance its image among the non-aligned as the champion of disarmament (confidential interviews, 1974). If propaganda in this case, is defined as the pursuit of objectives ulterior to the ostensible goal of actually encouraging "peaceful uses of the ocean floor" which the UN mandated in 1968 seabed negotiations attain (United States Arms Control Agency, 1969: 802), then those who assume that propaganda was the only Soviet objective are missing a major if not *the* major, intent of the Soviet stance. Viewed from the strategic context of the discussions, Moscow's positioning was consistent with the maximization of its interests, particularly, the elimination of the American submarine-surveillance capability. There was some prospect, albeit slight, that Washington could be induced to diminish its defensive investment in the seabed if subject to sufficient pressure. Early 1969 was a propitious time to attempt such an effort as the Nixon Administration was not necessarily bound to the defense-policy strictures of its predecessor. The maximalist strategy, the Soviet call for demilitarization, also acted as an information-gathering device, testing the strength with which the Nixon Administration was likely to hold the Johnson Administration's policies dictating that seabed arms control be limited to weapons of mass destruction. Finally, even if these objectives were not achieved, a maximalist posture provided Moscow with something to bargain away as part of a quid pro quo or as a gesture of good faith.

Likewise, when perceived from the perspective of bargaining strategy, we can better appreciate the Soviet rationale in proposing that verification be achieved through reciprocity. The stipulation was clearly the most controversial that Moscow offered. Taken literally, it would have required a party to place an object on the seabed before it could challenge the activities of another, a curious requirement that the Soviets were never to adequately explain.[4] However, when Moscow's behavior is assessed from the perspective of positioning strategy, a logic can be ascertained. The stance, from this perspective, offered two advantages: first, it made it difficult for other parties to estimate what the Russian minimum disposition would be. This allowed Moscow flexibility. Perhaps, more significantly, it could be used by the Soviets as a bargaining chip, something to swap if the need arose.

When the United States positioned itself maximally on the issue of territorial limits, it availed itself of the same opportunities. Whether the Soviets conceived their stand on verification as part of a conscious strategy is uncertain. It is unlikely that the United States did in contemplating its position on limits. Rather, its posture appears to have been the result of the bureaucratic political process imposing the lowest common denominator of conflicting departmental interests. The leadership of the American delegation, for example, recognized that any call for demilitarization to begin at anything less than 12 miles was not likely to be acceptable to the Committee's membership whose terri-

4. The Soviets argued (United States Arms Control Agency, 1970: 156) that their position was guided by the principals of the Antarctic and outer-space treaties. However, American diplomats attempting to gain clarification of the position in the context of the seabed were unable to fathom the Russian's rationale (Leonard, 1974).

torial limits were greater (Leonard, 1974). Furthermore, this group saw little reason why this delimitation could not be accommodated. The United States Navy reflected other interests. From the Navy's point of view, any demarcation other than the three-mile line would establish a bad precedent. It could undermine Washington's effort to maintain transit rights through the world's strategic straits unimpeded. It might also diminish the allowable zone within which the United States could exercise defensive activities unimpeded (Foss, 1964: 32-36; Hollick and Osgood 1974: 78-80; Winnefeld and Builder, 1971: 19-25). Recognition that these contrasting views posed a dilemma may have contributed to the initial American decision to take an informal integrative position on the issue. The tack appears to have been designed to stimulate the early adoption of a common denominator to resolve the issue.

In addition to the three maximalist positions adopted, it was also noted above that equitable stances were embraced by the United States on the issue of the comprehensiveness of the weapons ban and its verification by the Soviet Union on the issue of territorial breadth. The American position on verification, i.e., the call for its establishment on the basis of unilateral observation, was adopted simply because Washington's decision makers felt it was a fair resolution of the issue consonant with the doctrine of freedom of the high seas which was universally accepted. (Leonard, 1974; confidential interviews, 1974). The U.S. position on comprehensiveness and Moscow's stand on territorial limits can largely be attributed to the strategic context of the talks, i.e., the United States' interest in preserving its submarine-monitoring devices and the Soviet Union's stake in demarcating an agreement consistent with its 12-mile territorial limits. By so positioning themselves, the superpowers availed themselves of the principle benefits of equitable positioning, common benchmarks for conflict resolution and consequential reductions in the possibilities of deadlock, time and opportunity losses.

EFFECTIVENESS OF POSITIONING

Reaction to the two drafts by the other conferees varied. Moscow's military allies appeared comfortable with the entire Soviet draft (Sachs, 1970: 26, 114-115, 118-119, 132-133). The nonaligned were sympathetic to select portions. With the exception of Brazil, the nonaligned were satisfied with the Soviet call for a total prohibition of military activity, although there was some sentiment that exceptions to the all-encompassing nature of the prohibition might be necessary. (Sachs, 1970: 142, 154-156, 144, 149, 152; Conference of the Eighteen Nation Committee on Disarmament 1969: 411: 8). No objections were raised to the geography of the Soviet prohibition. However, strong exception was taken by virtually all these countries to Moscow's call for verification to be based on reciprocity (Sachs, 1970: 144, 149, 152, 212-213).

Washington's military allies displayed still another pattern of reaction to the proposals before them. Britain and Italy were comfortable with the American proposition that the scope of prohibition be limited to weapons of mass destruction (Sachs, 1970: 147, 204). Canada responded by detailing a list of both conventional and nuclear weapons and related systems that should be prohibited (Sachs, 1970: 192-193). All three were at odds with their alliance leader on the issues of the prohibition's geography and verification. In lieu of a prohibition that would begin at the three-mile line, Britain advocated that it begin 12-miles out to sea while Canada and Italy favored the establishment of defensive zones with monitoring devices extending two hundred miles out to sea and two hundred fathoms deep respectively. (Sachs, 1970: 147, 192-194, 204-205). On the question of verification, neither the American nor the Soviet proposal received support from the Western allies.

Bargaining over the two draft treaties followed their submission until October 7, 1969 when the superpowers jointly submitted a draft treaty (United States Arms Control Agency, 1970: 473-475). The document failed to manifest the impact of maximalist-positioning employed by either superpower. Rather, the Soviet Union acquiesced to the American call for the prohibition to be limited to nuclear weapons and other weapons of mass destruction, and agreed that verification be based on observation and consultation. The United States acquiesced—albeit, in somewhat ambiguous language—to the Soviet call for the prohibition to exclude the 12-mile zone adjacent to the coastal state's shoreline.[5] The new draft formed the basis for a year of further bargaining be-

5. The geography article stated, "For the purpose of the Treaty the outer limit of the contiguous zone referred to in Article I shall be measured in accordance with the provisions of Section II of the 1958 Geneva Convention on the Territorial Sea and the Contiguous Zone in accordance with international law" (United States Arms Control Agency, 1970: 473).

tween the superpowers, several nonaligned states, and Canada over provisions to insure that the treaty not impinge on signatories' territorial or jurisdictional claims over the seabed. Three more joint-draft treaties were formally submitted during the period (U.S. Arms Control Agency, 1970: 507-509; 1971: 185-188, 475-479), the final one concluding the negotiation on September 1, 1970.

CONCLUSIONS

The seabed-arms control negotiation put to the test contending hypotheses concerning the utility of maximalist-and equitable-positioning strategies. Ostensible advantages of maximalist-positioning lay in the contention that target parties will be moved to modify their positions through the power of suggestion inherent in the posture or through the concessionary quid quo pros it allows. At the very least, it provided the employer a means to test a target party's commitment to its own position. Challenging these notions, equitable strategies assert that positioning in a manner that is obviously unacceptable to a target party when an equitable alternative is available, at the very least costs time, and moreover, increases the possibility that the negotiation will deadlock. In arms control negotiation, time spent may be an opportunity cost for restraining new weapons development.

The seabed negotiation appears to support the equitable school's critique of maximalist bargaining. Maximalist-positioning undertaken by the Soviets in advocating total prohibition and verification through reciprocity and by the Americans in advocating a three-mile prohibition geographic clause failed either directly or indirectly to move target parties. The strategy did result in several months expenditure of time that might have been avoided. Only the Soviet position on verification attained the rather modest objective of stimulating conferees to indicate what they did not want: the Soviet proposal.

By contrast, had equitable-positioning been undertaken by all sides at the outset of the negotiation, at least the comprehensiveness and geography clauses could have been resolved expeditiously. The parameters of what was commonly acceptable were largely known in advance of the formal negotiations; the likely scope from the 1968 discussion and the ad hoc committee to study the ocean floor that resulted in Soviet and American submission of draft resolutions and the probable geographic coverage from the international trend toward the extension of the maritime territorial claims 12 miles out to sea. Equitable-positioning could not have easily resolved the question of verification because there was no commonly recognized norm of equity. Nonetheless, the American suggestion that verification be based on observation and consultation was designed to be equitable; although it failed to be totally acceptable to other participants, its good faith was manifested by the fact that it provided the foundation for the construction of the final verification article.

In sum, the seabed-arms control negotiation would have been concluded more expeditiously, the outcome being roughly the same, had the United States and the Soviet Union at the outset adopted equitable-positioning strategies on the three focal points of negotiation rather than opting for preferences commonly recognized as anathema to the other. Whether the same conclusion is applicable to arms control or other negotiation generally is a matter that remains to be explored in other case studies.

Bennett Ramberg is a Research Fellow at the Center for Arms Control and International Security, University of California at Los Angeles. He is the author of The Seabed Arms Control Negotiation: A Study of Multilateral Arms Control Conference Diplomacy *(Denver: University of Denver) 1978 and* Destruction of Nuclear Energy Facilities in War: A Proposal for Legal Restraint *(Princeton: Center of International Studies) 1978.*

8. An Application of a Richardson Process Model

SOVIET-AMERICAN INTERACTIONS IN THE TEST BAN NEGOTIATIONS 1962-1963

P. TERRENCE HOPMANN
THERESA C. SMITH
Department of Political Science and
Quigley Center of International Studies
University of Minnesota

Richardson models have often been used to describe reactive processes in arms races. This paper argues that, following the work of Otomar Bartos, negotiations may also be analyzed as a reactive process rather than as a process of discrete position changes. Four variants of the basic Richardson model were employed to determine whether the Partial Test Ban negotiations exhibited such an interactive pattern. In all four equations for the behavior of both the United States and the USSR the stimulus variable provided the greatest explanatory power, supporting the notion that these negotiations were reactive. Several important differences emerged, however, between the Test Ban negotiations and most arms races. On balance, the data gave strong support for the basic assumption of Richardson models, namely that negotiations may be treated as a highly reactive process.

NEGOTIATIONS AS AN INTERACTIVE PROCESS

THE DEBATE ABOUT RECIPROCITY IN NEGOTIATIONS

Recently there has been substantial discussion among theorists of the negotiation process about how best to characterize the process through

AUTHORS' NOTE: *The authors are grateful for the research support of the Graduate School and the Office of International Programs at the University of Minnesota. They would like to thank Timothy King and Kathleen Burek for their contributions to the preparation of this paper and Dina Zinnes and Harold Guetzkow for their helpful comments on an earlier draft.*

which actors seek to achieve negotiated agreements on issues where conflicts of interest are present. In a recent work on this topic, Bartos (1974: 27) has argued that "any model of negotiation has to deal with the *interactions* between the opposing sides, and it has to make assumptions about the nature of this interaction." In a chapter in this book, Bartos has reaffirmed this position by asserting that "reciprocity" plays a crucial role in negotiations. In his book, Bartos suggests three specific models of the interactive process, namely a Richardson (1960) model, a Bush-Mosteller (1955) stochastic process model, and a Markov-chain model.

Bartos also argues that the interactions between negotiators may be of two general types. In the first instance there is a positive reciprocation among actors in that one negotiator responds by roughly imitating the behavior of his opponent. Thus (Bartos, 1974: 38): "the more the opponent lowers his demand, the more the negotiator lowers his." The second case involves an exploitative relationship, where a negotiator exploits his opponent's concessions by toughening his own positions. Both of these cases involve reciprocal interactions, although in the latter the relationship between demands and concessions is inverse.

Bartos devotes his greatest attention to applying a model of arms races developed by Lewis F. Richardson to the case of negotiations, and he utilizes laboratory experiments to test the assumptions of such a model. In its simplest form Richardson's model states that, for two adversary nations, rates of armaments (dx/dt and dy/dt) are an additive linear function of the opponent's weapons (y or x), a country's own arsenal (x or y), and grievances (g or h). Opponent's weapons are modified by a perceptual coefficient (k or l), called the "defense coefficient" by Richardson. The domestic-arsenal terms are qualified by coefficients representing fatigue and expense of maintaining one's own arms (α or β). Specifically, for two opposing nations, we have:

(1) $dx/dt = ky - \alpha x + g$

(2) $dy/dt = lx - \beta y + h$

Smoker (1965), Caspary (1967), Saaty (1968), and others have used these equations to describe the diverging trajectories of adversaries' weapons acquisitions. Theoretically, these equations might also describe a converging process in which the trajectories approached some finite limit. However, a convergence model has had few applications to arms races since, apparently, nations have seldom approached a maximum limit on absolute amounts appropriated for the military, nor have they frequently begun a downward spiral converging at zero armaments. But there are converging processes in international relations, and one of Bartos' major contributions has been to suggest that negotiations may indeed entail such convergence.

Although Bartos' laboratory research required some significant modifications of the basic Richardson model in order to apply it to negotiations, his work does represent an initial step towards the application of a model which treats negotiations as a reciprocal interaction process. Furthermore, his experimental evidence does suggest that, with some modifications, a Richardson model can reveal important aspects of negotiations. For example, Bartos (1974: 143) has found "Richardson's assumption that negotiators tend to reciprocate to be more correct than the assumption that they exploit each others' concessions." In addition Bartos (1974: 174) found that the modified Richardson model has a mathematical "equilibrium in concessions rather than in demands." This gave further support to the notion that negotiations involved a reciprocal trading of concessions in order to reach agreement.

However, this treatment of negotiations as a process of reciprocal interactions has recently come under attack. Zartman (1975: 70) has criticized Bartos and others on the grounds that their theories are inadequate in terms of "their ability to be operationalized and their utility in explaining real situations." In his chapter in this book, Zartman has further criticized this approach as deterministic and for its "lack of correspondence with the way things take place" in the real world of international negotiations.

The first criticism suggests that the essential concepts of Bartos' model cannot be operationalized with regard to actual negotiations. However, several schemes have been developed and employed for coding texts of actual international negotiations (see Jensen, 1968; Hopmann, 1972, and 1974; and Walcott and Hopmann, 1975) which include the principal variables in Bartos' conceptualization of the negotiation process.

The second criticism, that these models are deterministic, has some validity, especially when referring to formulations of the variety developed by Richardson. From a policy perspective, it is generally valuable to identify manipulable variables through which policymakers can intervene in a process and affect outcomes. Of course, some of the variables used in this approach are in fact manipulable, including concession rates. The use of a deterministic model only implies that the general strategy was decided in advance and did not change significantly throughout the course of the negotiations; otherwise the coefficients would change during the negotiations. Furthermore, it is useful to be able to identify significant determinate trends in every process, and the reciprocal-interaction approach to negotiations may be valuable in spite of its deterministic formulation if it in fact helps to describe, explain, and predict what actually occurs in real world negotiations.

This leads directly to Zartman's most serious criticism of this formulation, namely that it is not a valid description of how negotiations actually occur in the real world of international relations. As Zartman (1975: 71-72) states:

> Unlike experimental subjects and poker players, negotiating diplomats do not simply throw out bids in an effort to close the gap between themselves and the other party. . . .As a result, theories about negotiation as an incremental process of converging bids do not conform to reality and experiments in these terms are not simulations but, at best, as-if analyses.

On the contrary, Zartman argues that the major task of negotiations is to overcome basically different conceptualizations of the issues as held by different parties. Such changes are not likely to occur incrementally, in his view, but are rather likely to involve revolutionary changes in values or conceptualizations of the problems by both parties. In his chapter in this book, Zartman summarizes his position by arguing that "negotiation is a matter of finding the proper formula and implementing detail." Mutual concession-making, he suggests, takes place primarily with regard to detail rather than basic formulas.

Although Zartman is undoubtedly correct that the negotiating process is more complex than a simple exchange of concessions, we are somewhat skeptical about whether his alternative formulation of the process sheds greater light on the nature of the process. For one thing, he seems to have oversimplified Bartos' analysis of the negotiation process. The fact that Bartos has found that negotiations contain an equilibrium in concessions does not necessarily imply that incrementally converging bids are *all* that characterize the process. While some conceptual issues must undoubtedly be resolved before the give-and-take about details can take place, there is nothing inherently contradictory between such a process and one of mutual concession-making. The preceding holds as long as one does not make the assumption that all concessions are of equal importance and as long as one acknowledges that certain kinds of concessions may be contingent upon reconceptualizations of the issues under negotiation or of the environment of the negotiations. The process of reconceptualization of issues requires mutual interaction just as does the process of compromise on details.

Futhermore, we doubt that agreement on a formula must always precede negotiation on details. In many negotiations, agreement on a formula is virtually impossible to achieve, either because negotiators find themselves in an uncomfortable position talking about vague goals and formulas or because negotiators become overly committed to formulas and hence cannot appear to concede at this level. On the contrary, agreements often proceed from negotiations on detail, where the solutions emerge from a process of interaction rather than being imposed by some abstract and general formula.[1] Cross, in his chapter in this book, refers to such a process when he proposes treating negotiations as a "search process." In particular he notes that: "In the face of imperfect understanding of one another's preferences, each party is exploring a list of issues, some of which are already under discussion and some of which would have to be introduced, for pairs of items on which concessions may be profitably exchanged." A recent laboratory simulation by Hopmann and Walcott (1976) illustrates this process of search in a problem designed to parallel the negotiations leading up to the Partial Nuclear Test Ban Treaty.

The issue posed in the debate between the conceptualizations of the negotiation process by Bartos and Zartman is essentially an empirical one, namely a question of determining which conceptualization corresponds better "with the way things take place" in the real world. While Zartman is essentially correct in his assertion that Bartos has not tested his models against real world data, this does not necessarily mean that his formulation is invalid or that it can be supplanted with Zartman's alternative treatment of the process.

Indeed, a recent study by Hopmann and King (1976) has found that considerable reciprocity was exhibited between the Soviet Union and its two Western opponents, the United States and the United Kingdom, in the negotiations in 1962-1963 leading up to the Partial Nuclear Test Ban Treaty. Generally, they found high positive correlations between the behaviors of the three nuclear nations both inside and outside of the negotiations during this period. Within the negotiations, more than 45% of the behavior of each nation was explained by the behavior of its

1. These arguments are based largely on Hopmann's interviews with delegates from most nations participating in the negotiations at SALT, the Conference of the Committee on Disarmament, the Conference on Security and Cooperation in Europe, and on Mutual Balanced Force Reductions in Europe.

negotiating opponent towards itself. Hopmann and King (1976: 105) thus concluded: "the behaviors of the three nuclear powers within the test ban negotiations were highly symmetrical over time; that is, each nation tended to change its responses roughly 'in kind' with changes in the stimuli directed toward it from other actors both inside and outside of negotiations."

Thus, our aim in this paper is to investigate whether some variants of Richardson's basic model may be applied to real-world negotiations, namely those leading to the Partial Nuclear Test Ban Treaty of 1963. In attempting to make such an application, one must keep in mind that the original arms-race models of Richardson do not predict the outbreak of war; in a similar way, the equations in this paper cannot be expected to predict the outcome of negotiations. While the structure of the model may determine if positions converge, making agreement *possible,* it indicates nothing further about probable outcomes, partially because the bounds of the system are unknown. Therefore, while the model may specify eventual convergence, no actual agreement will take place if this theoretical convergence occurs beyond the point where real-world conditions have limited the negotiations or forced a breakdown in talks. The Richardson formulation, as we adapt it, is simply a description of the negotiation process and will not tell us whether negotiations will succeed or fail.

THE MODELS

The models considered in this paper include three variables. In a manner similar to Spector (1977b), we hypothesize that negotiations are likely to be influenced by both individual factors and by environmental ones. However, we have broken the environmental variables into two categories, those internal to the negotiations and those occuring externally in the general interactions among states. We have summarized the individual variables with reference to perceptions or definitions of the situation, which reflect how the personality of the negotiator impinges on his attitudes and beliefs about the environment. Following Richardson, we have treated the environmental variables as involving the interactions among states, with the behavior of the other serving as an environmental stimulus. We treat the perception variable as corresponding roughly to Richardson's notion of grievance.

The three principal variables in our study are thus: (1) the behavior of each nation within negotiations towards its opponent; (2) the actions of each nation toward its opponent outside negotiations; and (3) the perceptions by each nation's negotiators of the actions of the other nation both inside and outside negotiations.

With respect to the first two behaviors, we make one further distinction. A stimulus (S) refers to the behavior of the opposing nation towards the nation whose behavior is being analyzed, while a response (R) refers to the behavior of the nation under consideration towards its opponent. The basic objective of our model is to explain the internal behavioral responses of each negotiating nation (INR) in terms of three independent variables: (a) the external behavior of the opposing nation towards them (EXS); (b) the internal behavior of the other nation towards them (INS); and (c) their perceptions of the combined behavior of the other nation towards them (PER).

In this study we examine four models, each of which is fitted for both the United States and the Soviet Union, making eight equations in all. The first three are of theoretical importance, while the fourth is included to assess the statistical impact of omitting theoretically important variables. These models are presented below:

(1) $\dot{x} = a\dot{y} - b\dot{x}_l + c\dot{z}_l + d\dot{w}$
(2) $\dot{x} = a\dot{y} - b\dot{x}_l + d\dot{w}$
(3) $\dot{x} = a\dot{y} + c\dot{z}_l + d\dot{w}$
(4) $\dot{x} = a\dot{y} + d\dot{w}$

Where:

$\dot{x} = \triangle INR$, the change in internal response,

$\dot{x}_l = \triangle INR(L)$, the change in internal response (lagged),

$\dot{y} = \triangle INS$, the change in internal stimulus,

$\dot{z}_l = \triangle EXS(L)$, the change in external stimulus (lagged),

$\dot{w} = \triangle PER$, the change in perceptions,

and a, b, c, and d are the corresponding coefficients to be estimated.

Although these equations owe their inspiration to Richardson, they differ from his formulation in two ways. First, they are more complex because they involve first derivatives (operationalized as first differences) throughout, rather than only on the left side of the equation. The derivatives are used since it is hypothesized that changes in negotiating responses are not related so much to aggregate levels of stimuli and perceptions but to the rate of change in these variables over time. As operationalized, this means that changes since the previous time period are particularly important in determining current responses. Second, these equations contain new variables, since there are considerations relevant to negotiations which are of little or no interest to arms racing, especially the distinction between internal and external environments. Furthermore, grievances or perceptions are treated as a variable and not as a residual constant as in Richardson's work. In our equations, a regression constant is computed, but it remains uninterpreted since it has no clear substantive meaning.

The first set of equations above contains all of the variables considered in this study, including the impact of change in lagged-external events ($\dot{z}_l$ or $\triangle EXS(L)$) which is added to traditional Richardson formulations. The second model is identical to the first except that the external environment was excluded, thus making it, conceptually, the closest to traditional formulations of the Richardson model. The third model is identical to the first except that the lagged-internal response variable ($\dot{x}_l$ or $\triangle INR(L)$) has been omitted. This enables us to test the hypothesis that negotiations may differ from arms races in that past behavior is not an important constraint for the former. The fourth set of equations, computed to serve as a basis for comparison, is the simplest. This set contains only the internal stimulus ($\dot{y}$ or $\triangle INS$) and perceptions or grievances ($\dot{w}$ or $\triangle PER$).

METHODOLOGY

THE DATA

In order to examine our analytical models empirically, it was necessary to develop indicators for each of the three variables, namely the behavior of each nation toward the other within the negotiations, the behavior outside the negotiations, and the perceptions by each nation's negotiators of the actions of the other nation. The operationalization of the variables and the data-collection procedures are essentially the same as those employed by Hopmann and King (1976: 115-122), and the reader is referred to that article for more detailed descriptions.

The first variable involves the within-the-negotiations behavior of the United States and the Soviet Union toward one another, i.e., INS and INR. In this study, these behaviors are treated along a continuum from soft-bargaining behaviors that generally represent movement towards convergence and cooperation to hard-bargaining behaviors which usually entail movement toward divergence and conflict. It must be emphasized that this dimension is somewhat broader than the simple notion of concession rates used by Bartos and many other studies of the negotiation process.

The data for these internal behaviors were obtained through a categorical content analysis of the verbatim transcripts of the meetings in Geneva of the Eighteen Nation Disarmament Conference from March 14, 1962 through June 21, 1963 (ENDC/SCI/PV. 1-50; ENDC/PV.96-147). Shortly after these meetings, the negotiations were transferred to a secret conference in Moscow where the final agreement was drafted; however, all of the basic provisions of the treaty had been discussed previously at length in the more open sessions in Geneva. Each statement made by one nation toward or about another was classified in a set of categories developed by Hopmann (1972: 222), partially on the basis of the conceptualization of bargaining developed by Schelling (1960). These codings were then divided into two broad categories: (1) soft-bargaining behaviors included making new proposals, making concessions, issuing promises, indicating agreement on specific issues, and acknowledging the contributions of the other party to an agreement; (2) hard-bargaining behaviors included making retractions of previous proposals and concessions, issuing threats, making commitments, indicating disagreement on specific issues, and making accusations about the contributions of the other party toward the failure of negotiations. Then a ratio of the proportion of soft to hard bargaining was computed on a monthly basis as the index of negotiating behavior.

The second variable dealt with the actions of the other nation outside of the negotiations (EXS), treated along a scale of cooperation and conflict. The actions of the United States and the Soviet Union toward one another during the period from January 1, 1962 through August 30, 1963 were identified from three sources: *The New York Times Index, Keesing's Contemporary Archives,* and the *New Times,* published respectively in the United States, Great Britain, and the Soviet Union. The fact that sources from countries participating in these events were used could conceivably create some overlap with the third variable, perceptions, if the interpretation of these events reflected a particular national viewpoint. Yet all sources were used to record actions in each direction between the United States and the Soviet

Union; when the same events were reported differently in the various sources, a composite and neutral statement was abstracted from all sources. Since all sources were combined in our analyses, it is hoped that the selection of statements is relatively free of the perceptual screen of any single nation. This assumption is generally supported by the data in Table 1 which indicate that there are no high correlations between perceptions and external behavior.

The events abstracted from these three sources were scaled by four judges along dimensions of conflict and cooperation developed by Corson (1970). The average score of the judges was taken as a measure of the direction and intensity of the interaction. Summary scores were then computed on a monthly basis, providing the composite degree of cooperation and conflict exhibited by each nation toward the other.

The third set of variables concerned the perceptions by each nation of the other (PER), treated on a scale of affect ranging from positive to negative. Randomly sampled pages from the verbatim transcripts of the ENDC negotiations were subjected to content analysis using the Stanford political version of the General Inquirer (Holsti, 1969: ch. 7). The dictionary employed for the content analysis is based on the "semantic differential" developed by Osgood et al. (1957: 72), although special attention was directed to the dimension of positive and negative affect. Thus, perceptions refer to the affect that an actor assigns to the actions of the other towards itself, summarized on a monthly basis. In order to employ these data in a Richardson-process model, we have had to treat them as though they were interval data. We must acknowledge that this is making a somewhat stronger assumption about the nature of the measurement than was initially intended. Indeed, throughout this paper we are working with data which are perhaps softer than those generally employed in analyses using Richardson-process models, where defense budgets or the deployment of certain kinds of armaments are generally used. We feel that this limitation is partially offset by the fact that these data appear to be quite valid indicators of the theoretical concepts which we want to analyze. Thus, we believe that the use of these data is justified given the exploratory nature of this research, and with the added proviso that use of the data should be accompanied by some caution about drawing excessively powerful conclusions from the results.

ANALYTICAL METHODS

To appraise the applicability of Richardson's model to negotiations, we used linear-multiple regression (LMR) analysis. This technique is appropriate because our goal is to test the applicability of a linear-additive model, and multiple regression fits a linear function calculated to minimize squared error. Thus, we have estimated the coefficients a, b, c, and d for each of the four models described previously for the United States and the Soviet Union, treated separately.

A linear-simultaneous solution procedure applied to the equations for both countries might have been superior to linear-multiple regression here because it allows for interactive effects across equations in estimating all the coefficients. However, use of this technique has been postponed since any amount of curvilinearity that existed in the data would pose more serious problems for simultaneous estimations than for Ordinary Least Squares (OLS). We also note that apparently Richardson (1960: 87-90) used OLS techniques in his analysis. We suspect that some adjustments for curvilinearity, especially in the external-behavior and perception variables at approximately the time of the Cuban missile crisis in October 1962, might provide a better fit. However, in that case, we would still estimate the equations separately since the computational details of simultaneous-curvilinear estimation remain to be worked out by statisticians.

Linear-multiple regression analysis makes a number of significant assumptions which must be evaluated in connection with its use. Of considerable importance, LMR requires that all relationships among variables be linear. To check for major deviations from linearity, we ran scatterplots and computed Pearson's r for all pairs of variables; the latter data are reported in Table 1. Some of the scatterplots showed considerable dispersion resulting in low r's, but in no case did it appear that a clear curvilinear relationship existed. In two cases, using discontinuous curves over some part of the range might have improved the fit. In the absence of any theoretical reason for expecting the relations to take such complicated forms, however, this was not considered to be a sufficiently compelling reason to abandon the simplifying assumption of linearity for application in this analysis.

Additional problems in the use of LMR might appear if multi-collinearity or serial correlation exist in the data, since the assumptions

TABLE 1
Pearson's r's for all Country-Specific Relationships[a]

	ΔUSINS	ΔUSINR	ΔUSPER	ΔUSEXS(L)	ΔUSINR(L)	ΔRUINS	ΔRUINR	ΔRUPER	ΔRUEXS(L)
ΔUSINR	.585								
ΔUSPER	.770	.204							
ΔUSEXS(L)	.441	.577	.387						
ΔUSINR(L)	-.020	-.085	-.005	-.108					
ΔRUINS	.654	*	.327	.519	-.094				
ΔRUINR	*	.585	.770	.441	-.020	.654			
ΔRUPER	.271	.030	.255	-.028	.142	.035	.271		
ΔRUEXS(L)	-.103	-.110	.277	-.161	-.135	-.058	-.103	.064	
ΔRUINR(L)	-.210	.069	-.219	-.066	.585	.015	-.210	.049	.139

*Cells marked with asterisks indicate that, in effect, correlations between the two variables would be automatically perfect since these are the same variables; i.e., RU response is the same as US stimulus and vice versa.
a. US = United States — RU = Soviet Union

of LMR would not be met. However, assessing compliance with these assumptions is a complicated matter which can be discussed more effectively after analysis of the results.

Linear-multiple regression analysis yields R^2, a value for the maximum variance explained using some linear-additive combination of the independent variables. The beta weights give an indication of the relative importance of the independent variables in determining this combination. Unlike Richardson, we leave the beta weights unlabeled as there are no obvious theoretically derived concepts which correspond to them. Also by adding an explicit grievance variable that receives its own beta, we have added an additional coefficient to Richardson's version of the model. Unlike Richardson, we leave the regression constant uninterpreted. Since these are not standardized data, this constant still appears in the equations which are estimated, though not in any of the four models set forth. It has no substantive interpretation but represents the point where the regression line intersects the y axis.

RESULTS

VARIANCE RESULTS

In order to compare each of the four variants of Richardson's basic model, several criteria were used. First, we calculated the R^2 and its level of significance for each equation. However, values of R^2 are not directly comparable due to the different number of variables in each equation. We have thus also calculated Rao and Miller's (1971: 15-21) corrected $\bar{R}^2$, an analog of R^2 adjusted for sample size and the number of parameters estimated. The values computed for each equation may thus be compared with one another using $\bar{R}^2$. Finally, we have examined the differences between R^2 and $\bar{R}^2$ to provide an indication of how much explanatory power is being added to an equation through the addition of new independent variables. All of these data are summarized in Table 2.

The data indicate first that the basic model explains the most variance at moderate levels of statistical significance, though the results are stronger in the American than in the Soviet case. Dropping the impact of the external environment in the second model had somewhat

TABLE 2
Regression Analysis—Multiple R's for all Equations

Model	Nation	R^2	p	$\bar{R}^2$	$\bar{R}^2 - R^2$*	Form of Equation
1a)	US	.645	.087	.442	−.203	$\Delta INR = a\Delta INS - b\Delta INR(L) + c\Delta EXS(L) + d\Delta PER$
1b)	USSR	.546	.184	.287	−.259	
2a)	US	.363	.193	.172	−.191	$\Delta INR = a\Delta INS - b\Delta INR(L) + d\Delta PER$
2b)	USR	.500	.064	.425	−.075	
3a)	US	.644	.033	.552	−.092	$\Delta INR = a\Delta INS + c\Delta EXS(L) + d\Delta PER$
3b)	USSR	.496	.122	.328	−.168	
4a)	US	.360	.086	.244	−.116	$\Delta INR = a\Delta INS + d\Delta PER$
4b)	USSR	.461	.034	.336	−.098	

*This figure represents the reduction in R^2 brought about by making the $\bar{R}^2$ correction for number of variables in the equation; the negative values mean that the R^2 declined by the amount indicated.

TABLE 3
A Comparison of Beta Weights for Models 1 and 3

Model	Country	ΔINS	$\Delta INR(L)$	$\Delta EXS(L)$	ΔPER
1a)	US	.902	−.024	.432	−.659
3a)	US	.902	—	.435	−.660
1b)	USSR	.645	−.225	−.051	−.263
3b)	USSR	.641	—	.254	−.082

different effects for the two countries. In the case of the United States, comparing models 1a and 2a, we find that model 1 produced better results for both R^2 and $\bar{R}^2$. Thus, in the American case, there seems to be little reason for removing the impact of the external environment. For the USSR, however, although R^2 was lower in equation 2b than in 1b (a natural result considering that an independent variable was dropped from the equation), the value of $\bar{R}^2$ was enhanced in the version without the external environment. Thus, in the Soviet case, one may conclude that the inclusion of the external variable provides little improvement and, in terms of parsimony, a loss in explanatory power.

Turning to the third model where the lagged internal behavior of one's own nation was removed, we find that the results are generally stronger than in the first model. This is reflected in an actual increase in the corrected $\bar{R}^2$ in equations 3a and 3b over 1a and 1b, implying reduced error variance and more accurate prediction without $\Delta INR(L)$. This was particularly remarkable in the case of the United States where R^2 was barely reduced by removing its own past behavior and where $\bar{R}^2$ was substantially increased. This suggests that the small increase in R^2 when $\Delta INR(L)$ is added is probably an artifact of linear-multiple regression, because adding anything to an equation will increase R^2 slightly. In preferring model 3 to model 1, we are suggesting a substantial revision of the initial Richardson formulation where past behavior was an important factor. Removing this variable leaves us open to the charge that the coefficients estimated in model 3 are biased because a theoretically relevant variable has been removed. However, since most of the consequent changes in the betas, as reported in Table 3, are in the second and third decimal places, we consider this possibility comparatively unimportant.

When models 3 and 2 are compared, there are quite different results for the two countries. In the case of the United States, equation 3a is preferable to 2a on all criteria. Thus, the inclusion of external events rather than past behavior appears to be essential in the American case if a loss of substantial information is to be avoided. On the other hand, in the case of the USSR, equation 2b was consistently better on our criteria than 3b, suggesting the somewhat greater importance of past behavior rather than external constraints in their case.

Turning finally to the fourth model, we find not unexpectedly that the reduced number of variables has lowered R^2 in comparison with all other versions while producing some of the best results in terms of statistical signficance. When compared with equations 2a and 2b, this model produced slightly better results for the United States on adjusted $\bar{R}^2$. When compared with equation 3a for the United States, equation 4a was distinctly weaker on both R^2 and $\bar{R}^2$. For the USSR, however, equation 4b generally produced stronger levels of significance and a higher $\bar{R}^2$ than 3b.

Looking at these results on a country-by-country basis, it appears that equation 3a is the best predictor for the United States. It produces the highest $\bar{R}^2$ and thus the least error variance. It is also a close second to equation 1a in R^2 and exceeds equation 4a in level of significance. In short, in the United States case, the role of past behavior may be dropped with little cost, but also dropping the influence of external events (as in the case in model 4 relative to 3) involves a considerable loss in terms of both R^2 and $\bar{R}^2$, as expected.

The choice of the best model for the Soviet Union is not as clear as for the United States. The model which generally did the best for the United States, the third, does not emerge on top for any criteria for the USSR. Although equation 1b has the highest R^2, this is an artifact of the larger number of independent variables in this equation in comparison with all others. Thus, dropping the role of external events in the models for the USSR, as is the case in equation 2b in comparison with 1b, involves some sacrifice in unadjusted R^2, while substantially improving the corrected $\bar{R}^2$ and the level of significance. On the other hand, dropping the effects of past behavior in equation 3b in comparison with 1b improves the level of significance and $\bar{R}^2$ only slightly. As will be noted below, this may be the result of the presence of a lagged endogenous variable in models 1a and 2 in contrast to model 3. However, it does appear that past behavior is a more important constraint in the Soviet case than in the American one. This may be due largely to significant domestic constraints, especially party and bureaucratic forces, that may promote greater consistency over time than is exhibited by the United States. However, if maximum explained variance is desired, a choice between models 2 and 4 might be made by testing the significance of the difference between the R^2s.

SOME STATISTICAL CONSIDERATIONS

At this juncture, a discussion of the degree to which our data met the assumptions of ordinary-least-squares (OLS) regression is necessary. Time-series data equations including lagged-endogenous variables—lagged forms of the dependent variable—very often exhibit serial correlation in the errors, or autocorrelation. In our data, this problem potentially arises in models 1 and 2 where $\Delta INR(L)$ appears as an independent variable in equations in which ΔINR is the dependent variable. When OLS methods are used without transformations, this may produce biased estimates of error variance. This usually results in underestimating the magnitude of true error variance, thereby overestimating betas of the lagged-endogenous variables, overestimating R^2, and overestimating the significance levels of both. Alternative estimation methods are then recommended, involving generalized-least squares (GLS), pseudo-GLS, or OLS on a transformed model. Many of these methods are quite cumbersome. They require knowledge of the underlying error structure, which is usually unavailable and cannot be determined empirically in small samples such as the one used in this study. One may make assumptions about the error structure, but an incorrect assumption regarding errors in GLS will be likely to produce more inaccurate and imprecise results than those given by OLS, especially for simple models such as ours with one exogenous, independent variable (see Hibbs, 1974: 296). The alternative to making risky assumptions is to resort to an involved two-stage estimation procedure, but these are generally inaccurate in small samples.

This discussion suggests that where preliminary inquiries are conducted using small samples, unless there are strong theoretical reasons for assuming one error pattern over another, GLS may be no more revealing or may even produce greater distortion than OLS. We have thus employed OLS in our analyses, mindful of its limitations. Since in this study the lagged-endogenous variables are neither positively nor heavily weighted, there is little reason to suspect that OLS has exaggerated their influence or that a GLS treatment would produce radically different results in this respect. In fact, as the data presented

TABLE 4a
The h Statistic for Equations Containing INR(L)

Equation	Country	h Statistic	p =
1) ΔINR = aΔINS − bΔINR(L) + cΔEXS(L) + dΔPER	1a) US	.66217	.2266
	1b) USSR	−2.193	.0122
2) ΔINR = aΔINS − bΔINR(L) + dΔPER	2a) US	.54272	.2912
	2B) USSR	−.60410	.2578

above indicated, the lagged-response variables are *not* influential even when a technique is used which may be expected to *overstate* their true importance. Another consequence of this bias is that remaining variables may be underemphasized, so possibly the internal stimulus, external stimulus, and perception variables are even more important than they appear in predicting responses in the negotiations.

Since time-series data frequently exhibit serial correlation, it is important to test for its presence in applications of these models. However, the usual statistic, Durbin-Watson's d, is inappropriate for the first two models because the lagged-endogenous variables may have produced biased estimates of error variance, and thus artificially diminished indications of the presence of serial correlation. Durbin has adapted a similar statistic to the case of LMR with lagged-endogenous variables (Durbin, 1970: 419). His new statistic, h, tested as a standard normal deviate, is calculated for the first two models with the results reported in Table 4a. These data indicate that only equation 1b may safely be assumed not to be affected by any problems of serial correlation. Given the equivocal probabilities for equations 1a, 2a, and 2b, the existence of autoregression in those data cannot be denied or affirmed with any substantial confidence.

Since there are other sources of serial correlation besides lagged endogenous variables, the third and fourth models were also tested for autocorrelation, using the standard d statistic (Durbin and Watson, 1951: 173-177). Some difficulties arose in calculating whether these equations were affected by serial correlation, because the sample size in our study ranging from 12 to 14 monthly periods is below the normal minimum of 15. Since the probability distribution involved begins to diverge at sample sizes below 15, our results based on slightly smaller samples must be approached with some caution. Nevertheless, the data reported in Table 4b indicate that the data for model 3 for both the

TABLE 4b
The d Statistic for Equations Without INR(L) for p=.05, n=15

	Country	d	d_u	d_L
3) $\triangle INR = a\triangle INS + c\triangle EXS(L) + d\triangle PER$	3a) US	1.4399	1.74	.82
	3b) USSR (inconclusive)	2.4566	1.75	.82
4) $\triangle INR + a\triangle INS + d\triangle PER$	4a) US	1.963	1.54	.95
	4b) USSR (no autoregression)	2.392	1.54	.95

United States and the Soviet Union fell into the indeterminate range, implying that the hypothesis that some autoregression exists can neither be accepted nor rejected at the .05 level of significance. In the fourth model for both countries, on the other hand, the data indicate that at the .05 level we can reject the hypothesis that there is some serial correlation in the data. In no case, therefore, can we affirm conclusively the presence of serial correlation in our equations, although in a number of cases the ambiguous results suggest the necessity for some caution in interpreting our findings.

Finally, we have examined our data for the presence of multicollinearity, since LMR is not an adequate estimation technique if any of the independent variables are linear functions of other independent variables already in the equation. We have first examined the simple correlations among all of the variables, and Table 5 summarizes those zero-order correlations which were greater than .50. However, high simple correlations alone do not provide a sufficient reason to reject LMR (Rao and Miller, 1971: 48). Thus, a further check on multicollinearity was made by regressing all independent variables, singly and in additive combination, on all other independent variables in the models for each country. The results, reported in Table 6, show little if any multicollinearity in the Soviet data, but a substantial amount appears in some of the data for the United States. In this case $\triangle PER$ and $\triangle INS$ are strongly related (r = .77), and $\triangle EXS$ (L) is moderately correlated with $\triangle INS$ (r = .44). In the latter case, however, $\triangle EXS$ (L) is not actually a source of multicollinearity, because adding it to the equation (3a compared to 4a) raised the corrected $\bar{R}^2$ from .244 to .552, whereas a multicollinear variable would reduce $\bar{R}^2$. Although, clearly, $\triangle PER$ and $\triangle INS$ are strongly related, they are also essential to the

TABLE 5
Summary of Highly Correlated Variables in the
Data on the Basis of Simple r's

	USINS	USEXS(L)	RUINS
USINR	.585	.577	.645
USPER	.770		

model for theoretical reasons. Thus, no equation excluding one of them was computed, so that no discussion of their separate effects on $\bar{R}^2$ or on the standard error of coefficients is possible. With this possible exception, therefore, we have concluded that multicollinearity does not appear to be a major problem affecting our results.

RESULTS FOR BETA WEIGHTS

We also want to determine which variables contribute most to explaining changes in the negotiation process. To answer this question we must look at the standardized beta coefficients appearing in Table 7. The overwhelmingly obvious conclusion from this table is that ΔINS is the most heavily weighted and most significant component in each equation for each country. In theory, that should not be very surprising considering that this is essentially a reactive model in which the stimulus would presumably play an important role, but it does provide dramatic evidence of the interactive nature of these negotiations. This variable seems to have had more effect on American than on Soviet behavior, with the coefficients for the USSR generally being lower.

The second variable, ΔINR(L), has an unexpectedly negligible effect for the United States (beta = -.024, p = .92 in equation 1a), and for the Soviet Union it exerts only a small and problematical negative effect (beta = -.225, p = .41 in equation 1b). It is, of course, true that this measure does not imply that past behavior has no influence whatsoever, but simply that the effects of one's own prior response on the present response do not emerge as strongly weighted in a regression analysis which predicts response from some linear composite of the independent variables. Since the model allows only linear nonmultiplicative effects on ΔINR, we are justified in maintaining that, under the present assumptions, ΔINR(L) is not an important consideration in these negotiations, especially for the United States. Additionally,

TABLE 6
Multiple R Check for Multicollinearity[a]

Equation	United States		Soviet Union	
	R	R^2	R	R^2
PER=INS	.77	.60*	.13	.02
PER=INS + EXS(L)	.77	.60†	.08	.01
EXS(L)=PER	.39	.15	.06	.00
EXS(L)=PER + INS	.45	.20	.09	.01
INS=EXS(L)	.44	.19	-.06	.00
INS=EXS(L) + PER	.79	.62†	.07	.00

a. In those equations where there is only one independent variable, R = r, and the same R, R^2, and p value are obtained regardless of which variable is designated as the independent variable.
*Significant at the .001 level.
†Significant at the .02 level or better.

for statistical reasons already mentioned, OLS usually *overstates* the importance of lagged-endogenous variables. This makes it all the more surprising that $\triangle INR(L)$ is not an influential contributor to the process of predicting $\triangle INR$.

This finding is noticeably different from that obtained in most applications of Richardson models to arms races, where a country's prior arming behavior generally emerges as heavily weighted. In the case of arms races, this may be explained largely by the influence over armament programs exerted by heavily entrenched military-industrial-bureaucratic complexes that assure continued development and procurement of arms. However, in arms control negotiations the vested interests in agreement, while perhaps vigorous at times, may not be steady or influential over long periods of time, fluctuating with such factors as the ebb and flow of public opinion, the cycles of election years and economies, the appearance of domestic dissent, and so forth. Another possible explanation for this apparent inconsistency in behavior over time may be that negotiators are pursuing a deliberate strategy of keeping their positions unpredictable, though not wildly so, in order to achieve an accord which maximizes their own gains. Some of the advantages to negotiators of such a strategy have been suggested by Schelling (1960: especially chs. 7-8). Finally, these findings also appear to be consistent with Jensen's (1968) observations regarding

TABLE 7
Betas on Variables Explaining $\triangle INR$[a]

Model	Country	$\triangle INS$	$\triangle INR(L)$	$\triangle EXS(L)$	$\triangle PER$
1a)	US	.902 (.042)	-.024 (.920)	.432 (.132)	-.659 (.105)
1b)	USSR	.645 (.039)	-.225 (.411)	-.051 (.849)	.263 (.337)
2a)	US	.753 (.108)	-.060 (.818)	—	-.209 (.635)
2b)	USSR	.651 (.016)	-.199 (.395)	—	.184 (.431)
3a)	US	.902 (.029)	—	.435 (.102)	-.660 (.082)
3b)	USSR	.641 (.034)	—	.254 (.342)	-.082 (.753)
4a)	US	.762 (.088)	—	—	-.219 (.600)
4b)	USSR	.648 (.014)	—	—	.181 (.431)

a. Significance levels indicated in parenthesis.

the early stages of the test ban negotiations, which he found to be characterized by an "approach-avoidance" conflict. In such conflicts, the parties would gradually approach one another's positions as agreement would appear attractive from a distance. But as their positions grew closer the costs of agreement would loom higher in their perceptions so that avoidance tendencies would set in and they would tend to back off from agreement. Of course, in the partial test ban negotiations, these tendencies were eventually overcome, making it possible to consumate an agreement.

Looking at the beta coefficients next for $\triangle EXS(L)$, we find that they make a statistically significant contribution at the .10 level only in the case of equation 3a, involving the United States. For the USSR the effects of this variable are generally negligible (for example, in equation 1b the beta coefficient = -.051, p = .849). Thus while the Soviet behavior was apparently more affected by previous positions than was the case for the United States, the United States was more affected by the external environment.

Finally, turning to the perception variable, we found that it was generally negatively related to U.S. behavior, being the strongest in equation 3a (beta coefficient = -.660, p = .082). On the other hand, for the USSR the ΔPER variable generally exerted a weak, positive effect, though it never reached the .10 level of significance. The strong negative relationship for the impact of this variable in the American case may be somewhat curious, especially since in terms of simple r's, American perceptions and actions were weakly but positively correlated (r = .204). However, when a partial correlation between ΔPER and ΔINR for the United States was calculated controlling for actual Soviet behavior towards the United States, namely ΔINS, the relationship became strongly negative (-.479). The strong positive relationship of ΔPER to ΔINS (r = .77) in the American case may have masked the negative relationship between ΔPER and ΔINR when the stimulus was not controlled for. Thus, although American behaviors were symmetrical to actual Soviet behaviors, they were, in fact, negatively related to their own perceptions of Soviet behaviors. This may be indicative of an exploitative relationship similar to the type suggested by Bartos, although it is somewhat different in this case in that the potential exploitation involved the relationship between American *perceptions* of Soviet actions and American responses, rather than the relation of actual Soviet actions to American responses, which was positive. However, the data do suggest the possibility that American negotiators may have pressed their advantage and become tougher when they *perceived* the Soviet Union becoming softer in its negotiating behavior. They may have thus hoped to gain a more desirable outcome from a temporarily more genial opponent. Conversely, they engaged in more positive actions themselves when they *perceived* Soviet behavior hardening, perhaps because the failure to do so might have been perceived as sealing the fate of the negotiations. Although our data are consistent with such an interpretation, they are not necessarily proof of an exploitative relationship in these negotiations. Furthermore, no such relationship appeared for the Soviet Union.[2]

CONCLUSIONS

The substantial and statistically significant R^2s obtained in these analyses indicate that a model similar to a Richardson process is

2. For the USSR, the following simple r's were found:
$r_{\Delta INR - \Delta PER}$ = .035; $r_{\Delta INS - \Delta INR}$ = .645; $r_{\Delta PER - \Delta INR}$ = .271

capable of capturing much of the variation in the behavior of the superpowers in the negotiations leading to the Partial Nuclear Test Ban Treaty of 1963. For the United States, all models proposed in this paper except 2a were statistically significant at better than the .10 level, and for the Soviet Union equations 2b and 4b were significant at the same threshold. This demonstrates that Richardson-type models can describe at least some increasingly cooperative interactions as well as competitive ones. In looking at the contributions of specific variables to the model, several other fundamental conclusions stand out.

First, in all cases the most significant factor contributing to each variant of the model for both countries was the internal stimulus, the behavior of the other actor within the same negotiations. This factor made a contribution which was significant at better than the .05 level in all variants of the model except for the United States in model 2, where the p value approximates .10. In this respect, our results were basically similar to those obtained in Richardson models of arms races. Contrary to the arguments of Zartman (1975), these data clearly demonstrate that the negotiations of the Partial Nuclear Test Ban Treaty were characterized by a process of mutual interactions, including a generally tit-for-tat exchange of soft and hard bargaining moves heading gradually, though not always consistently, towards agreement. Thus, the negotiation process was strongly characterized by a process of mutual interactions between the two major parties. This is not to assert that cognitive change and the development of new formulas for agreement were not relevant. Although our data do not speak to this point directly, a substantive interpretation of these negotiations would tend to indicate that some such processes were at work. However, these data would certainly seem to suggest that even processes such as cognitive change, the reformulation of objectives and principles, and other cognitive aspects of negotiation can be treated in an interactive model which considers the role of both individual and environmental variables.

Second, the negotiations on the Partial Nuclear Test Ban Treaty were not strongly affected by past behaviors. In this important respect they differed from an arms race. Our results, though, were consistent with Bartos' (1974: 166) findings from an experimental setting. He found that negotiations were essentially "future oriented" in that one's past behavior was not a forceful constraint on present behavior. Bartos investigated specifically whether persistence in bargaining positions was more typical than oscillation of positions. He calculated whether responses by his simulated negotiators were or were not consistent over time, i.e., whether or not they reversed themselves when their options included lowering their offers, repeating them, or raising them. His data (Bartos, 1974: 112-113) revealed that negotiators overall tended to repeat their demands 51% of the time, reversing themselves almost as often as they maintained their positions. Thus, he concluded that "fluctuating demands" rather than "smooth demands" characterized the behavior of the negotiators.

Third, we found in the case of the United States that the behavior of the USSR towards it outside of negotiations made a significant contribution to an equation accounting for the negotiating behavior of the United States within the Eighteen Nation Disarmament Conference. On the other hand, Soviet behavior within the negotiations was not accounted for at a significant level by American actions towards the USSR outside the negotiations. Not surprisingly, these findings were consistent with those of Hopmann and King (1976: 140) using a correlational analysis of the same data.

Fourth, we found that perceptions of grievance, treated as a variable rather than as a constant, had some impact on the negotiating behavior of both countries, though of a quite different nature. In the case of the USSR, the impact of perceptions of American behavior was generally positive though rather weak. In the case of the United States, perceptions of Soviet actions strongly affected American behavior, but always in a negative direction. We speculated, although our evidence on this point is by no means conclusive, that this may be indicative of some exploitative behavior in these negotiations. The data suggest that the Americans tended to toughen their negotiating stands when they perceived the Soviets in more positive terms, while relaxing their stands when they perceived the Soviets as tougher.

Further research along these lines would benefit from an increased sample size, preferably over several kinds of arms-limitation negotiations. This would add to the scope and generality of the findings. Applying a Richardson-type model to bargaining using different operationalizations and different data sources would also add to the potential generalizability of these results. Finally, the research might be further extended through the use of curvilinear and other estimation procedures not employed in our present analysis. On the basis of the one case analyzed in this paper we would certainly not claim to have resolved definitively the debate between interactive approaches to negotiations typified by Bartos' research and the "formula-detail" approach advocated by Zartman. But we do feel that our overall results indicate that models of interactive processes similar to those formulated by Richardson, which Bartos found to be applicable in a laboratory setting, may be potentially applicable to real-world international negotiations as well.

P. Terrence Hopmann is Director of the Quigley Center of International Studies and Associate Professor of Political Science at the University of Minnesota. He is coauthor of Unity and Disintegration in International Alliances, *and has written numerous articles on alliance cohesion and on international negotiation processes for scholarly journals and anthologies. In 1975-1976 he was a Fulbright-Hays research scholar in Belgium.*

Theresa C. Smith is an Assistant Professor of Political Science at Saint Cloud State University. She received her Ph.D. from the University of Minnesota in 1977, where she did research on the relationship between arms-racing and the outbreak of war.

9. Argumentation in Foreign Policy Settings

BRITAIN IN 1918, MUNICH IN 1938, AND JAPAN IN 1970

ROBERT AXELROD
*Department of Political Science and
Institute of Public Policy Studies
University of Michigan*

This is a study of argumentation in three different kinds of high level, confidential, foreign policy settings: a collegial setting, a bureaucratic setting, and a bargaining setting. The causal and value assertions of the participants were coded using the detailed records of these three settings. The data show to be inadequate a defense/attack model of argumentation in which the participants support their own arguments to make them resistant to attack, while attacking the weak spots in others' stated positions. In fact, there are few assertions which are supported by specific evidence, almost no mutually supported causal arguments, and the assertions which were attacked were no less emphasized than the assertions which were not attacked. More in accord with the data is the novel-arguments approach in which the key factor in persuasive argumentation is the development of arguments which others have not already taken into account.

Argumentation is a vital part of the policy process when power is shared and when problems are so complex that the participants are not

AUTHOR'S NOTE: I wish to thank my research assistant and principal coder, Stan Bernstein; my programmers, Ernest Beffel, Leslie Forman, David Gow, Gary Raffel, and Edward Shulaker; my auxiliary coders, Jane Barnard, Joan Kmenta, and Barbara sure that their own initial positions are necessarily the best ones. When a policy problem arises, a person's or organization's interests in one or another possible course of action is often far from obvious. Interests must be discovered; or to put it another way, they must be developed piecemeal.

Each of our standard approaches to decision-making recognizes this problem, but each does little to solve it. The unitary rational-actor model (Allison, 1971) and the statistical models of decision-making take for granted that the utilities of the entire organization are given in advance. The organizational-process model discusses the role of standard operating procedures and the tendency of decision makers to satisfice rather than optimize their interests, but it does not get into the details of how the consequences of alternatives are estimated. The bureaucratic-politics model treats the policy outcomes as emerging from organizational interests as represented by actors in roles. This is a useful start, but it leaves open the questions of how the role occupants come to see their own interests, and how the somewhat converging and somewhat conflicting interests seen initially by the role occupants get developed through interactions.

The development of interests in a policy choice is done by seeking the causal links between the alternatives and utility. This is what a means-ends analysis is about. Some of these links, or causal paths, come immediately to mind for the decision maker. But he or she is usually aware that not all of them come to mind right away. So, special measures are taken to become aware of more of them—to develop a richer understanding of the consequences of choice, whether collective choice or individual choice within a collective format.

In actual practice, policy makers have several methods for developing these interests, including simply ruminating on them, making lists for themselves, asking their subordinates to write reports, and calling meetings to discuss the issue. This study is concerned with the argumentation process in meetings which are called to deal with major foreign policy problems.

Lewis; and my translators, Steve Reed and Yoko Sakuma. For their help in developing the ideas that went into this paper, I also wish to thank James Beniger, Michael Champion, Michael Cohen, Robyn Davis, Alexander George, Mark Granovetter, Bernard Grofman, Ditsa Kafry, Arnold Kanter, Daniel Okimoto, John Padgett, Tom Palfrey, Seizaburo Sato, Paul Sniderman, and William Zimmerman. I am grateful to Ichiro Suetsugu, Secretary General of the Japanese Council on National Security, for permission to use the transcripts of that group, and to Akio Watanabe and Schien Yoshida for leading me to them. Finally, I wish to thank the National Science Foundation which supported this research under grant SOC74-19773, and the Center for Advanced Study in the Behavioral Sciences where this work was completed.

Meetings serve many functions, but the functions that are most relevant for developing one's interests in a policy choice are:

(1) the opportunity to talk, since self-expression helps the development of one's own thoughts,
(2) the opportunity to listen to arguments offered by others, and
(3) the opportunity to persuade others of one's own current viewpoint.

A simple paradigm would be that people in committees have initial positions based on the arguments that they have developed on their own or heard before the meeting. Then, they express themselves (not necessarily all that they know or without distortion) to convince others that their initially favored view is best. But they also listen to see if *they* should be persuaded. That is to say, each recognizes that *he* may want to change.

March and Simon (1958) warn that the appearance of rational discussion may be exaggerated to minimize organizational conflict. Still, rational discussion is not to be dismissed. It is a vital aspect of the policy process. As Neustadt (1960: 23) points out in speaking of the president, "despite his status he does not get action without argument. Presidential *power* is the power to persuade." In general, argumentation is important when issues are complex, and its importance is heightened when power is shared.

One of the forms of policy-making in which argumentation plays a vital role is negotiation. After all, most of what happens in negotiation is the assertion of arguments by one side, and the response with other arguments by the other side. Negotiators themselves frequently see negotiations as a search process. They realize that they have only an imperfect understanding of one another's preferences so they pay attention to the other's arguments for several reasons, including a desire to find pairs of items on which concessions may be profitably exchanged (Cross, 1977). The nature of the agreement itself is often based on a formula and details for its implementation (Zartman, 1977). Exactly which formula emerges and how its details are specified is determined through the process of argumentation. Thus an understanding of argumentation is important not only in a decision-making context with flexible preferences, but even in a negotiating context with relatively stable preferences.

This paper is a study of argumentation in high level, confidential, foreign-policy meetings. There will be no attempt to examine the full context of these meetings nor to evaluate the quality of their outcomes.

Instead, the focus will be on a systematic analysis of the process of argumentation within the meetings themselves. This is not to deny the significance of nonverbal cues within the meetings or the significance of messages between the meetings. It is only to say that much can be learned from what is available: the arguments within the meetings.

The goal is to gain a better understanding of how argumentation is actually conducted among elite decision makers, and thereby achieve a better understanding of the policy process itself, including both decision-making and negotiations.

THE SETTINGS

Three quite different types of policy groups can be identified. The first is a collegial group in which the members derive their authority not from any organizational constituency, but rather from their personal attributes such as their reputation and their skills in argumentation. The second type of group is the one more typical of American foreign-policy decision-making, in which the members are chosen on the basis of their formal roles in the organizational units which have a stake in the policy issues at hand. This is the kind of group which can be most easily described with the bureaucratic-politics paradigm (Allison, 1971), in contrast to the relatively collegial process more favored by those who found merit in the operations of the ad hoc Executive Committee during the Cuban Missile Crisis, such as George (1972, 1975) and Janis (1972). The third kind of setting is a bargaining session in which the participants use threats and promises as well as arguments to infuence each other under conditions of substantial conflict of interest (March and Simon, 1958: 129-135; Walton and McKersie, 1965: 11-125; Lindblom, 1965: 33). Negotiation plays a different role in each of the three types of groups. It is subsidiary in a collegial group, significant in a bureaucratic group, and central in a bargaining group.

The data for this study are derived from the detailed records of one instance of each of these three types of settings. The advantage of selecting three quite different kinds of settings is that it allows one to compare and contrast the modes of argumentation which may appear. If some findings apply to all three such diverse groups, this is good reason to believe that they may have broad applicability. Conversely, if a specific finding applies to only one group but not to the other two, then the differences between the groups can be consulted to see what might account for the difference. Let us now turn to the three settings selected for analysis.

The Japanese Council on National Security in 1970 was a clear instance of a collegial group, the British Eastern Committee of 1918 was a typical bureaucratic group, and the negotiations between Chamberlain and Hitler leading to the Munich agreement of 1938 was a salient example of a bargaining setting. Each of these settings involved a small number of participants, at a high level, dealing with policy problems of great importance, under conditions of uncertainty, in the face of differing values and beliefs, where arguments were made and decisions taken without public surveillance.

The Japanese Council on National Security represents a case of collegial deliberations. The Council was a semiofficial advisory group to Prime Minister Eisaku Sato in 1970. Its chairman, Tadao Kusumi, was a close associate of the Prime Minister, and the other members included some of Japan's leading defense intellectuals. It was a collegial group in that the members did not represent specific organizational units or political factions. They had considerable group solidarity based on their earlier work together on Okinawan reversion, and their group cohesiveness was probably reinforced by the norms of Japanese groups (Nakane, 1970). Their main task was to propose a realistic plan for Japanese defense arrangements over the next several years. Recognizing the likelihood of American pullbacks from Asia, and accepting the domestic and international limitations on the growth of Japanese military strength, they focused on the question of deterring potential adversaries and on the role of American bases in Japan. The outcome was a proposal for crisis-stationing: most of the bases would be run by Japan with arrangements for American forces to return in times of crisis. One indication of the significance of the group is that two weeks after they decided on this recommendation, the Director General of the Self-Defense Agency announced for the first time that in times of emergency Japan would let the United States use two air bases that had just been turned over to Japan (Japan Times, December 26, 1970).

The British Eastern Committee represents a case of a standing committee with representation from the major bureaucratic units within the government that had a stake in foreign policy. Being a standing committee of the Imperial War Cabinet it could effectively determine British policy within the range of its authority, the Middle East. From among the many problems it addressed, the one which has been selected for analysis was the question of what to do about British involvement in Persia at the end of World War I. The main line of the discussion was whether Britain should withdraw and let Persia "stew in her own juice," continue her active policy of indirect control of the Persian army and finances, or try to conciliate the government and the people of Persia by employing a softer line. The decision after two meetings in December 1918 was to continue the firm British policy, and if necessary to show the Persians that "within the velvet glove is an iron hand" (Eastern Committee, 1918).[1]

The negotiations in September 1938 between Britain and Germany that led to the Munich agreement represent a case of bargaining between nations rather than between individuals or bureaucratic sections within a single nation. It was an extreme case of high conflict of interest and great stress. Hitler had threatened to dismember Czechoslovakia, a nation whose existence was guaranteed by France and indirectly by the United Kingdom. The British Prime Minister, Neville Chamberlain, offered to come to Germany to negotiate with Hitler. The two men met with only a translator on September 15 and again on September 22, and then with five aides on September 23-24, 1938. The main issues of debate were the conditions and timing of the surrender of the Sudeten region of Czechoslovakia. The outcome was the avoidance of an immediate war. This end was forced by the imposition of British and French governmental pressures on the Czechoslovakian government to accept the solution agreed upon by Chamberlain and Hitler.

All three of these settings have highly detailed records of their deliberations. The records of the Japanese Council on National Security are still confidential, but the verbatim transcripts of the meetings have been made available for this study. All sections dealing with policy on foreign policy and defense matters (excluding those dealing exclusively with the estimation of American credibility) were translated and analyzed. The minutes of the Munich negotiations, while written in the third person, are also highly detailed. Both the British and the German versions were published after World War II, and the British version has been used in this analysis (Woodward et al., 1949: 342-351, 463-473, and 499-508). The records of the British Eastern committee consist of verbatim transcripts which have been declassified only recently (Eastern Committee, 1918).

---

1. For more background on the British Eastern Committee and its deliberations on Persia, see Axelrod (1976: 74-95).

TURNING DOCUMENTS INTO DATA

For the purpose of this study, each document was coded sentence by sentence and even phrase by phrase to identify the causal and value assertions made by the speakers. For a full discussion of the documentary coding rules, see Axelrod (1976: 82-84), and for the text of the coding rules themselves, see Wrightson (1976). The fundamental idea is that each causal assertion is coded in terms of its three components: cause, connector, and effect. For example, consider the statement, "Security augments the ability of the Persian government to maintain order." The cause is regarded as "the amount of security in Persia," the effect is regarded as "the extent of the ability of the Persian government to maintain order" and the connector is "+" since there is a positive impact of the cause variable on the effect variable. As an example of a negative causal relationship, consider the statement, "the ability of the British to put pressure on the Persian government inhibits the [extent of the] removal of the better local governors in Persia." Here the connector is "-" since an *increase* in the ability of the British to apply pressure is asserted to cause a *decrease* in the removal of the better governors.[2]

Value assertions are those assertions whose effect variable is the utility of a participant. Thus, saying that "chaos in Persia is bad for Britain" is a value assertion, and is coded as if it were "chaos in Persia causes a lowering of British utility." Occasionally assertions (usually assertions of value) are so obvious as not to have to be stated explicitly. In this case they are regarded as assumed assertions. For example, the statement that "the bankruptcy of Persia would harm British security interests in the area" would be coded as two statements: one explicit causal assertion about the effect of bankruptcy on British security interests, and one assumed value assertion about the effect of British security interests on British utility.

Consistency of the coding was achieved by having all of the documents coded by the same person. Reliability was affirmed by comparing the work of this coder with the coding of each of two other coders of known reliability on a test document of 7300 words.[3]

---

2. Other connectors that are used include: 0 for "no effect," ⊕ for "zero or positive effect," ⊖ for "zero or negative effect," M for "matters" (i.e., positive or negative effect), and U for "universal" (i.e., any effect is possible).

3. The results are as follows, stated in terms of the average of the current coder with each of the two previous coders. The agreement score on the number of explicit codable assertions in each of the 226 sentences was .82 according to Robinson's measure of agree-

(Note 3 continued at bottom of p. 183)

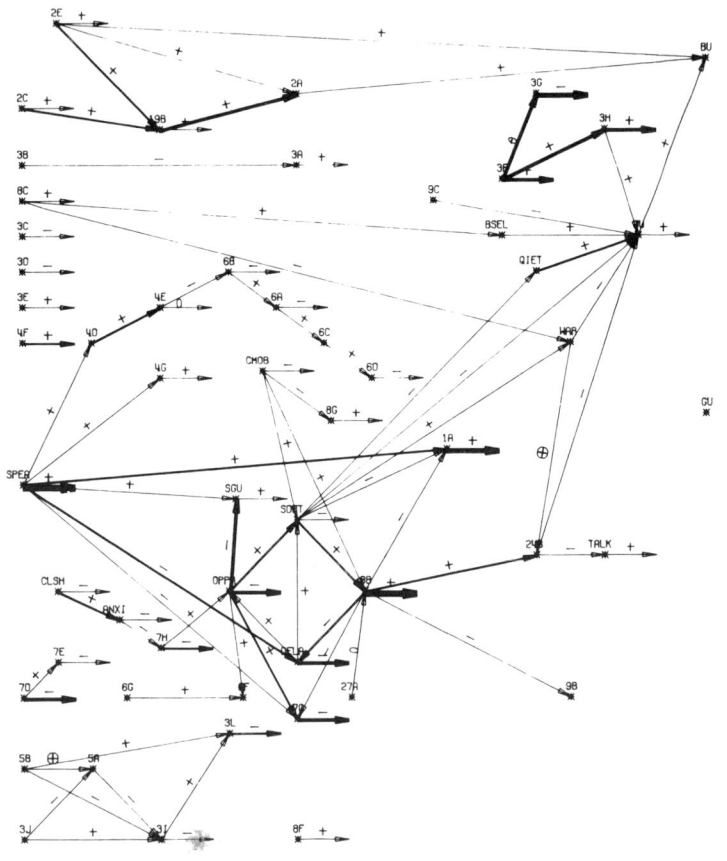

BU— British utility
GU—German utility
JU—Joint British and German utility
ANXI—Anxiety of inhabitants of frontier districts
BSEL—British policy to support the principle of self-determination in the Sudetenland
CLSH—Number of armed clashes on Czechoslovakian-German frontier
CMOB—Czechoslovakian mobilization
DELA—Delay in implemenation of solution to Sudeten question
OPPR—Oppression of Sudeten Germans
QIET—Joint policy to keep political situation quiet during meetings
SDET—Further deterioration of situation in Sudetenland
SPEA—German policy to arrange peaceful return of Germans in Austria and Czechoslovakia
TALK—Direct talks between Hitler and Chamberlain

Figure 1: A Dyadic Model of Negotiation

1A—Improvement of Ango-German relations
2A—Hitler's flexibility to define a solution to the problem
2C—German policy to free Germany from treaty of Versailles
2E—Fulfillment by Hitler of promises to Germans (variables 2C, SPEA, 4F)
3A—Racial basis of Nazi party and Germany
3B—German policy of imperialist domination of non-Germans
3C—German policy to unite all Germans in Europe in Germany
3D—German policy to unite German national groups far from Reich with Reich
3E—German policy to exclude controversy provoking wound-opening territorial demands (e.g., with France)
3F—Negotiated settlement of German demands
3G—Expansion of German territorial demands
3H—Germany properly executes negotiated terms
3I—German policy to limit naval fleet to proportion of British naval power
3J—Germany and Britain determination not to make war
3L—German disadvantage vis-a-vis Britian in a war
4D—Demands for secession by Polish, Hungarian, and Ukranian minorities
4E—Dismemberment of Czechoslovakia
4F—German policy to establish German right to colonies
4G—Austrian-German utility
5A—Possibility of war between Britian and Germany
5B—British policy to warn of possibility of war given certain (hostile) acts
6A—Czechoslovakia as spearhead in side of Germany
6B—Czechoslovakia alliances with others countries (versus Germany)
6C—Increase in size of German air force (beyond intended size)
6D—German military expenditures
6F—Sudeten German resistance to oppression
6G—Growth of power and prestige of German Reich
7D—British policy that Germany and Britain direct appeal to Czechoslovakian parties for armistice
7E—Admonitions for calm to Sudeten-German victims
7G—Outrage to German pride
7H—German inactivity in response to Sudeten oppression
8B—Germ policy to solve the Sudeten question by war
8C—British policy to announce agreement to separation of Sudetenland and Czechoslovakian constitutional revision
8F—Implementation of Sudeten-German separation
8G—German policy to accept British temporary armistice
9B—Ability to stop war machine of Germany
9C—French and British readiness to go to war over the Sudentenland
SGU—Utility of Sudenten-Germans
WAR—Potential for war over Sudetenland
19B—German popular support
24B—War (end of peace in Europe)
27A—World-wide support of Germany

ment (1957). This means that 82% of the variance in 226 pairs of observations is accounted for by the within-pairs sums of squares. For those assertions that were identified by both coders, complete agreement on three parts of the assertion (i.e., the part of the sentence that contained the cause, the part that contained the sign, and the type of sign) occurred 88% of the time. Agreement on the identification of variables across assertions occurred 81% of the time. Agreement on the direct effect of each variable on utility (whether explicit or assumed) occurred 75% of the time. When a direct effect on utility was noted by two coders, the agreement on the sign was 90%. For further details on the reliability check procedures see Axelrod (1976: 84-86).

Since the effect variable of one assertion can be the cause variable of another assertion, arguments can be represented as chains of assertions. The easiest way to visualize the complex structure that can result is to represent the concept variables (whether causes or effects) as points, and represent the connectons between them as arrows from the cause concept to the effect concept. Figure 1 is an illustration of Hitler's arguments made during the first meeting of the Munich negotiations. To help keep this large graph legible, the many arrows which go to German utility are represented as short horizontal arrows with no effect variable at their head. As another visual aid, the thickness of arrows is drawn proportional to the number of times the same cause and effect variable are mentioned in an assertion. This graph represents each of the 55 concept variables and 149 assertions Hitler made in the first meeting with Chamberlain.[4]

Table 1 gives some of the basic characteristics of the three settings. Altogether 2191 assertions using 662 different variables were coded. A sense of the size of this data set can be obtained by noting that Figure 1, which shows the arguments used by Hitler in the first meeting of the Munich negotiations, contains only about one-fifteenth of the assertions in the entire data set. As can be seen from Table 1, each text is approximately the same length in English, but the collegial-Japanese setting yielded half again as many assertions as did either of the other two settings. Per thousand words of English text, the Japanese setting had both more causal statements and more value statements than the other two. Thus, the basic notions of causation and utility on which the coding scheme is based were found to be highly applicable in this non-Western setting.

THE DEFENSE/ATTACK MODEL

A plausible image of partisan discussion is that the participants defend their own point of view and attack the arguments of others who have differing policy preferences. In this image, the participants try to build a defense for their own arguments by supporting their assertions with evidence. Or they use mutually supporting arguments to bolster their causal arguments so that if one line of defense fails another will be available. Moreover, in the defense/attack model they

---

4. A careful study of the graph will show that there are two cycles, or causal loops, involving the variables SDET, 8B, DELA, and OPPR. Such cycles are comparatively rare, and most graphs in the three settings are entirely free of them. For the cognitive implications of the lack of cycles, see Axelrod (1976: 231-239).

TABLE 1
Three Settings

	Japanese Council on National Security	British Eastern Committee	Anglo-German Munich Negotiations
type of setting	collegial	bureaucratic	bargaining
word of English text	15,300	18,600	14,000
speakers	14	9	4
concept variables	302	186	174
assertions	928	610	653
explicit	741	523	531
assumed	187	87	122
causal assertions per 1000 words of English text	33.3	16.1	23.8
value assertions per 1000 words of English text	27.4	18.1	22.8

seek out and attack the undefended spots in their opponents' arguments in order to overcome them. This defense/attack model may be appealing because of its conflictual nature, but, as we shall now see, it is not very helpful in explaining the data from any of the three cases at hand.

(1) First consider the use of specific examples. For instance, a Japanese participant illustrated his point that the requirement of prior consultations could inhibit timely American reponse to a crisis by mentioning the Soviet invasion of Czechoslovakia in 1968: "Czechoslovakia or something, something new comes up and it [prior consultations] could become very difficult." In fact, however, very few of the hundreds of explicit assertions are supported by specific examples which are cited as evidence (see Table 2, line 1a). This is somewhat surprising since one would expect that between practical men of politics, concrete historical evidence would be a powerful way of supporting an assertion. An excess of ideological or abstract thinking does not account for this lack of historical evidence, since the most ideologically oriented of all the speakers in the three settings (Hitler and Ribbentrop) actually used proportionally more historical examples than did the other speakers. And so did the speakers who would be expected to be the most abstract thinkers, the members of the Japanese Council on National Security who were professors.

To be generous in the counting of the support by evidence, we might want to include those assertions which are claimed to be generally

TABLE 2
Defense/Attack Model

	Japanese Council on National Security	British Eastern Committee	Anglo-German Munich Negotiations
1. Proportion of explicit assertions for which there is:			
a. historical evidence	5%	1%	5%
b. claimed generality	1%	.4%	1%
c. unsupported emphasis	21%	16%	17%
2. Number of mutually supporting causal arguments	3	1	0
3. Average emphasis (by major speakers) of:			
a. attacked assertions	.26 (n=57)	.11 (n=57)	.43 (n=7)
b. other assertions	.22 (n=747)	.13 (n=507)	.19 (n=634)

true even if no specific evidence is cited in their support. For example, in justifying his warning about the inviolability of the Anglo-German Naval Agreement, Chamberlain used the form of claimed generality in saying to Hitler, "When two peoples are on the point of conflict with one another they must be perfectly clear in advance of the consequences of such a conflict" (Woodward et al., 1949: 346). The picture remains unchanged, however, when these instances of claimed generality are counted (Table 2, line 1b). There are still no more than 6% of all assertions that are supported by either method. This is in sharp contrast to the much larger proportion of assertions which are emphasized without support, either by indications that the speaker firmly believes the statement to be true, or by indications that the speaker thinks the assertion is important (see Table 2, line 1c).[5]

5. The definitions of the four types of emphases are as follows. Specific evidence is the number of specific examples which are cited by the speaker as evidence of the operation of the coded causal principle. Claimed generality is an indication of the speaker's belief that the relationship between cause and effect variables is regular, trustable, or of wide or constant application. Certainty is an indication that a speaker firmly believes the assertion he is making. Importance is an indication that the speaker thinks an assertion is important. It is possible to have more than one indication of a single kind of emphasis and/or

(2) The very rare use of mutually supporting causal arguments is another fact that is inconsistent with the defense/attack conception of partisan discussion. An argument about how one concept variable affects another is mutually supported if there are two or more independent nontrivial paths (i.e., paths with no intervening variable) by which the first concept is asserted to have an impact on the second concept. The paths are nontrivial if they involve one or more intermediate concepts, and they are independent if they do not share any of these intermediate concepts. While there are many mutually supporting arguments about how concept variables are good or bad (i.e., how they impact on utility), there are, in toto, only four such mutually supporting *causal* arguments about how one concept variable impacts on a concept variable other than utility (see Table 2, line 2).

(3) The defense/attack image would also suggest that people attack the undefended weak spots in their opponents' arguments, i.e., they tend to attack those assertions that had not already been emphasized. To check this, the major speakers were compared to each other, and each disagreement about how one concept variable affected another was noted.[6] The results of this analysis (Table 2, lines 3a and 3b) show that assertions that are attacked by someone in the same meeting had been no less emphasized than assertions which are not attacked.

In summary, the defense/attack image of argumentation is not very helpful in explaining several important kinds of information: the infrequency of assertions being supported with specific evidence, the infrequency of mutually supported causal arguments, and the lack of greater emphasis on assertions which are attacked compared to assertions which are not attacked. And the above findings are true in all three settings: the collegial-Japanese setting, the bureaucratic-British setting, and the bargaining setting of the Munich negotiations.

---

more than one type of emphasis for a given assertion. It is also possible for a given single indication of emphasis to apply to more than one assertion. The reliability of the four types of emphases (specific evidence, claimed generality, certainty, and importance) was checked by having one-quarter of the text of each setting independently coded for emphasis by a second coder. The overall intercoder reliability was .70 with no important differences across emphases types or settings.

6. Major speakers are those who had more than 40 explicit assertions. There are six of this type in the Japanese setting, four in the Eastern Committee and two in Munich; they account for 87%, 89%, and 98% respectively of all assertions in their settings. A disagreement on assertions takes place when two assertions about the same cause and the same effect variables have inconsistent signs, such as when one person says "A promotes B" and the other says "A retards B."

THE NATURE OF DISAGREEMENTS

Since the defense/attack model is an inadequate description of what is happening in these meetings, perhaps a better understanding can be obtained by focusing on the nature of specific disagreements the participants have with each other. The most helpful unit of analysis for this purpose is the relationship. A relationship is an asserted connection from a given concept variable to another concept variable, regardless of how many times this connection is asserted, or by how many different speakers, or what the sign of the connection is asserted to be. There is a disagreement over a relationship when there are two or more speakers who use that relationship and their signs are inconsistent.

The striking thing is that there are a very large number of different relationships used in each setting, but only a small proportion of them are disagreed over. There are between three and five hundred different relationships used by the major speakers in each of these settings, resulting in a great richness to the policy discussions in these settings. But there are only a handful of relationships on which the speakers disagree: 29 or 6.0% in the Japanese Council on National Security, 20 or 6.0% in the Eastern Committee, and 6 or 1.5% in the Munich negotiations (Table 3, line 1).

In analyzing these disagreements, it is useful to distinguish between causal and value relationships. As can be seen from Table 3, more than half of the relationships are value relationships, and one of this type is two or three times more likely to be disagreed over than a causal relationship. But even value relationships are not very often disagreed over; less than 11% of them in each of the three settings. Thus, both types of relationships and all three settings show a low level of disagreement considering that these are face to face, high level, confidential meetings on complex foreign-policy problems.

One potential explanation for this low rate of disagreement is that the participants can disagree with each other without ever having to state directly their disagreement. For example, one person might say that A promotes B and C, both of which are good for Japan, while the other person might say that A promotes D which is bad for Japan. They do not disagree on any of the causal relationships or on any of the value relationships, but the conclusions implicit in what each has said differ concerning the impact of A on Japanese utility. Taking into account all of the possible effects which can be inferred from the

TABLE 3
Disagreements Among Major Speakers

	Japanese Council on National Security	British Eastern Committee	Anglo-German Munich Negotiations
1. Percent of all relationships disagreed over	6.0% (n=483)	6.0% (n=335)	1.5% (n=403)
2. Percent of causal relationships disagreed over	3.9% (n=285)	3.6% (n=222)	.9% (n=235)
3. Percent of value relationships disagreed over	9.1% (n=198)	10.6% (n=113)	2.4% (n=168)

assertions made by each speaker,[7] there can obviously be many more disagreements between speakers than there are disagreements on single relationships. The number of inferrable effects is also greater, however. Altogether, less than 6% of the effects which can be inferred from the assertions are disagreed over in each setting, and in Munich, only 1.6% are disagreed over. Therefore, the low proportion of relationships which are disagreed over is not due simply to the possibility that disagreement is more common among what can be inferred compared to what is directly stated.

What is especially striking is that the proportion of disagreement, among both causal and value relationships, is lowest in the Munich negotiations. After all, those negotiations were between the leaders of two nations potentially on the verge of war. What seems to account for the low rate of value disagreement is that Chamberlain sometimes says that an increase in a specific concept variable would be good (or bad) for Britain, and Hitler says it would be the opposite for Germany, but neither says what they think it would be for the other. Thus they do not directly disagree, even though they differ on what should be done about it. If this type of disagreement is included, then the rate of value disagreement in Munich is 12%, virtually the same as in the other two

---

7. For the mathematics of computing these "total effects," see Axelrod (1976: 61-64, 343-348).

groups.[8] This still leaves unanswered, however, why there is also such a low rate of disagreement among the 235 causal relationships in Munich.

As we have seen, people in all three settings do not disagree with each other at a very high rate. It also happens that they rarely disagree with something they themselves have already said. This is true even though each setting involves several hundred relationships and two or more meetings on the same subject separated by at least a week.[9] In the collegial-Japanese group this disagreement with something one has already said happened only 19 times, in the bureaucratic-British setting it happened a mere 8 times, and in the bargaining of the Munich setting it happened only three times. Moreover, most of these 30 self-disagreements cannot be attributed to the lapse of time between meetings since 23 of them included self-disagreement within a single meeting.

There are many possible reasons for a person saying something which is inconsistent with a prior statement, including the consideration of a changed context but not its specification, the desire to show agreement with another, and, of course, the actual changing of the mind. The comparatively large number of times one of the Japanese speakers disagreed with himself might well be due to the sense of common purpose of the group, which in turn was promoted by the nature of its advisory role, the strong sense of membership in a shared enterprise, and probably the cultural differences between Japanese and Western groups (Nakane, 1970). The heightened sense of common purpose in the Japanese group probably made it easier for a participant to be less careful about monitoring the consistency of his arguments, easier for him to change his mind, and easier for him to admit a change to others.

CONCLUSION

We now have seven principal findings regarding argumentation in three high-level foreign-policy groups:

8. This is based on n = 115, the number of value relationships there would be in the Munich setting if the British, German, and joint utility were regarded as a single-utility variable.
9. The Japanese setting used portions of five meetings spread over six months; the Eastern Committee had two meetings on Persia, separated by 10 days; and the negotiations leading to the Munich settlement took place in three sessions over a period of a week.

(1) Assertions are infrequently supported by specific evidence.

(2) Causal arguments are almost never mutually supporting.

(3) Assertions which are attacked are no less emphasized than assertions which are not attacked.

(4) Hundreds of different relationships are used in the meetings, but few are disagreed over.

(5) Causal relationships are even less likely than value relationships to be disagreed over, even when unstated implications are taken into account.

(6) There is relatively less disagreement over causal relationships in the Munich negotiations than in the collegial and bureaucratic groups. This was because both the Munich negotiators expressed their own preferences but tended to avoid assertions about what would be good or bad for the others.

(7) Speakers rarely disagree with something they themselves have already said, but this happens most in the collegial-Japanese setting, and least in the Munich negotiations.

These findings, and especially the first three, indicate that the defense/attack conceptualization is not a very adequate way to conceptualize argumentation in policy meetings.[10]

More in accord with the data now available is an orientation developed by Burnstein and Vinokur (1973).[11] Their idea is that to be persuasive an argument must be (1) perceived to be valid by the target and (2) not already known and taken into account by the target. In short, a persuasive argument is a valid argument which is novel. Using the novel-arguments theory, and assuming that the participants in high-level foreign-policy meetings have initial positions which they are trying to persuade others to adopt, and assuming that they have a judgment about what arguments others will regard as valid, several predictions could be made. In particular, there would be little need for offensive or defensive behavior other than offering arguments which others might not yet have taken into account. Such a prediction does indeed seem to be consistent with the data at hand.

---

10. This conclusion is not due solely to the fact that assertions are a very small unit of analysis. The result that there is little support and only infrequent disagreement may be partly attributable to the small unit of analysis. The small unit of analysis can not be the sole explanation of the failure of the defense/attack model, however, since disagreement is not more frequent when potential inferences are taken into account. In any case, attacks do not disproportionally tend to be made against the weak spots in the other's arguments.

11. Their theme is developed further with evidence from small-group experiments in a number of subsequent studies: Vinokur and Burnstein (1974), Burnstein and Vinokur (1975), Vinokur et al. (1975), Burnstein and Vinokur (forthcoming).

The novel-arguments approach also suggests the importance of the very factors that have been stressed by a wide variety of policy analysts: diversity, openness, creativity, acceptance of interpersonal conflict, and avoidance of premature closure.[12] Unfortunately, the novel-arguments approach is not yet specific enough to be able to take us very far in two of the most important tasks that confront the analyst of elite policy-making: the understanding of how decisions emerge from the deliberations of policy groups and the advising on how the policy process can be improved. Moreover, the low rate of disagreement raises the important question of whether high-level policy makers are simply failing to process each other's arguments, or whether they are being strategically sophisticated in ways we do not as yet fully understand.

What is now available for the first time is a set of systematic data on the specific arguments and their structure from several different kinds of high-level foreign-policy settings. The results from this data have already shown that one conception of argumentation is inadequate, and that another conception is potentially useful. In the future, these quantitative results from a collegial, bureaucratic, and bargaining setting can serve to lessen our dependence on anecdotal evidence. By providing the means to evaluate models of the way elite policy groups operate, these results may even inspire the development of new conceptions of how argumentation is conducted, how interests are developed, and how policy is made.

Robert Axelrod is Associate Professor in the Department of Political Science and the Institute of Public Policy Studies of the University of Michigan. He is author of the works The Conflict of Interest *and* Structure of Decision. *He spent 1976-1977 at the Center for Advanced Study in the Behavioral Sciences.*

---

12. See especially Lindblom (1965; 1968), Argyris (1967), George (1972; 1975), Janis (1972), and Cohen and March (1974).

10. Bargaining as Trial and Error

THE CASE OF THE SPANISH BASE NEGOTIATIONS 1963-1970

BRIAN H. TRACY
HAUS RISSEN

Rather than a single unified process, bargaining is seen to comprise two distinct but complementary processes of change (convergence and structuring) and one termination process (arbitration). Initial structuring activity transforms issues into a set of identifiable exchange relationships with a measurable disparity of demands (the convergence set), giving the bargaining relationship sufficient structure so that convergence can proceed. When necessary, the parameters of that convergence set will be altered to provide a more satisfactory formula for agreement. The history of the United States-Spanish base negotiations from 1968 to 1970 reveals that the initial formula for agreement was overhauled twice before it assumed a form capable of accommodating both parties' interests. Several concluding observations assess the utility of the trial and error approach for the analysis of international negotiations.

In the past decade, a scattered and speculative body of bargaining literature has matured into a set of complex and at times elegant theories of the bargaining process. Still, these advances in theory offer little direct assistance to the analyst of international negotiations or to the practitioner involved in making day-to-day bargaining decisions. It appears that an engineering feat, linking theory and practice, is needed. The following study is one attempt at such an engineering approach.

I

Is there only one "bargaining process"?

An affirmative answer to this question is generally taken for granted. The mere existence of several schools of bargaining theory suggests, however, that the answer is not so obvious. In important aspects, the principal approaches to bargaining differ so radically from one another that it is difficult to bear in mind that they are studying the same phenomenon.

Two approaches are generally recognized as having particular relevance: the convergence model and the strategic choice model (see Young, 1975; Zartman, 1971, 1974; Tracy, 1975). The convergence model, especially the Cross (1965, 1969) learning variant, is an extraordinarily well-developed and convincing analysis of the elements and mechanism of convergence of demands within stable parameters. It points out the importance of changing expectations and of the time costs of bargaining. The bargaining process is dynamic and serves a productive as well as a distributive function. The demand/expectations/adjustment convergence model shows the interrelatedness of the principal elements of the bargaining process and offers a number of solid and provocative propositions about the nature of the convergence process. The convergence approach, however, views bargaining as taking place almost entirely within fixed and stable parameters, thus minimizing or eliminating the role of manipulation or restructuring of those parameters. There is little sense of preliminary bargaining. And convergence bargaining is limited to consideration of only one issue or exchange at a time. In short, the restrictive assumptions that underlie the convergence approach preclude consideration of significant aspects of bargaining behavior.

In the strategic bargaining approach, players make maximizing decisions about how to manipulate or restructure the basic variables defining the bargaining relationship, often by integrating salient aspects of the environment into that process (Schelling, 1960; Young, 1967, 1975; Zartman, 1971, 1976; Snyder, 1971; Jervis, 1970). Special concern is directed to a variety of strategic moves—far-ranging moves that have such an impact on the course of the bargaining process as to preempt almost all future activity. Each player thus tries to manipulate his opponent's decision-making structure so that the opponent's best choice is also in one's own best interest. Since one's best choice depends on the expected behavior of the opponent, it becomes necessary to try to outguess the opponent. In order to cope with the complexities of potentially infinite regress reasoning, bargainers resort to a series of control moves that limit the range of alternatives open to the opponent. Agreement is finally reached on a salient outcome point.

The strategic choice model offers no sense of an overall process. There is a subsequent reliance on one-shot sequences or game-defining moves, with but slight consideration given to how the moves interrelate and proceed toward resolution. This is in part necessitated by reliance on static and severely simplified structures. Accepting regress reasoning as a central tenet, bargainers can get so entangled in the intricacies of strategic calculations that even a one-move decision becomes enormously complex.

The two bodies of literature see the problem of bargaining from different perspectives; these perspectives in turn generate assumptions and models that are applicable to the particular aspect of the problem examined, but which account for only a portion of bargaining behavior.

These two approaches to the bargaining problem may represent bodies of theory surrounding two very different, if complementary, processes of change within what we call bargaining. This observation provides the basic hypothesis of this essay, namely that it is not possible adequately to represent bargaining by any single process. The outcome is rather the result of the interaction of several separate bargaining processes. Each process proceeds logically—within its capacities of perceiving, coding, and processing reality and translating the resulting synthesis into action—toward resolution of the bargaining conflict. Consequently, any hope of finding a "solution" to a generalized bargaining problem lies in identifying which processes comprise what we know as bargaining, how they interact, and what effect each has on the course of bargaining.

What processes are involved in bargaining and what functions do they have?

An attempt to integrate these two approaches runs into substantial obstacles. Merely the assumptions of two different forms of rational decision-making suggest that the two approaches cannot be meshed. For one cannot assume that a bargainer will think and act according to two different assumptions about rationality in the same context.

Minor aspects may change, but basic assumptions about rationality must persist and lend consistency to the bargaining process. To arrive at a single working definition of rationality, it appears that a choice is in order.

At least in the foreseeable future, the problems associated with regress reasoning are unlikely to be overcome. Therefore, simple maximization decisions may provide a firmer foundation for current bargaining research. Adoption of this type of rationality, however, does not automatically imply that the convergence model is accepted *in toto*. For it may well be possible to operationalize that part of the strategic model having to do with active choice (in changing basic parameter values) so long as that choice is not tied to behavior or logic which results in an outguessing regress.

The convergence model and a strongly-revised form of the strategic choice model may, then, be integrable. While the former describes calculations internal to the convergence process, the latter describes calculations that shape the shifting boundaries of the process.

This "structuring" approach (as it will be called) differs substantially from the strategic process described above. While the latter concentrates on influencing the other's behavior, the structuring approach concentrates on influencing the course of the bargaining process. A player would then evaluate perceived alternatives in relation to his own choice situation and in relation to an emerging bargaining structure. Instead of concentrating on outguessing his opponent's choice structure, his energies would be directed toward forming expectations about and perhaps altering the structure of the convergence process.

Structuring activity is defined, then, as those bargaining moves which establish or alter the parameters that define the convergence process. Where the Cross expectations model allows for adjustments to be made only within the existing parameters of that process (with a few exceptions), the structuring approach sees that some of the basic defining variables are subject to alteration and adaptation.

Rather than simple, tactical decision, structuring moves involve decisions by individual bargainers about the larger course of the bargaining process. Structuring involves defining and simplifying the elements of any bargaining process so that both parties can, so to speak, agree on what to agree or disagree about. The net effect of these moves is to expand or limit the range of outcomes that are possible, shifting the locus of probable outcome points.

A third bargaining process, arbitration,[1] is acknowledged by both the strategic and convergence theorists and is incorporated into some of their theories. Arbitration, as defined by Cross (1969: 92-95), involves identification and adoption of a particularly salient outcome point by both the parties involved, as a substitute for further bargaining. The potential outcome point must therefore be distinguishable from a bargainer's bid. And, in general, it must result from the suggestion of an impartial third party, even one so broadly defined to include prominent situational factors (i.e., salience) as well as other individuals.

Since arbitration is discussed within both convergence and strategic literature, it seems to be compatible with both. Rather than a subpart of those processes, however, arbitration has a unique set of organizing assumptions, inherent logic, concepts and mechanisms of change that justify its designation as a separate and distinct process of bargaining. Despite this, arbitration plays a smaller role than either of the two other processes. Whereas structuring and convergence are processes of change, arbitration is only a *termination* process.

The complementarity of these processes is reflected in the role each plays in relation to an emerging bargaining structure. The bargaining structure is both the result of bargainers' actions and the pertinent environment for future decisions. It serves as the principal standard for the bargainers' evaluation of the consequences of alternative courses of action. Players make maximizing decisions in relation to their perception (expectations) of the present and likely future evolution of this structure.

It may thus be possible to interpret this emerging structure as a collective good (Frohlich, Oppenheimer, and Young, 1971); it becomes a positively valued entity in itself because it is the vehicle necessary for the attainment of desired goals.

The central feature of the bargaining structure is the emerging convergence set. During preliminary bargaining, an amorphous group of interests and preferences is transformed into a commodity that can be bartered and perhaps eventually traded at a specific exchange rate. Convergence can only take place once interests and objectives have been filtered and accommodated through preliminary

---

1. The term "arbitration" is misleading because it suggests a legalistic solution to a nonjudicial process. Nevertheless, it is difficult to find an alternative to this term proposed by Cross that is sufficiently preferable to merit changing the notation of this bargaining process.

structuring to the point where they can be dealt with as an exchange. When this occurs, it is possible to identify (1) those issues or exchange relationships whose fates are linked to one another, and (2) the range of bids on each of these issues. If these phenomena are followed over time, a picture of an evolving "convergence set" emerges. The establishment and subsequent alteration of this convergence set provides the basic structure of the bargaining process. The step at which issues can be reduced to a two-dimensional exchange relationship characterized by a measurable disparity in current demands marks a qualitative transformation of the bargaining process.

A secondary feature of the bargaining structure is the set of accompanying working arrangements that bargainers devise to influence their future behavior. These arrangements commonly define (1) the code of conduct delimiting the range of acceptable bargaining tactics, (2) the accompanying enforcement system of penalties that will—definitely, probably, or possibly—befall the bargainer who violates the code of conduct, and (3) the number and type of decision rules that prevail. A decision rule establishes the conditions under which exchange will take place between a participant's resources and a probability of victory.[2] Taken together, the code of conduct with its enforcement system and the decision rules help give form and substance to the bargaining process.

Bargaining thus consists of two dynamic processes of change and one termination process. All activity taking place within the parameters of the convergence set is termed convergence. All activity outside that process is called structuring, insofar as it is concerned with preserving or altering the basic variables of the convergence set. Hence, by definition as well as by reflecting the major approaches to bargaining, these two processes appear to account for the basic dynamics of change and adaptation within bargaining. In addition, all bargaining is seen to terminate through arbitration.

---

2. Decision rules are concerned not with the entire range of bargaining behavior but with that segment of behavior and resources directly related to decision-making. For example, in the democratic mode, decision rules may determine whether a chief executive is elected by an absolute majority, a simple majority, or a plurality of votes. In a spoils system, decision rules will often set the "going price" for political appointments. As such, they define how power can be applied to the bargaining process.

How do the bargaining processes interact?

Do they operate simultaneously[3] or sequentially? And, if sequentially, in what sequence and why? There appears to be a logical or natural sequence that these processes will follow: structuring activity to establish the convergence set, convergence of demands over time, ending in settlement through arbitration.[4] But few bargaining or negotiation processes run so according to plan. Rarely can bargainers construct a convergence set on their first attempt that proves durable and flexible enough to carry them to agreement. When one or both bargainers become aware that the course that the convergence process is taking is not only unacceptable but perhaps beyond recourse within the current bounds of the convergence process, they are faced with the choice of either breaking off negotiations or seeking to alter one or more of the parameters of the convergence set. Recognition of the inadequacy of the present convergence set invites either abandonment of the entire bargaining relationship or a shift from convergence to structuring activity so that future progress can be made. The "process" of bargaining is thus a history of the alternating dominance of structuring and convergence activity, terminating in nonagreement or in agreement through the arbitration process.

Furthermore, insofar as a revised convergence set proves more capable of accommodating the bargainers' interests and thereby increasing chances for agreement, the efficiency of the entire bargaining process may be enhanced. Occasional restructuring of the convergence process through trial and error can serve as a necessary realignment of that process, preventing the overall bargaining process from reaching the breakdown boundary prematurely. The eventual bargaining

---

3. For example, two simple processes that take place at a circus are a man riding a bicycle in a circle and a man juggling plates. Knowing a few details, it is easy to predict where the bicycle or the plates will be at any moment. Yet if one man rides a bike in a circle and juggles the plates (two simultaneous processes), it becomes an enormously difficult task to predict the location of a plate for any given moment. I am indebted to Dr. William Ascher for this example. For an excellent elaboration of this concept, as applied to the politics of modernization, see Brunner and Brewer (1971).

4. Although present in early studies of phases in wage-rate negotiations, this approach is most clearly developed in Zartman's formula/detail approach (1975 and in this issue).

structure that carries the bargainers to agreement is based not principally on considerations of reason or justice that can somehow be foretold at the outset; it is based more on practical experience gained through trying out a number of proposed formulae. Bargainers evaluate the convergence set by utilitarian considerations of whether it promises to facilitate concession toward agreement within an acceptable time frame.

The decision task for bargainers consists of two steps. First, the bargainer must decide whether to accept or to attempt to change the set of variables defining the convergence process. Second, he must make a value-maximizing decision within one of the three subsidiary processes (structuring, convergence, or arbitration).

There are consequently four processes that make up what we know as bargaining. The first is a major choice of whether or not to change the boundaries of the convergence process. It is a channeling decision that triggers one of three subroutines. The second decision takes place within the bounds of one of the three subroutines.

The subroutines are complementary and mutually correcting processes. No bargain could be achieved with only one of them. The convergence process provides for the stabilizing of expectations that permits agreement to be reached. Structuring provides for flexibility that ensures that the eventual outcome will accommodate the interest of both players. Arbitration facilitates the selection and adoption of a particular outcome point, saving the bargainers the cost of further convergence or structuring.

The interaction among these bargaining processes provides the dynamism for the process of learning and adjustment that we call bargaining. One process will be activated by a bargainer's decision based on his evaluation of the adequacy of the current convergence set. Serving as the bargainer's formal representation of those aspects of the environment which they consider relevant to the solution of their bargaining relationship, the bargaining structure takes on the role of the pertinent decision environment. It becomes, in a sense, a third unit of the bargaining process. It is influenceable only by each of the two bargainers or by elements from the larger environment— which will affect the structure in ways that are partly predetermined by rules of screening that are part of the structure itself.

The principal dynamic is one of initial expectation that the current structure will be sufficient to reach agreement, comparison of these expectations to the experience of bargaining, and continous reevaluation in light of the new information gained. If the new information fits sufficiently well with the anticipated information, the bargainer will respond by choosing to operate within the convergence set. If the new information is disadvantageous or disagreeable, he may seek to rectify the situation by employing a structuring move. If the new information is quite attractive, he may choose to abandon that structure and adopt an arbitrated outcome. This amounts to an expectations/adjustment model on a different scale than that of the convergence theorists.

In addition to this generalized understanding of shifts among bargaining processes, it is possible to hypothesize some conditions under which these shifts may be likely to occur.[5] A bargainer will tend to shift modes in a given fashion whenever several of these conditions overlap or when he perceives one of the conditions in a particulary acute manner. One case has been fairly well spelled out already (Cross, 1969: 92-95). Given a convergence or structuring situation, a bargainer may accept a potential arbitrated solution if (1) the convergence process has narrowed the range of demands considerably, (2) the bargainer has high costs associated with the passage of time, and (3) there exists one prominent potential arbitration solution—whether suggested by a third party, a "division of the difference" rule, or a salient facet of the environment.

On the other hand, a bargainer in a convergence situation will be inclined to try a structuring move (1) if his bargaining costs are low or significantly lower than those of his opponent, (2) if he is relatively indifferent to agreement, or (3) if a convergence deadlock has been reached and/or he gets into a "chicken dilemma." This last term suggests that bargainers can find themselves in a dilemma where concession is regarded not as a cooperative gesture but as evidence of one's own weakness (Swingle, 1970). The resulting situation is a sort of Prisoner's Dilemma of concession rates. A bargainer wishing

---

5. Following are the criteria used to determine when a shift takes place. A shift to structuring occurs when one of two parameters defining the convergence set is changed: (1) the number of exchange relationships successfully coupled to or decoupled from the convergence set (Jervis, 1970: 139-224) or (2) time costs, especially changes in bargaining deadlines (affecting both players' costs) or radical shifts in one player's security point, due to changed conditions in the negotiating environment. A shift to convergence takes place when, after structuring activity, players undertake concession moves within the context of stable parameters defining the convergence set. A shift to arbitration takes place when partial or general agreement is reached among the bargainers.

to move toward agreement but hoping to avoid the adverse effects of a concession may opt instead to restructure the convergence set.

Given a prevailing structuring process, a player may decide to switch the bargaining relationship to the convergence subroutine (1) if his time costs and his indifference curve are high, (2) if he desires to gain information about the opponent's behavior in order to form confident expectations or to get an indication of the approximate range of demands, (3) if he has confident expectations that the existing parameters of the convergence set will lead to an acceptable agreement, and (4) if, given low time costs, he perceives no way of restructuring the bargaining relationship because of constraints imposed by the bargaining structure. These hypotheses will be reviewed at the end of this article. In the following section, this "trial and error" framework is employed to trace the dynamics of change and adaptation in one international negotiation.

II

The United States-Spanish military pact, signed on 26 September 1953 and renewed ten years later in slightly revised form, provides the background for the seven-year case study examined here. The Pact of Madrid comprised three agreements: a defense agreement authorizing the establishment and maintenance of four military bases on Spanish territory, to be jointly utilized by Spain and the United States but remaining under Spanish sovereignty; a military defense assistance agreement requiring the United States to provide military equipment and supplies to Spain and to make funds available to Spain for purchase of additional U.S. military equipment; and economic assistance for Spain. In 1963, the defense and military assistance agreements were renewed for five years with only minor modifications.[6]

---

6. The United States agreed to consider a threat to Spain (as distinct from the bases) as a matter for "common concern" and stated that the United States-Spanish defense ties would become part of the security arrangements for the Atlantic and Mediterranean areas. The final level of military aid grants was set at $100 million, plus another $50 million in arms that Spain would have to purchase herself, and $100 million in Export-Import Bank loans.

PRELIMINARY BARGAINING

Three issues came to dominate the preliminary stages of negotiation: whether and under what terms the United States would continue to utilize the Spanish bases, the nature of the U.S. defense commitment to Spain, and the amount of aid that Spain would receive.

The ink was hardly dry on the 1963 agreement as both countries began preliminary structuring moves for the next renewal negotiations in 1968. Both Spain and the United States began to establish their security points—those points at which they would be indifferent to renewal or termination of the base nonagreement. Each sought to convince the other that his own indifference curve was quite high because of the liabilities associated with agreement and the existence of other attractive options to agreement.

Spain's overall tactic was to threaten a policy of nonalignment or of closer political alignment with France and Western Europe to replace ties with the United States. The American strategy was to question seriously the continuing utility of the Spanish bases, given recent technological advances and Spanish limitations on the use of the bases, and to plead that its hands were tied by a Congress increasingly wary of foreign involvements.

Spanish Foreign Minister Castiella developed a negotiating stance that sought to balance Spanish policy between military ties with the United States, economic and strategic ties to Western Europe, improved trade relations with the Soviet Union, and overtures to the Arab Nations. In talks with Americans Castiella stressed that many Spaniards were growing increasingly aware of the dangers to Spain of American military presence and that the bases themselves were regarded as a symbol of Spanish inferiority.[7]

The initial U.S. strategy on the renegotiations was to proceed as if the 1963 base agreement would be renewed without change. There were no attempts to raise new issues that would require negotiations on any broader scope before it became obvious in early 1968 that

---

7. The Spaniards feared not only being drawn involuntarily into a U.S.-Soviet nuclear dispute (in which several of Spain's major cities would be directly threatened because of their close proximity to the bases), but also a repeat of the type of nuclear accident that spilled four nuclear bombs on Spanish soil and waters after a SAC B-52 bomber collided with its KC-135 aerial tanker plane and crashed near the village of Palomares in January 1966.

Spain would not accept a simple adoption of the previous agreement. Only after the 1967 Arab-Israeli war did the United States begin seriously to reconsider the role that the Spanish naval and air bases served in the defense of the West.[8]

Up until 1968, the United States claimed that it was difficult to respond seriously to Spanish complaints and demands for revision since they were so vague. In July, 1968, however, Spain managed to bring its demands together in written form for presentation to the United States. Spain requested that existing Executive Agreements be replaced by a treaty of formal mutual defense guarantee. The United States had already indicated that a full-fledged treaty, which would require Senate ratification, was impossible. But it hinted that some kind of joint cooperation or declaration might be possible (New York Times, July 14, 1968: 9). Linked to the extent of defense commitment was the issue of prior consultation. Spain insisted that the United States should obtain Spain's consent before introducing new weapons into Spain or initiating major changes in strategic policy.

Spain also sought renewed American efforts to have Spain invited to join NATO and increased military cooperation between Spanish and NATO forces. But the U.S. government, quite sensitive to domestic reports that it was planning to save the Franco government from a domestic uprising, was anxious to limit the financial and political costs of such close cooperation.

The third major issue of the negotiations involved the amount of assistance to be given to Spain in exchange for U.S. rights in using Spanish bases. The Spanish armed forces first requested large amounts of military equipment without placing a specific price tag on the total. When these demands were formally presented to the United States in the July 1968 memorandum, the U.S. sought to discredit them from the beginning. The Johnson administration reminded the Spanish armed forces that much of their equipment was on temporary lease and valued the list of Spanish-requested new equipment at $1.2 billion,

---

8. A study was prepared for the Joint Chiefs of Staff on the functions and uses of the Spanish bases with respect to the Mediterranean area. "The report, which has not been published, appears to have defined the main task of the air bases as providing aircraft for 'sensitive missions' in the eastern Mediterranean. It may also have mentioned the United States space monitoring installations on Spanish territory that the Spaniards have claimed as serving a strategic purpose almost as important as the naval base at Rota" (Story, 1973: 156, citing U.S. Senate, 1970a). This study seems to have considered several alternatives to the existing Spanish bases and to have found those alternatives severely lacking.

even though the Spanish objected, claiming that the estimated figure was a gross exaggeration (Story, 1973: 166). Spanish military assistance had run at about $40 million yearly.

The second part of the U.S. assistance issue involved the amount of U.S. investments in Spain. These private investments played a large role in Spain's economic growth during the 1960s. At the beginning of 1968, President Johnson announced stringent curbs on overseas investments and military spending as part of an American dollar-protection program to reduce the rapidly worsening balance of payments deficit. Spain was included on the list of developed countries to which the restrictions would apply most strictly. Because of severe economic problems, Spain proposed that she be granted the same type of treatment as Finland and Greece, where American investment would be allowed to continue at 65% of the then-present levels. Although the United States stood firm in refusing to weaken its balance of payments regulation in order to exempt Spain, it did agree in early August to a case-by-case study of potential U.S. direct private investment in Spain and the likely dollar outflow (New York Times, August 11, 1968: 1, 2).

By August 1968, the major points of conflict between the two states had been specified and the range of difference of demands had been established. The situation was sufficiently structured that bargainers could form confident expectations. The exchange relationship that evolved consisted of one overall, composite exchange relationship between, on the one hand, U.S. use of Spanish bases and the particular terms of use, and, on the other hand, the extent of the U.S. defense commitment and military cooperation with Spain and the extent of financial compensation awarded to Spain. By the summer of 1968, the bounds of the convergence were established. The range of divergence in these initial demands defines the bounds of the contract zone, setting the stage for the give-and-take of convergence bargaining.

The distinction between the preliminary and main phases of bargaining is particularly clear. Following the American suggestion that Spain present her demands formally, the establishment of the convergence set took place in a period of less than one month in the summer of 1968. Until then, structuring moves dominated the bargaining relationship.

What factors account for this shift from structuring to convergence bargaining? First of all, the September 26 deadline was approaching—both parties were under increasing time pressure. Second, they were

TABLE 1
Convergence Set

Issue	U.S.	Spain
Base rights:		
use of bases	full; conditional on price	conditional on price
use in wartime	full	subject to prior consultation
Defense support:		
defense commitment	some joint declaration	full-fledged alliance
military cooperation	marginal increases in effort	close integration of forces with those of U.S. and NATO
Financial support:		
military assistance	$100 million	$1.2 billion
investment ceiling	case-by-case study	Finland/Turkey alternative (65% of 1967)

unable to move toward agreement so long as neither could identify the other's demands well enough to form expectations about his probable behavior. There was no basis for evaluating contending claims. Finally, both nations wanted to reach agreement on extending the base agreement because the alternatives were undesirable.

THE MAIN EVENT

Once the parameters of the convergence set had been established in August 1968, the two parties began bargaining earnestly in order to try to reduce the range of conflict on each of the issues, so that agreement could be reached by the September 26 deadline. Foreign Minister Castiella headed a negotiating team to Washington for serious negotiations in September. Initially, neither side made major concessions. In the last ten days before the September 26 deadline, however, Spanish negotiators cut their demands from $1.2 billion, to $745 million, to the "rock bottom" price of $700 million in military aid. The United States stuck by its position of $100 million in military aid over the next five years but offered minor concessions. It agreed to sell an extra $100 million in arms to Spain on credit, to furnish $100 million in Export-Import Bank loans, and to provide $40 million for a Spanish naval construction program. In addition, the U.S. negotiators reminded Spain of the $40 million that its forces spent in Spain each year (New York Times, September 28, 1968: 6).

Since a considerable gap existed between the demands in late September, both parties agreed to an extension of the negotiations into the six-month grace period. If agreement were not reached during that period, the previous base agreement provided that the United States would be required to withdraw its forces from Spain within the year following the new deadline. Conditions that led to the decision to extend the negotiations were (1) moderate time costs, (2) perceptions that the convergence process offered little hope of agreement within the given parameters, and (3) a readily-available alternative, provided for in the previous agreement. Both sides could now afford to undertake further restructuring moves to again try to arrive at a convergence set satisfactory enough to lead to agreement.

Within a month following the extension of the negotiations, Castiella was back in Washington for a one-day meeting with Secretary of State Rusk. The two decided that much of the explanation for the lack of convergence lay in misperceptions caused by differing concepts of the military threat posed to the Iberian peninsula. It was therefore decided that, in order to set a figure for the proper amount of military assistance to Spain, it would be necessary for talks to be established between the armed forces of Spain and the armed forces of the United States.[9]

In early November, the United States attempted to break the continuing deadlock in negotiations by initiating a series of carefully prepared political gestures. The United States sought to convey the impression that, while budgetary and balance of payments limitations prevented it from offering more aid, it was willing to meet part of the Spanish political price for the bases. This met part of the Spanish complaint that "the West gives us little, takes what we have to offer and, on top of that, makes us use the delivery entrance," as one official

---

9. This amounted to a fractionalization of bargaining; the parties sought to establish a common definition of the environment in order to determine the proper bounds for convergence bargaining. In Zartman's (1975) terms, bargaining on the details would be postponed until there was common agreement on a "referent principle."

phrased it (New York Times, November 10, 1968: 4). In effect, this amounted to the unilateral introduction by the United States of political and status-cultural considerations into the convergence set. This American move served to add a compensatory exchange value on which the United States could afford to concede something that Spain wanted, and the loss to the United States would be comparatively small.[10]

At approximately the same time, the United States suggested that it would be willing to discuss the dismantling of the air bases at Torrejon in order to placate public opinion in Spain and give Spain an apparent compensating factor for reducing its demands. And the United States hinted that once the Vietnam war had ended, the question of the extent of military aid to Spain would likely be reconsidered. Whether as a reciprocal gesture or not, Spain reduced her asking price to $400 million in early November (New York Times, November 8, 1968: 5).

Meanwhile, Foreign Minister Castiella's position was worsening within Spain. He had undertaken renegotiations of the base agreement primarily in political terms, seeking something approaching full partnership. The military leaders felt threatened by the possibility of the bases being closed. By November 1968, their beliefs that Castiella had miscalculated led to increased criticism. It seemed that Spain might be confronted with the undesirable choice of either closing the bases or making significant additional concessions. The military officials who met with General Wheeler therefore openly expressed their dissatisfaction with Castiella's bargaining strategy. The Spanish military officers, like the Americans, were opposed to the implicit alternative of a neutralist foreign policy for Spain. This emerging rift in Spain confirmed U.S. expectations (New York Times, November 21, 1968: 21).

In late February, the "Burchinal affair" broke out. By the time it was over, it had intensified congressional and public criticism of

10. The political gestures involved a visit by Secretary of State Rusk to Madrid on November 16 after he attended NATO talks in Brussels (the first visit on this level since 1965); a visit by Chairman of the Joint Chiefs of Staff, General Wheeler to talk about the level of military aid needed; a visit by German Chancellor Kurt Kiesinger to Madrid to demonstrate the importance that Western Europe attached to Spanish partnership in the defense of Western Europe; and a letter from Secretary of State Rusk saying that American investments in Spain would rise (although no specific promises or means of implementation were given).

the potential Spanish base agreement. Columnist Flora Lewis revealed that the military negotiator, Major General David A. Burchinal,[11] in trying to agree on defining the common threat to Spain and the United States, had signed a minute which suggested that the United States would defend Spain from vaguely defined threats from northern Africa such as Algerian aggression or a "proxy" war in Spain's colonies backed by the Russians. In addition, Burchinal agreed to a minute that referred to Spain as "an integral part" of Western Europe, implying that the United States might be obliged to defend Spain under the NATO agreement. General Burchinal was reputedly working under the close supervision of high Pentagon officials without the knowledge of the State Department. The State Department was incensed and called for Burchinal to return to Washington for a high level review of the whole affair. Eventually, the note that had already been signed by Burchinal was qualified by the addition of a "preparatory note" which reduced the sense of American commitment. Many members of Congress were outraged.

The Spanish government was also alarmed by what it regarded as a deliberate leak. The leak may well have been intentional.[12] In this way, the Nixon administration (or more probably the State Department) sought to counter what it saw as an undesirable evolution of the existing bargaining structure. The effect was to sabotage the content of the tentative agreement between the American and Spanish armed forces. The U.S. indifference curve was shifted upward as congressional, press, and public reaction was greatly disturbed both by the content and by the means used to arrive at the military minute. Consequently, the range of potential outcomes on the military assistance issue can be seen to have shrunken considerably by this point.

Spanish Foreign Ministry fears that the leak was deliberate were reinforced by the general relaxed attitude of the State Department toward the negotiations. This unhurried attitude seemed based on a State Department assessment that (1) the bases were useful but

---

11. Burchinal was Deputy to NATO Supreme Commander General Lyman Lemnitzer and was second in command over all NATO forces in Europe and over all American forces in Europe.

12. Several American sources seem to confirm that the leak was deliberate. See, for example, U.S. Senate (1970a: 2368). Spanish officials tried to determine whether the leak had come from officials involved in the old administration or from the Nixon administration (which would have had ominous implications for the ongoing negotiations).

not essential, (2) the Spanish military had no desire to have the bases removed, (3) the military's judgment would prevail with General Franco, and (4) it would be a political liability to sign an agreement with Spain during the state of exception declared earlier in the year.

Due to the tough bargaining policy of the United States, there was little convergence in the negotiations prior to late March 1969. The result of five and a half of the six months' extension was not a convergence of expectations but rather a solidification of the points of divergence. But as the March deadline approached, a shift to convergence took place. Time costs were acute since no provision existed for extension of the negotiations past the end of the six-month grace period. And, although Spain was pessimistic, the United States seemed to think that last-minute compromises would lead to acceptable agreement by the deadline.

The Spanish government at this time tried to calm American congressional and public criticism of Spain's dictatorial policies. It rescinded the state of exception on March 22, several weeks earlier than planned.

In fact, by this point the Nixon administration was concerned mainly with the economic value of military hardware and the political costs of a military commitment to Spain. The essential decision had been made to maintain American use of the bases. A Pentagon study revealed that the price of disbanding an overseas military installation, moving men and equipment and recasting strategy, often proved to be greater than the cost of remaining at that overseas base (New York Times, March 23, 1969: IV, 3). Since Spain had effectively agreed to secure continued American use of the bases in the fall, the demands of both sides were not too distant. But questions of the terms of use and the amount of political and economic commitment also remained to be answered.

Foreign Minister Castiella arrived in Washington and met with Secretary of State Rogers on March 25, 1969, the day before the deadline. During a brief flurry of compromise as the deadline approached, the United States offered to provide $175 million in military aid over the five-year period (New York Times, May 27, 1969: 2). But the offers and counteroffers remained divided by a seemingly unbreachable gap. Neither side felt capable of further concessions. In short, the parties found themselves in a chicken dilemma where the only escape lay in alteration of the parameters of the bargaining relationship. Castiella proposed an extension of the negotiations past the deadline, an offer that was accepted immediately by the United States. Soon thereafter, the two countries announced an "agreement in principle" to extend the agreement for U.S. military base rights in Spain for five more years. The details of this agreement in principle would be worked out in the coming months. In fact, the only agreement that had been reached was an interim agreement on the nature of the convergence set and subsequent working arrangements.[13]

While holding hearings on U.S. commitments abroad, the Senate Foreign Relations Committee in mid-April decried what it termed a "quasi-commitment" to defend the Franco regime, possibly even in the event of a civil war. It disclosed that a high-ranking American military officer (later revealed to be General Earle Wheeler) had assured the Spanish government that "[t]he presence of American armed forces in Spain constitutes a more significant security guarantee than would a written agreement" (New York Times, April 18, 1969: 1). This revelation helped spark the initiation of a "national commitments resolution" designed to prevent the emergence of such quasi-commitments into full-blown defense commitments.

Senator Fulbright may, however, have provided a means of escape from the convergence deadlock. A comment he made during the hearing was apparently picked up by Aguirre de Carcer, Director of North American Affairs in the Spanish Foreign Ministry. He devised a compromise formula that proposed a broad program of cooperation with the United States in such fields as space tracking, peaceful nuclear development, education, culture, civil aviation, and investment. In short, Spain was to be paid in civil rather than in military kind (Story, 1973: 178). Finally, the details of a new military relationship were to be the subject of continuing negotiations. This proposal was greeted with interest in Washington but it was unclear for many months whether the State Department would agree to the proposed formula.

In the meantime, however, both parties were faced with the task of producing an interim agreement which would at least temporarily take the wind out of the sails of domestic forces opposed to additional concessions. Spain proposed in early May a plan to extend American

---

13. The Johnson adminstration apparently badly miscalculated the seriousness of Spanish demands. Not until March 1969 was the situation deemed important enough to get high level attention. By then it was too late. "With the United States unable to offer a substantially increased political or economic commitment, and with Spain committed to nothing less, the only possible solution, short of rupture, was the kind of extension agreed upon" (New York Times, June 22, 1969: 11).

rights to use military bases for eighteen months rather than five years as previously planned. This amounted to a provisional extension of the 1963 base agreement that would serve to appease congressional criticism.[14] It would be accompanied by a request for $52 million in American military aid over the eighteen-month period, equivalent to a prorated figure of the latest American offer.

This process of convergence bore fruit within a month. Spain and the United States signed an agreement in Washington on June 21, 1969. In return for the continued use of Spanish bases for the next fifteen months (eighteen months after the March 26 deadline), the United States agreed to supply Spain with $50 million in arms and up to $35 million in Export-Import Bank credits with which Spain could make additional arms purchases. This shift to arbitration stemmed from very high time costs and the existence of a prominent and acceptable outcome point.

In the first ten months following the interim agreement, the bargaining relationship was relatively dormant. The Department of Defense announced that it planned to deactivate the air base at Moron, leaving only the Rota and Torrejon installations in full use. In a cabinet reshuffle following a financial scandal, Foreign Minister Castiella was replaced by Gregorio López Bravo. In a major foreign policy speech delivered soon after the new cabinet was formed, Vice President Carrero Blanco made it clear that better relations with the Common Market and with the United States would be the basis of Spanish foreign policy.

Shortly after the Libyan coup in September 1969, the United States hastily had to evacuate Wheelus Air Base. The only other base in that area of the world that could provide a combination of clear weather and adequate ground facilities was the base complex in Spain. In February 1970, the United States announced that it was transferring the Wheelus operations to the Spanish base at Saragossa.

The United States and Spain began preparations for the formal negotiations which were to recommence in April. The United States informed the Spanish government that it definitely wanted to retain the use of the bases for another five years—a shift from the American uncertainty of the previous year. The final decision to retain use of the bases had apparently been made in February 1970, after more

---

14. It is conceivable that this suggested extension resulted not from the Spanish Foreign Ministry but from a National Security Memorandum prepared on the American bases in Spain during April.

than a year of debate in the Nixon Administration. The Department of State also told Spain that it was willing to consider a general aid program as compensation for the use of the bases, as proposed by Spain the previous spring (New York Times, March 20, 1970). With the issue of base usage resolved except for contractual details, demands had narrowed to the point where an arbitrated solution was possible.

In early April, a list of military equipment desired by Spain was submitted to Washington; it was scaled down considerably from previous demands since Spain had decided to seek broader forms of aid and cooperation. The extent of the shift in Spanish demands from military aid to educational, scientific, and economic aid suprised the American negotiators (New York Times, April 12, 1970: 23).

Foreign Minister López Bravo arrived in Washington in April to begin formal renegotiations. Several days after his arrival, a preliminary accord was reported on the scientific, economic, and educational issues.

The visit of Secretary of State Rogers to Madrid in late May[15] proved to be a mild disappointment for both sides. Secretary Rogers informed the Spanish government that the United States could extend no new security guarantee to Spain. Foreign Minister López Bravo countered with the Spanish demand: the agreement would have to include either a firm security commitment for assistance in case of attack or a quite sizable increase in the level of American military aid, including eighteen F-4 Phantom bombers, tanks, and armored cars. While Spain never expected to get both, she clearly wanted one or the other (New York Times, May 30, 1970: 3). Spanish officials and press were angry at continued U.S. intransigence on the defense commitment issue because they felt Spain was being asked to bear unilaterally the burden of the increased security threat resulting from the existence of the bases.

In place of an increased security guarantee, the United States offered its long-range support for the admission of Spain into the North Atlantic Alliance. Despite an impasse on the question of the security

15. May 1970, kicked off by the Cambodian incursion and the Kent State and Jackson State shootings, was a traumatic month for the United States. The Senate Foreign Relations Committee demanded that it be consulted on the potential agreement. The Subcommittee on United State Security Agreements and Commitments Abroad decided to reconvene for hearings on the Spanish bases. The Nixon Administration therefore decided to delay signing the agreement until at least all American troops were withdrawn from Cambodia at the end of June and Congressional and public hostility and subsided (New York Times, May 25, 1970: 15).

commitment, there had been movement on other fronts by the end of May:

> According to reliable sources, the United States would furnish two submarines and six destroyers, all used, but in operating condition. The army would receive machinery to expand and improve its arsenals.
>
> The agreement would cover a broad range of educational and economic cooperation.
>
> A project to train Spanish graduate students in the United States has been approved in principle but any firm agreement may have to await passage of a new Spanish educational law. In addition, the Spanish are talking of a program whose minimum cost is $42 million while the maximum American proposal is for about $25 million.
>
> The United States has also offered financial assistance to scientific research institutions here, and a survey is being conducted by an American scientific official to determine needs.
>
> In addition, there will be joint declarations on economic cooperation and trade policy and an American offer to help with highway planning [New York Times, May 28, 1970: 12].

In late July 1970, Undersecretary of State Johnson returned to the Senate Foreign Relations Committee to brief it on the terms of the forthcoming base agreement with Spain. He disclosed that the United States had pledged to "support the defense system" of Spain and to make its defense policies compatible with those of Spain. In exchange, Spain had reduced her request for aid to a mere $20 million in direct grants over the next five years and $125 million in Export-Import bank loans, plus some surplus weapons and ships. He stated that American negotiators were able to keep the aid level reasonable only by increasing the U.S. commitment to the defense of Spain (New York Times, July 25, 1970: 2).

Senator Fulbright attacked the proposed agreement as costing the United States $400 million instead of the $150 million claimed. And he demanded that a defense commitment such as that extended to Spain be submitted to the Senate for approval as a treaty. Under this pressure, the Administration hastened to sign the agreement with Spain (New York Times, August 4, 1970). Even though the official deadline was a couple of months distant, both governments felt themselves under strong time pressure, not only because of the desire to undercut possible congressional opposition, but also because of previous bad experiences with cliffhangers. Comprehensive agreement was also facilitated because the revised convergence set had allowed for a progressive narrowing of demands to the point where an arbitrated solution was possible.

The Agreement of Friendship and Cooperation was signed in Washington on August 6, 1970 (U.S. Senate, 1970b). The essence of the agreement is contained in Chapters VI and VIII on economic and defense cooperation. Here it is possile to ascertain the final trade-off of costs and benefits to each of the parties.

The United States is committed to "support the defense system" of Spain. The United States increased its defense cooperation with Spain, establishing a Joint Committee on defense matters. Along with this, the United States agreed to provide Spain with an air defense system tied into that of the North Atlantic Treaty Organization. It was revealed several years later that the United States had also committed itself to making joint scenarios for defending Spain's Moroccan enclaves of Ceuta and Melilla, the Canary Islands, and Spanish Sahara.[16]

The United States agreed further to contribute to the modernization of Spanish defense industries, to train Spanish technicians, and to grant a considerable amount of used military equipment to Spain.[17] In addition, the bases and other military facilities (which cost almost $400 million to build) were themselves to be turned over to Spain; this included the Rota-Sargossa pipeline. Finally, the United States apparently agreed to increase its political and diplomatic contacts with Spain.[18]

For her part, Spain agreed to allow the United States to continue to use Spanish bases and other military facilities. Any major alteration

16. The United States proved reluctant to draw up these scenarios, angering Spain (Washington Post, March 24, 1963: A19).

17. The armed forces were scheduled to receive 36 second-hand Phantom jets, more than 100 tanks and half-tracks, 25 helicopters, heavy artillery, two KC-130 tanker planes, six C-130 transport planes and smaller equipment. Some of these arms would be purchased with $125 million in Export-Import Bank loans provided by the United States. The Navy would be loaned two conventional submarines, five destroyers, four minesweepers, three landing craft, a munitions ship, and an oil tanker (Painton, 1970: 82).

18. Within two years, Secretary of State Rogers, Secretary of Defense Laird, and Secretary of Commerce Stans all visited Spain. President Nixon included Spain in his fall 1970 European trip and spoke of Spain as a "pillar of peace." Admiral Moorer, Chairman of the Joint Chiefs of Staff, visited in June 1971 and was a guest at a parade celebrating Franco's victory over the Republicans. A month later, Vice-President Agnew was in Madrid for Spain's National Day celebrations. In addition, Prince Juan Carlos was received with honors normally reserved for a head of state when he visited the United States in February 1971.

or construction would, however, require joint agreement. A more serious limitation is that the use of the bases in the event of an "external threat or attack against the security of the West . . . will be the subject of urgent consultations between the two Governments, and will be resolved by mutual agreement in light of the situation created" (U.S. Senate, 1970b: 6). In other words, the use of the bases in wartime or other emergencies is subject to consulation and approval by Spain. The wording is similar to that found in American agreements with Greece and Turkey. It was reported that Spain had made clear to the United States that it would not permit use of its bases for U.S. military operations involving the Arab states and Israel. This prohibition also included the use of the air bases during fighting between the United States and the Soviet Union in a conflict growing out of an Arab-Israeli war. Spain was known to be anxious to protect her interests in North Africa (New York Times, August 14, 1970: 23). The existence of this qualification was denied by the Department of State. And, it was emphasized (but not clarified), the United States and Spain both retain "the inherent right of self-defense."

According to Undersecretary of State Johnson, the new agreement did not change a previous United States-Spanish accord that the United States would not overfly Spain with nuclear weapons (U.S. Senate, 1970b: 6).

The format and terms of the new agreement bear little resemblance to what might have been predicted from looking at the bounds of the initial convergence set in the summer of 1968. The negotiations had gone through a number of shifts in process and working arrangements. The bargaining had been hard and frustrating; eventually, though, a satisfactory formula for convergence had been found so that the two state could move toward agreement.

OVERVIEW

The history of the United States-Spanish base negotiations can be analyzed in terms of the convergence and structuring activity which, by a trial and error process, shaped the evolution of the convergence set.

The conflicting demands of Spain and the United States can be broken down into specific issues or exchange relationships and traced over time. Figure 1 shows the point of initiation, the duration, and the point of resolution of each of the major issues in these negotiations.

It permits identification of the issues or exchange relationships involved in the bargaining relationship at any particular moment. The convergence set consists of those issues which have been transformed into exchange relationships and whose fates have been linked to the outcome of the overall negotiations. The dotted lines refer to issues in dispute which are as yet poorly defined or whose status is uncertain because of insufficient information. Lack of information concerning an initiation or termination point is indicated by a question mark.

This chronological picture of issues at stake, however, misses much of the bargaining action. To get a closer look at the dynamics of the negotiations, it would be desirable to be able to identify the range of demands over time for each of the exchangeable values and to be able to account for their interrelation. The convergence diagrams in Figure 2, derived from the previous history, attempt to portray graphically the convergence of demands for each of the major issues in the convergence set. Of course, it is impossible to quantify and to measure the intervals between specific demands within some of the exchange relationships; using the rule of thumb, the diagrams are at best a subjective rendition of the trends and highlights of this convergence activity. Only those issues whose outcomes were resolvable only in conjunction with the overall base rights issue are depicted.[19]

The major issue, that of American use and terms of usage of the bases, was a "lumpy" issue. The question of limits on the use of the bases only slightly detracts from the "all or nothing" quality of this issue. Resolution of the other issues was dependent on the expectations each player had about the "stake" of the opponent in maintaining the bases. The result of this peculiar situation was that the range of demands on this issue, while somewhat inferable, was not securely established until almost the end of the negotiations.

On the defense commitment issue, the initial demands ranged from a full-fledged alliance to preservation of the status quo (fair phrases, but little substance). The first slight peak shows the August 1968 U.S. counteroffer, the second shows General Wheeler's remark that American troops stationed in Spain constituted a stronger commitment than a piece of paper, and the third peak marks the February 1969 accord signed by General Burchinal. Spanish demands declined slowly but steadily.

The question of the amount of defense cooperation that the United States was willing to extend to Spain likewise peaks at the Burchinal

19. A dotted line implies an estimate because of sketchy information.

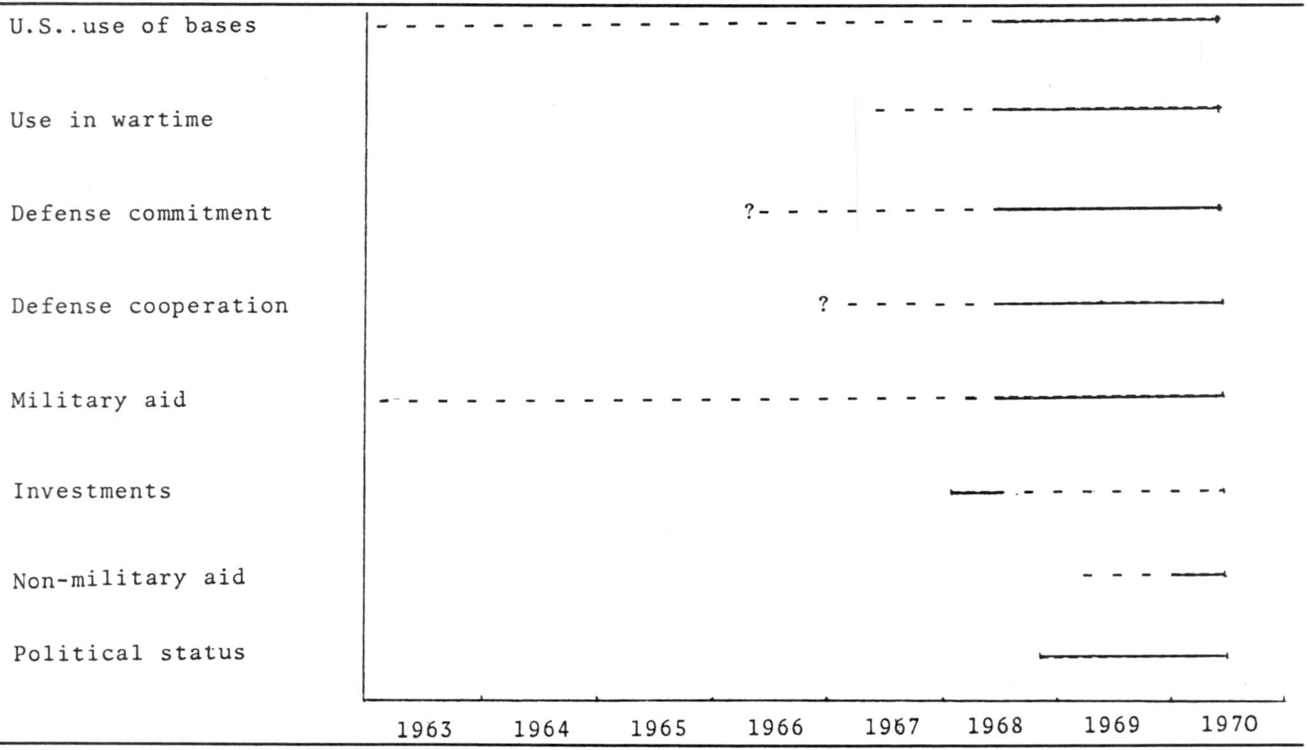

	1963	1964	1965	1966	1967	1968	1969	1970
U.S. use of bases		----	----	----	----	----	----	----	
Use in wartime					----	----	----	----	
Defense commitment				?---	----	----	----	----	
Defense cooperation				?	---	----	----	----	
Military aid	----	----	----	----	----	----	----	----	
Investments						----	---	---	
Non-military aid							---	---	
Political status							----	----	

Figure 1: Duration of Issues

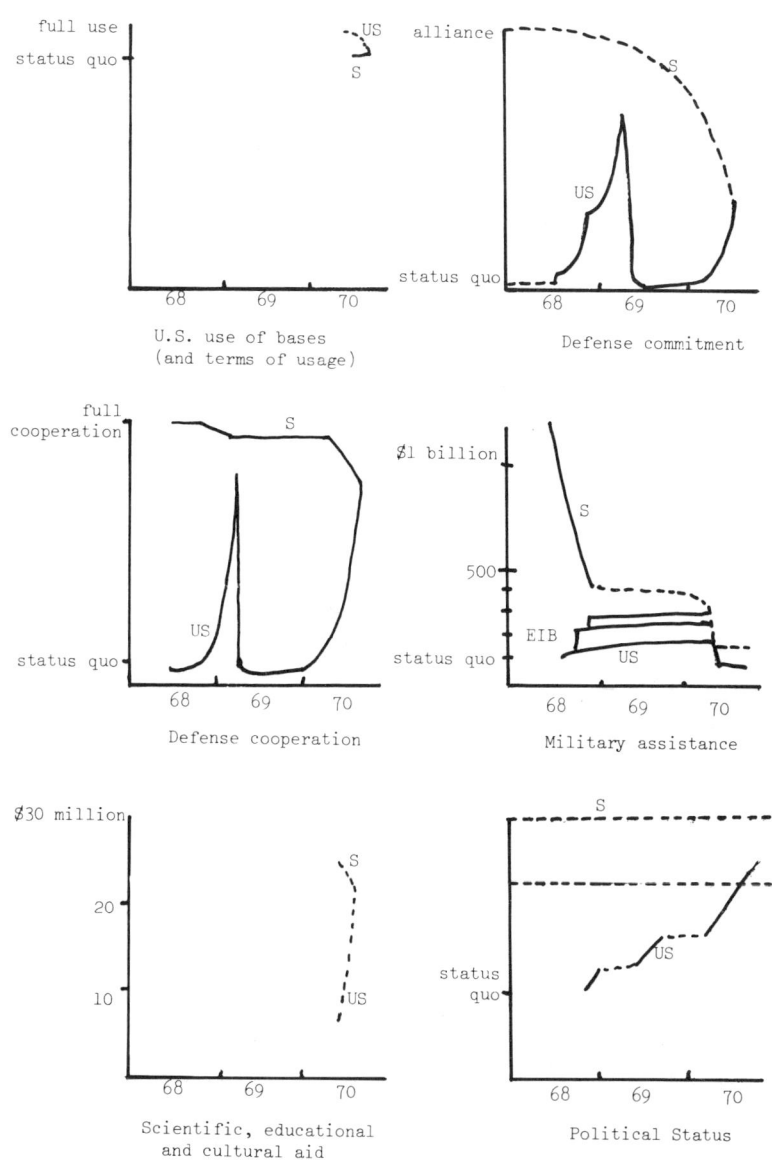

Figure 2: Convergence of Demands on Major issues

minute. The final months of the bargaining show large American concessions.

The military assistance issue became quite complicated. In addition to the "hard" question of military equipment, it involves the "soft" question of Export-Import Bank loans (with which Spain could purchase additional equipment) as well as a November 1968 hint that the United States would reconsider its aid level once its involvement in the Vietnam war declined. The Spanish demand curve is quite interesting here. Within four months in 1968, Spanish demands plummeted from an estimated $1.2 billion to $400 million worth of military equipment. From that point on, Spain felt it could concede little more. By the spring of 1970, however, Spain had decided to request only a small amount of military aid, shifting a good portion of her demand for financial compensation to the new issue of nonmilitary aid. When this greatly reduced demand was presented to the United States, its offer curve (which had been almost stationary) fell correspondingly.[20]

Very little information is available on the range of demands over time concerning U.S. nonmilitary aid to Spain.

Finally, there is the peculiar issue of political status: how openly would the United States demonstrate its friendship with and approval of the Franco regime? Spain was unable to make any public "demands," but it was clear that she sought warmer demonstrations of American friendship than she had received in the last several years. The United States was apparently willing to pay the domestic and international costs of closer association. American political gestures rose in number and in magnitude, culminating with plans for President Nixon's visit in fall 1970.

A pattern of concession emerges. U.S. use of the bases was secured by concessions within and trade-offs among five distinct exchanges. The two issues on which the United States remained fairly intransigent (military assistance and defense commitment) were resolved substantially in its favor. In order to economize in these areas, however, the United States was forced to make large concessions in the areas of defense cooperation, political status, and nonmilitary aid.

Structuring activity was not confined to the introduction and resolution of issues and the extension of deadlines; much structuring was designed to limit the range of alternative outcomes within parti-

---

20. This figure, including equipment given or loaned to Spain and Export-Import Bank loans, probably amounted to close to $200 million. Since much of the American military equipment that was transferred to Spain was used or surplus, its dollar value is difficult to assess.

cular exchange relationships. Similar to "strategic moves" but not relying on regress reasoning, these structuring moves assumed many forms. Spain and the United States both engaged in threats that they would terminate the defense partnership if the price was too high or too low (depending on their respective points of view). Spain's threat to adopt a neutralist stance lasted only until the spring of 1969. As interim agreement was reached, both the United States and Spain backed away from these overt threats.

The United States presented Spain with a fait accompli in the January 1968 decision to limit American investments in Spain. Spain's ban on American overflights with nuclear weapons or during an Arab-Israeli conflict amounted to a similar fait accompli. Finally, if the leak about the Burchinal accord was intentional, it amounted to a quite successful closing off of any potential alternatives of substantial military aid or defense commitment to Spain. Each of these faits accomplis proved to be definitive.

Commitments and obligations were also used effectively. The U.S. obligation to supply Southeast Asia with military hardware took priority over the Spanish arms request; nonetheless, the United States hinted that it might be willing to reconsider Spain's needs once the Indochina war was over. In addition, the United States made it clear to Spain that its responsibilities to Western Europe took precedence over its relations with Spain.

The expenditures required for the conduct of the war in Indochina and the growing deficit in the U.S. balance of payments imposed such burdens that the United States could claim simple incapacity to meet the Spanish demands. The Nixon Doctrine amounted to a commitment to a scaled-down American overseas military posture, with the slack to be taken up by her allies. A month after it was announced, Secretary of State Rogers gave his word to the Senate Foreign Relations Committee that no new or expanded security guarantee would be given to Spain. This commitment was quite convincing in light of the congressional consensus for "no more Vietnams" and the congressional suspicions produced by the Burchinal incident.

Foreign Minister Castiella pledged himself publicly to obtaining a significant upgrading of the 1963 defense agreement. By these public statements, the Spanish government placed its national pride on the line, a commodity which could not be honorably compromised. These conflicting commitments obviously contributed to the repeated situations of deadlock.

A number of other structuring moves, such as the introduction of new issues and the extension of deadlines, demonstrate the produc-

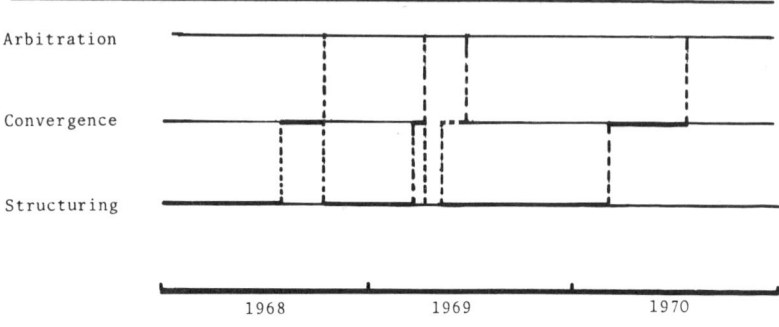

Figure 3: Shifts in Bargaining Process

tive aspect of bargaining activity as well. Whether positively or negatively valued, this assortment of structuring activities had a profound effect on the evolution of the convergence set.

Important as the convergence and structuring activities are, they tell only half the story. The history of the negotiations is the history of the *alternating* dominance of the convergence and structuring processes, ending in an arbitrated outcome. Figure 3 shows the periods of dominance and the points of shift from one process to another. Once the convergence set was established in the summer of 1968, the convergence process dominates for only about six weeks before the parameters of the convergence set are restructured by allowing the negotiations to extend into the grace period. Convergence bargaining does not resume until mid-March and lasts for only two weeks. The splitting of the bargaining process in the spring of 1969 results in simultaneous convergence and structuring activity. Nevertheless, convergence activity is limited to the need for a tactical, face-saving agreement while the principle differences are unresolved; it therefore seems justified to characterize this period as one of dominance of the structuring process. Once the United States agrees to the addition of the issue of nonmilitary aid to the convergence set in the winter of 1970, the bargaining structure has evolved to the point where it finally contains enough complementary convergence dynamics to accommodate the interests of both parties. Shifts to arbitration occur in the decisions to extend the dealines of the negotiations, in the June 1969 interim agreement, and at the time of the final agreement.

TABLE 2
Conditions Surrounding Shifts in Bargaining Processes

Shifts	Dates			
TO CONVERGENCE:	7/68	3/69	4/69	2/70
1) high time costs and indifference curve	+	+	+	(+)
2) to get information	+	NA	NA	NA
3) confident expectations of agreement	0	(+)	+	+
4) if low time costs, no alternatives	NA	NA	NA	NA
TO STRUCTURING:	9/68	3/69		
1) low time costs	+	+		
2) relative indifference to agreement	NA	0		
3) convergence deadlock or chicken dilemma	+	+		
TO ARBITRATION:	9/68	3/69	6/69	8/70
1) narrow contract zone	(+)	(+)	+	+
2) high costs	+	+	+	+
3) prominent outcome point	+	+	+	(+)

SYMBOLS: + confirmed
 − disconfirmed
 0 uncertain
 NA inapplicable
 ( ) qualified (i.e. somewhat confirmed or disconfirmed)

It appears that structuring activity far outweighs convergence activity. But this visual representation is a bit deceptive in that it fails to portray the intensity of bargaining, which was at its peak when bargaining costs were high and the convergence process was dominating.

According to the major hypothesis under review, certain conditions in the bargaining relationship will trigger a shift in process and thus facilitate agreement. Table 2 examines which of the predicted conditions was present when a shift occurred. At least one of these conditions is present in each shift; in most cases, several or all of the conditions were present. While this does not exclude alternative explanatory factors, it suggests that the predicted conditions may well have contributed to the shifts in dominance of the two processes. Furthermore, whenever one of the predicted conditions is absent, the shift is almost always accompanied by the presence of two or more of the other predicted conditions. This suggests that it is the constellation of factors and not any single one which determines the shift.

Brian H. Tracy is Lecturer in International Affairs and American Foreign Policy at HAUS RISSEN, an international institute for politics and economics located in Hamburg, West Germany.

REFERENCES

ACKOFF, R. L. and F. E. EMERY (1972) On Purposeful Systems. Chicago: Aldine.
ADAMS, J. S. (1976) "The structure and dynamics of behavior in organizational boundary roles," in M. E. Dunnette (ed.) Handbook of Industrial/Organizational Psychology. Chicago: Rand McNally.
ALLISON, G. T. (1971) Essence of Decision: Explaining the Cuban Missile Crisis. Boston: Little, Brown.
ARGYRIS, C. (1967) "Some causes of organizational ineffectiveness within the State Department." Occasional paper no. 2. Washington DC: U.S. Department of State.
ARROW, K. (1974) The Limits of Organization. New York: W.W. Norton.
ASHENFELTER, O. and G. JOHNSON (1969) "Bargaining theory, trade unions, and industrial strike activity." Amer. Economic Rev. 59: 35-49.
AXELROD, R. (1977) "Argumentation in foreign policy settings: Britain in 1918, Munich in 1938, and Japan in 1970." J. of Conflict Resolution 21, 4.
——— [ed.] (1976) Structure of Decision: the Cognitive Maps of Political Elites. Princeton, NJ: Princeton Univ. Press.
——— (1970) The Conflict of Interest. Chicago: Markham.
BARTOS, O. J. (1977) "Simple model of negotiation: a sociological point of view." J. of Conflict Resolution 21, 4.
——— (1974) Process and Outcome of Negotiations. New York: Columbia Univ. Press.
——— (1967a) "How predictable are negotiations?" J. of Conflict Resolution 11: 481-495.
——— (1967b) Simple Models of Group Behavior. New York: Columbia Univ. Press.
——— (1966) Concession-Making in Experimental Negotiation," pp. 3-28 in J. Berger, M. Zeldich, Jr., and B. Anderson (eds.) Sociological Theories in Progress. Boston: Houghton Mifflin.
BAUMOL, W. J. (1961) Economic Theory and Operations Analysis. Englewood Cliffs: Prentice-Hall.
BENTON, A. A. and D. DRUCKMAN (1974) "Constituent's bargaining orientation and intergroup negotiations." J. of Applied Social Psychology 4: 141-150.
BERMAN, M. R. and I. W. ZARTMAN (forthcoming) "How diplomats negotiate: formulas and concessions." International Organization.
BERNSTEIN, B. J. (1976) "We almost went to war." Bull. of Atomic Scientists 2: 13-21.
BOULDING, K. E. (1956) The Image. Ann Arbor: Michigan Univ. Press.
BRAITHWAITE, R. B. (1955) Theory of Games as a Tool for the Moral Philosopher. Cambridge, England: Cambridge Univ. Press.
BRAMS, S. J. (1975) Game Theory and Politics. New York: Free Press.

―――― and D. MUZZIO (1977) "Unanimity in the Supreme Court: a game theoretic explanation of the White House tapes case." Public Choice 30.

―――― and F. C. ZAGARE (1977) "Deception in simple voting games." Social Sci. Research 6.

BRAYBROOKE, D. and C. LINDBLOM (1963) Strategy of Decision. New York: Free Press.

BRUNNER, R. D. and B. D. BREWER (1971) Organized Complexity. New York: Free Press.

BURNS, E.L.M. (1970) A Seat at the Table. Toronto: Clarke Irwin.

BURNSTEIN, E. and A. VINOKUR (forthcoming) "Novel argumentation and attitude change: the case of polarization following group discussion."

―――― (1975) "What a person thinks upon learning he has chosen differently from others: nice evidence for the persuasive-arguments explanation of choice shifts." J. of Exper. Social Psychology 11: 412-426.

―――― (1973) "Testing two theories about group-induced shifts in individual choice." J. of Exper. Social Psychology 9: 123-137.

BURTON, J. (1969) Communication and Conflict. New York: Free Press.

BUSH, R. R. and F. MOSTELLER (1955) Stochastic Models for Learning. New York: John Wiley.

BUTLER, W. (1971) The Soviet Union and the Law of the Sea. Baltimore: Johns Hopkins Univ. Press.

CACI (1977) Long-Term Forecasts of Potential Middle East Peace Solutions. Arlington, VA: CACI-Inc. Federal.

CAMPBELL, J. C. [ed.] (1976) Successful Negotiation: Trieste 1954. Princeton, NJ: Princeton Univ. Press.

CARR, E. H. (1949) The Twenty-Years Crisis. London: Macmillan.

CARTWRIGHT, D. (1959) "Lewinian theory as a contemporary systematic framework," in S. Koch (ed.) Psychology: a Study of a Science. New York: McGraw-Hill.

CASPARY, W. (1967) "Richardson's models of arms races: description, critique, and alternative model." Inter. Studies Q. 11: 63-88.

CLAUSEWITZ, C. (1832-1969) On War (A. Rapoport, ed.). London: Penguin.

CODDINGTON, A. (1973) "Bargaining as a decision process." Swedish J. of Economics 75: 397-405.

―――― (1972) "On the theory of bargaining," in C. F. Carter and J. Ford (eds.) Expectations and Uncertainty in Economics. Oxford: Blackwell.

―――― (1968) Theories of the Bargaining Process. Chicago: Aldine.

―――― (1966) "A theory of the bargaining process: comment." Amer. Economic Rev. 56: 522-530, reprinted in Young 1975.

COHEN, M. D. and J. G. MARCH (1974) Leadership and Ambiguity. New York: McGraw-Hill.

Conference of the Committee on Disarmament (1970). Final Verbatin Records. Geneva.

―――― (1969) Final Verbatin Records. Geneva.

Confidential Interviews with Conference of Committee on Disarmament Participants (1974).

CONTINI, B. (1968) "Time in bargaining negotiations: some experimental evidence." Amer. Economic Rev. 57: 374-393.

COOPER, C. (1975) "The iron law of negotiations." Foreign Policy 19.
CORSON, W. H. (1970) Measuring Conflict and Cooperation Intensity in East-West Relations: a Manual and Codebook. Ann Arbor: Univ. of Michigan, Institute for Social Research. (mimeo)
CROSS, J. G. (1977) "Negotiation as a learning process." J. of Conflict Resolution 21, 4.
――― (1969) The Economics of Bargaining. New York: Basic Books.
――― (1965) "A theory of the bargaining process." Amer. Economic Rev. 55: 66-94.
DAHL, R. (1976) Modern Political Analysis. Englewood Cliffs, NJ: Prentice-Hall.
――― (1955) "Hierarchy, democracy and bargaining in politics and economics," in R. Dahl et al., Research Frontiers in Politics and Government. Washington DC: Brookings Institution.
DEAN, A. (1960) "The second Geneva conference on the law of the sea." Amer. J. of Inter. Law 54: 751-789.
――― (1958) "The Geneva conference on the law of the sea: what was accomplished." Amer. J. of Inter. Law 52: 607-625.
deCALLIERES, F. (1963) On the Manner of Negotiating with Princes. Notre Dame: Notre Dame Univ. Press.
deFELICE, F. B. (1976) "Negotiations, or the art of negotiating," in I W. Zartman, 1976.
DEUTSCH, M. (1973) The Resolution of Conflict. New Haven: Yale Univ. Press.
――― (1968) "Field theory in social psychology," in G. Lindzey and E. Aronson, 1968.
DOUGLAS, A. (1962) Industrial Peacemaking. New York: Columbia Univ. Press.
――― (1957) "The peaceful settlement of industrial and intergroup disputes." J. of Conflict Resolution 1: 69-81.
DRUCKMAN, D. (forthcoming) "The monitoring function in negotiation: two models of responsiveness," in H. Sauermann (ed.) Contributions to Experimental Economics. Tübingen: Mohr.
――― (1977a) "New directions and unexplored linkages in negotiation research," in J. A. Wall (ed.) Negotiation Research and Theory. Kent, Ohio: Kent State Univ. Press.
――― (1977b) "Boundary role conflict: negotiation as dual responsiveness." J. of Conflict Resolution 21, 4.
――― (1977c) Negotiations: Social-Psychological Perspectives. Beverly Hills: Sage.
――― (1976) "The person, role and situation in international negotiations," pp. 406-456 in M. G. Hermann (ed.) A Psychological Examination of Political Leaders. New York: Free Press.
――― (1973) Human Factors in International Negotiations: Social Psychological Aspects of International Conflict. Sage Professional Paper 02-020. Beverly Hills: Sage.
――― (1971a) "On the effects of group representation." J. of Personality and Social Psychology 18: 273-274.
――― (1971b) "The influence of the situation in inter-party conflict." J. of Conflict Resolution 15: 523-554.
――― (1968) "Prenegotiation experience and dyadic conflict resolution in a bargaining situation." J. of Exper. Social Psychology 4: 367-383.
――― (1967) "Dogmatism, prenegotiation experience, and simulated group representation as determinants of dyadic behavior in a bargaining situation." J. of Personality and Social Psychology 6: 279-290.

——— and R. MAHONEY (1977) "Processes and consequences of international negotiations." J. of Social Issues 33.

DRUCKMAN, D. and T. BONOMA (1976) "Determinants of bargaining behavior in a bilateral monopoly situation II: opponent's concession rate and similarity." Behavioral Sci. 21: 252-262.

DRUCKMAN, D., R. ROZELLE, R. KRAUSE, and R. MAHONEY (1974) "Power and utilities in a simulated interreligious council: a situational approach to interplay decision-making," in J. Tedeschi (ed.) Perspectives on Social Power. Chicago: Aldine.

DRUCKMAN, D., D. SOLOMON, and K. ZECHMEISTER (1972) "Effects of representational role obligations on the process of children's distribution of resources." Sociometry 35: 387-410.

DRUCKMAN, D., K. ZECKMEISTER, and D. SOLOMON (1972) "Determinants of bargaining behavior in a bilateral monopoly situation: opponent's concession rate and relative defensibility." Behavioral Sci. 17: 514-531.

DRUCKMAN, D. and K. ZECKMEISTER (1970) "Conflict of interest and value consensus." Human Relations 23: 431-438.

DURBIN, J. (1970) "Testing for serial correlation in least squares regression when some of the regressors are lagged dependent variables." Econometrica 38: 3.

——— and G. S. WATSON (1951) "Testing for serial correlation in least squares regression." Biometrika 38: 173-176.

Eastern Committee (1918) Minutes and Verbatim Annex, Cab 27/24. London: Public Record Office.

ECKHARDT, W. (1965) "War propaganda, welfare values and political ideologies." J. of Conflict Resolution 9: 345-358.

FARQUHARSON, R. (1969) Theory of Voting. New Haven: Yale Univ. Press.

FINK, C. F. (1968) "Some conceptual difficulties in the theory of social conflict." J. of Conflict Resolution 12: 412-460.

FORWARD, N. (1971) The Field of Nations. Boston: Little, Brown.

FOSS, W. (1964) "Why the three mile limit?" Navy 7: 32-36.

FRAZER, J. G. (1919) Folklore of the Old Testament. New York: Macmillan.

FREY, R. L. and J. S. ADAMS (1972) "The negotiator's dilemma: simultaneous ingroup and outgroup conflict." J. of Exper. Social Psychology 8: 331-346.

FROLICH, N., J. A. OPPENHEIMER, and O. R. YOUNG (1971) Political Leadership and Collective Goods. Princeton: Princeton Univ. Press.

FRYE, A. (1974) "Decision-making for SALT," pp. 66-100 in M. Willrich and J. Rhinelander (eds.) SALT: the Moscow Agreements and Beyond. New York: Free Press.

GARTHOFF, R. L. (1977) "Negotiating with the Russians: some lessons from SALT." Inter. Security 1: 3-24.

GEORGE, A. L. (1975) "Toward a more soundly based foreign policy: making better use of information." Commission on the Organization of the Government for the Conduct of Foreign Policy. Washington, DC: Government Printing Office: Appendix D.

——— (1972) "The case for multiple advocacy in making foreign policy." Amer. Pol. Sci. Rev. 56: 751-785.

——— et al. (1971) The Limits of Coercive Diplomacy. Boston: Little, Brown.

GRAVEL, M. [ed.] (1971) The Pentagon Papers. Boston: Little, Brown.

HACCOUN, R. and R. J. KLIMOSKI (1975) "Negotiator status and accountability source: a study of negotiator behavior." Organizational Behavior and Human Performance 14: 342-359.

HAMERMESH, D. S. (1973) "Who 'wins' in wage bargaining?" Industrial and Labor Relations Rev. 26, 1: 146-149.

HAMNER, W. C. (1974) "The influence of structural, individual and strategic differences on bargaining outcomes: a review," in D. L. Harnett and L. L. Cummings (eds.) Bargaining Behavior and Personality: an International Study.

HIBBS, D. A., Jr. (1974) "Problems of statistical estimation and causal interference in time series regression models," in H. L. Costner (ed.) Statistical Methodology 1973-1974. San Francisco: Jossey-Bass.

HICKS, J. R. (1932) The Theory of Wages. London: Macmillan.

HOLLICK, S. and R. OSGOOD (1974) New Era in Ocean Politics. Baltimore: Johns Hopkins Univ. Press.

HOLSTI, O. R. (1972) Crisis, Escalation and War. Montreal: McGill-Queens Univ. Press.

——— (1969) Content Analysis for the Social Sciences and Humanities. Reading, MA: Addison-Wesley.

——— et al. (1965) "Measuring affect and action," J. of Peace Research 1: 170-189.

HOMANS, G. C. (1961) Social Behavior. New York: Harcourt Brace Jovanovich.

HOPMANN, P. T. (1977) "Bargaining within and between alliances on MBFR: perceptions and interactions." Presented at the annual meeting of the International Studies Association, St. Louis, MO.

——— (1974) "Bargaining in arms control negotiations: the seabeds denuclearization treaty." Inter. Organization 28.

——— (1972) "Internal and external influences on bargaining in arms control negotiations: the partial test ban," in B. M. Russett (ed.) Peace, War and Numbers. Beverly Hills, CA: Sage.

——— and T. C. SMITH (1977) "An application of a Richardson-process model: Soviet-American interactions in the test-ban negotiation 1962-1963." J. of Conflict Resolution 21, 4.

HOPMANN, P. T. and T. KING (1976) "Interactions and perceptions in the test ban negotiations." Inter. Studies Q. 20.

HOPMANN, P. T. and C. WALCOTT (1976) "The impact of international conflict and detente on bargaining in international arms control negotiations: an experimental analysis." Inter. Interactions 2: 189-206.

IKLE, F. C. (1970) "American shortcomings in negotiating with communist powers," in Senate Subcommittee on National Security and International Operations, International Negotiation.

——— (1964) How Nations Negotiate. New York: Harper & Row.

——— and N. LEITES (1962) "Political negotiation as a process of modifying utilities." J. of Conflict Resolution 6: 19-28.

Institute for Strategic Studies (1969) The Military Balance 1969-1970. London: Institute for Strategic Studies.

JACKMAN, N. (1957) "Collective protest in relocation centers." Amer. J. of Sociology 63: 264-272.

JANIS, I. L. (1972) Victims of Groupthink: a Psychological Study of Foreign-Policy Decisions and Fiascos. Boston: Houghton Mifflin.

Japan Times (1970) December 26.
JENSEN, L. (1968) "Approach-avoidance bargaining in the test ban negotiations." Inter. Studies Q. 12: 152-160.
——— "Soviet American bargaining behavior in post-war disarmament negotiations." J. of Conflict Resolution 6: 522-541.
JERVIS, R. (1970) The Logic of Images in International Relations. Princeton: Princeton Univ. Press.
KAHN, A. S. and J. W. KOHLS (1972) "Determinants of toughness in dyadic bargaining." Sociometry 35: 305-315.
KALB, M. and B. KALB (1974) Kissinger. New York: Dell.
KELLEY, E. W. (1970) "Bargaining in coalition situations," in Kelley et al. (eds.) The Study of Coalition Behavior. New York: Holt, Rinehart & Winston.
KISSINGER, H. A. (1969) "The Vietnam negotiations." Foreign Affairs 47: 211-234.
——— (1961) The Necessity of Choice. New York: Harper & Row.
KLIMOSKI, R. J. (1976) "Representatives' negotiation behavior as a function of individual and group factors: a review of research." Columbus: Ohio State University. (mimeo)
——— (1972) "The effect of intragroup forces on intergroup conflict resolution." Organizational Behavior and Human Performance 8: 363-383.
——— and R. A. ASH (1974) "Accountability and negotiation behavior." Organizational Behavior and Human Performance 11: 409-425.
KNOUSE, S. and R. J. KLIMOSKI (1976) "An operant conditioning investigation of negotiating behavior." Presented at the nineteenth conference of the Midwest division of the Academy of Management, St. Louis, MO.
KNOWLES, K. G. (1954) "Strike proneness and its determination." Amer. J. of Sociology 60: 213-229.
KNOX, R. and R. L. DOUGLAS, (1971) "Trivial incentives, marginal comprehension, and dubious generalizations from prisoners' dilemma studies." J. of Personality and Social Psychology 20: 160-165.
KUHN, H. W. and A. W. TUCKER [eds.] (1953) Contributions to the Theory of Games 2. Princeton: Princeton Univ. Press.
KUHN, T. S. (1962) The Structure of Scientific Revolutions. Chicago: Univ. of Chicago.
LALL, A. (1966) Modern International Negotiations. New York: Columbia.
LAMM, H. and N. KOGAN (1970) "Risk-taking in the context of intergroup negotiation." J. of Exper. Social Psychology 6: 351-363.
LANDSBERGER, H. A. (1955) "Interim report on a research project on mediation." Labor Law Rev. 6: 552-560.
LEONARD, J. (1974) Interview.
LEVY-STRAUSS, C. (1949) The Elementary Structure of Kinship. Paris: Presses Universitaire Françaises.
LEWIN, K. (1968) The Conceptual Representation and Measurement of Psychological Forces. New York: Johnson Reprint.
——— (1951) Field Theory in Social Science: Selected Theoretical Papers. D. Cartwright (ed.) New York: Harper Bros.
——— (1936) Principles of Topological Psychology. F. Heider and G. Heider [trans.] New York: McGraw-Hill.
——— (1935) A Dynamic Theory of Personality: Selected Papers. D. Adams and K. Zener [trans.] New York: McGraw-Hill.

LINDBLOOM, C. E. (1968) The Policy-Making Process. Englewood Cliffs, NJ: Prentice-Hall.
——— (1965) The Intelligence of Democracy: Decision Making Through Mutual Adjustment. New York: Free Press.
LINDZEY, G. and E. ARONSON [eds.] (1968) The Handbook of Social Psychology. Reading, MA: Addison-Wesley.
LOVE, R. L., R. M. ROZELLE, and D. DRUCKMAN (1977) "Resolving conflicts of interest and ideology: a simulated political decision making." Presented at the annual meeting of the American Psychological Association, San Francisco.
LOWI, T. J. (1963) "Bases in Spain," in H. Stein (ed.) American Civil-Military Decisions: a Book of Case Studies. Tuscaloosa: Univ. of Alabama Press.
LUCE, R. D. and H. RAIFFA (1957) Games and Decisions. New York: John Wiley.
McGRATH, J. E. (1966) "A social psychological approach to the study of negotiation," in R. Bowers (ed.) Studies on Behavior in Organizations: a Research Symposium. Athens: Univ. of Georgia Press.
——— and J. W. JULIAN (1963) Interaction process and task outcomes in experimentally-created negotiation groups." J. of Psych. Studies 14: 117-138.
MALINOWSKI, B. (1922) Argonauts of the Western Pacific. London: Routledge & Kegan Paul.
MARCH, J. G. and H. A. SIMON (1958) Organizations. New York: John Wiley.
MARSHALL, C. B. (1965) The Exercise of Sovereignty. Baltimore: Johns Hopkins Univ. Press.
MARTIN, L. (1967) The Sea in Modern Strategy. New York: Praeger.
MAUS, M. (1925) The Gift. Paris: Presses Universitaires Françaises.
MAXWELL, G. and D. SCHMITT (1968) "Are 'trivial' games the most interesting psychologically?" Behavioral Sci. 13.
MITTELMARK, M. B., R. M. ROZELLE, and D. DRUCKMAN (1977) "Accountability and role behavior of bargainers." Presented at the annual meeting of the American Psychological Association, San Francisco.
MORLEY, I. E. and G. M. STEPHENSON (1970) "Formality in experimental negotiations: a validation study." British J. of Psychology 61: 363-384.
NAKANE, C. (1970) Japanese Society. Berkeley: Univ. of California Press.
NASH, J. F. (1953) "Two person cooperative games." Econometrica 21: 128-140.
——— (1950) "The bargaining problem." Econometrica 18: 155-162.
NEUSTADT, R. E. (1960) Presidential Power: the Politics of Leadership. New York: John Wiley.
NEWHOUSE, J. (1973) Cold Dawn: the Story of SALT. New York: Holt, Rinehart & Winston.
Newsweek (1972) October 30.
New York Times (1966) October 26: 20.
NICOLSON, H. (1964) Diplomacy. New York: Oxford.
NIERENBERG, G. (1973) Fundamentals of Negotiating. New York: Hawthorn.
Observations on International Negotiations (1971) Transcript of an informal conference, Greenwich, CT: New York: Academy for Educational Development.
OSGOOD, C. E., G. J. SUCI, and P. H. TANNENBAUM (1957) The Measurement of Meaning. Urbana: Univ. of Illinois Press.

PAINTON, F. C. (1970) "Changing course for Franco's Spain." US News and World Report, November 16.
PARDO, A. (1974) Interview.
——— (1968) "Who will control the seabed?" Foreign Affairs 41: 123-137.
PECQUET, A. (1738) De l'Art de Negocier avec les Souverains. Paris: van Duren.
PEN, J. (1952) "A general theory of bargaining." Amer. Econ. Rev. 1: 29-42.
Pentagon Papers: the Defense Department History of United States Decision Making on Vietnam: Senator Gavel Edition. Boston: Beacon Press.
PERRY, S. E. (1957) "Notes on the role of the national: a social-psychological concept for the study of international relations." J. of Conflict Resolution 1: 346-363.
PORTER, G. (1975) A Peace Denied: the United States, Vietnam and the Paris Agreements. Bloomington: Univ. of Indiana Press.
Presidential Science Advisory Committee, Panel on Oceanography (1966) Effective Use of the Sea. Washington, DC: Government Printing Office.
QUANDT, W. B. (1975) "The Middle East," in Wall, 1975.
RAIFFA, H. (1953) "Arbitration schemes for generalized 2-person games," in Kuhn and Tucker, 1953.
RAMBERG, B. (1978) The Seabed Arms Control Negotiation: A Study of Multilateral Arms Control Conference Diplomacy. Denver: Univ. of Denver.
——— (1977) "Tactical advantages of opening positioning strategies: lessons from the seabed arms control talks 1967-1970." J. of Conflict Resolution 21, 4.
RAO, P. and R. L. Miller (1971) Applied Econometrica. Belmont, CA: Wadsworth.
RAPOPORT, A. (1974a) "Prisoner's dilemma: recollections and observations," pp. 17-34 in A. Rapoport (ed.) Game Theory as a Theory of Conflict Resolution. Dordrecht: D. Reidel Publishing.
——— (1974b) Conflict in Man-Made Environment. Baltimore: Penguin.
——— (1966) Two-Person Game Theory. Ann Arbor: Univ. of Michigan Press.
——— (1965) "Models of conflict: cataclysmic and strategic," in Conflict in Society Symposium, London: CIBA Foundation.
——— (1960) Fight, Games and Debates. Ann Arbor: Univ. of Michigan Press.
RICHARDSON, L. F. (1960) Arms and Insecurity. Pittsburgh: Boxwood.
RIKER, W. H. (1962) The Theory of Political Coalitions. New Haven: Yale Univ. Press.
——— and W. J. ZAVOINA (1970) "Rational behavior in politics: evidence from a 3-person game." Amer. Pol. Sci. Rev. 64: 48-60.
ROBINSON, W. S. (1957) "The statistical measure of agreement." Amer. Soc. Rev. 22: 17-25.
ROKEACH, M. (1960) The Open and Closed Mind. New York: Basic Books.
ROSENTHAL, R. and R. ROSNOW (1969) Artifacts in Behavioral Research. New York: Academic.
ROSS, A. M. (1954) "The natural history of the strike," in Kornhauser, Dubin, and A. M. Ross (eds.) Industrial Conflict. New York: McGraw-Hill.
RUBIN, J. and B. BROWN (1975) The Social Psychology of Bargaining and Negotiation. New York: Academic.
SAATY, T. L. (1968) Mathematical Models of Arms Control and Disarmament. New York: John Wiley.
SACHS, M. (1971) Seabed 1969. New York: Worldmark.
——— (1970) Seabed 1968. New York: Worldmark.

SAWYER, J. and H. GUETZKOW (1965) "Bargaining and Negotiation in International Relations," pp. 464-520 in H. Kelman (ed.) International Behavior. New York: Holt, Rinehart & Winston.
SCHELLING, T. C. (1960) The Strategy of Conflict. Cambridge: Harvard Univ. Press.
SHAPLEY, L. S. (1953) "A value for n-person games," in Kuhn and Tucker, 1953.
SHEEHAN, E.R.F. (1976) "Step by step in the Middle East." Foreign Policy 22: 3-70.
SHAW, J. and C. THORSLUND (1975) "Varying patterns of reward cooperation." J. of Conflict Resolution 19.
SHAW, M. E. (1976) Group Dynamics: the Psychology of Small-Group Behavior. New York: McGraw-Hill.
SHERIF, M. (1936) The Psychology of Social Norms. New York: Harper & Row.
——— O. J. HARVEY, B. J. WHITE, W. R. HOOD, and C. W. SHERIF (1961) Intergroup Conflict and Cooperation: the Robber's Cave Experiment. Norman: Univ. of Oklahoma Press.
SIEGEL, S. and L. FOURAKER (1960) Bargaining and Group Decision-Making. New York: McGraw-Hill.
SMOKER, P. (1965) "Trade, defense and the Richardson theory of arms races: a seven nation study." J. of Peace Research 2: 161-176.
SNYDER, G. H. (1971) "Prisoner's dilemma and 'chicken' models in international politics." Inter. Studies Q. 15: 66-103.
SPECTOR, B. I. (1977a) "Psychological impacts on negotiation: an empirical analysis." Presented at the annual meeting of the International Studies Association, St. Louis, MO.
——— (1977b) "Negotiation as a psychological process." J. of Conflict Resolution 21, 4.
——— (1976a) "A social-psychological model of position modification: Aswan" in I. W. Zartman, 1976.
——— (1976b) "Power positions among nations: an analysis of responsiveness to foreign policy power strategies." Presented to the annual meeting of the Peace Science Society (International), southern section.
——— (1975) "The effects of personality, perception, and power on the bargaining process and outcome." Ph.D. dissertation, New York University.
STAHL, I. (1972) Bargaining Theory. Stockholm: Economic Research Institute.
STECH, F. (1977) "Communicated influence effects on duopoly bargaining behavior." Ph.D. dissertation, University of California at Santa Barbara.
STEIN, M. (1963) "Explorations in typology," in R. W. White (ed.) The Study of Lives. New York: Atherton.
STEINBRUNNER, J. D. (1974) The Cybernetic Theory of Decision: New Dimensions of Political Analysis. Princeton: Princeton Univ. Press.
STERN, L. W., B. STERNTHAL, and G. S. CRAIG (1975) "Strategies for managing interorganizational conflict: a laboratory paradigm." J. of Applied Psychology 60: 472-482.
STEVENS, C. C. (1963) Strategy and Collective Bargaining. New York: McGraw-Hill.
Stockholm International Peace Research Institute (1970) SIPRI Yearbook of World Armament and Disarmament 1969-1970. Stockholm: Almqvist and Wiksells.
STORY, J. (1973) "Spanish Foreign Policy 1945-1970." Ph.D. dissertation, Johns Hopkins University.

STROTZ, R. H. (1956) "Myopia and inconsistency in dynamic utility maximization." Rev. of Econ. Studies 23: 165-180.

SWINGLE, P. [ed.] (1970) The Structure of Conflict. New York: Academic.

SZULC, T. (1974) "How Kissinger Did It." Foreign Policy 15: 21-69.

TERHUNE, K. (1974) "'Wash-in,' 'wash-out,' and systemic effects in extended prisoner's dilemma." J. of Conflict Resolution 18.

——— and J. FIRESTONE (1966) "Studies of personality in cooperation and conflict." Presented at the North American Peace Research Conference of the Peace Research Society (International).

Time (1973) February 5: 13.

TRACY, B. H. (1978) "Bargaining as trial and error: the case of the Spanish base negotiations 1963-1970," in I. W. Zartman (ed.) The Negotiation Process: Theories and Applications. Beverly Hills: Sage.

——— (1975) "Bargaining models and base negotiations." Ph.D. dissertation, Johns Hopkins University.

TURK, H. and M. J. LEFCOWITZ (1962) "Toward a theory of representation between groups." Social Forces 40: 337-341.

United Nations (1960) Second UN Conference on the Law of the Sea. New York: United Nations.

——— (1958) UN Conference on the Law of the Sea. New York: United Nations.

U.S. Arms Control and Disarmament Agency (1971) Documents on Disarmament 1970. Washington, DC: Government Printing Office.

——— (1970) Documents on Disarmament 1968. Washington, DC: Government Printing Office.

——— (1969) Documents on Disarmament 1968. Washington, DC: Government Printing Office.

U.S. Committee on Government Operations, Subcommittee on National Security (1972) International Negotiation Part 7. Washington, DC: Government Printing Office.

——— (1970) International Negotiation: American Shortcomings in Negotiating with Communist Powers. Washington, DC: Government Printing Office.

U.S. Congress Committee on Armed Services, Preparedness Investigating Subcommittee (1962) Arms Control and Disarmament. Washington, DC: Government Printing Office.

U.S. Department of State, Bureau of Research and Intelligence (1974) National Claims to Maritime Jurisdictions. Washington, DC: Government Printing Office.

U.S. Senate (1970a) Committee on Foreign Relations, Subcommittee on United States Security Agreements and Commitments Abroad, Hearings.

——— (1970b) Agreement Between the United States and Spain. Report 91-1425. Washington DC: Government Printing Office.

VIDMAR, N. (1971) "Effects of representational roles and mediators on negotiating effectiveness." J. of Personality and Social Psychology 17: 48-58.

——— (1970) "Forces affecting success in negotiating groups," Behavioral Sci. 15: 154-163.

——— and J. E. McGRATH (1965) "Role assignment and attitudinal commitment as factors in negotiation." Technical report no. 3. Urbana: Univ. of Illinois.

VINACKE, W. (1969) "Variables in experimental games: toward a field theory." Psych. Bull. 71.

VINOKUR, A. and E. BERSTEIN (1974) "Effects of partially shared persuasive arguments on group-induced shifts." J. of Personality and Social Psychology 29: 305-315.

VINOKUR, A., TROPE, and E. BERNSTEIN (1975) "A decision-making analysis of persuasive argumentation and choice-shift effect." J. of Exper. Psychology 11: 127-148.

WADE, L. L. and R. L. CURRY (1971) "An economic model of socio-political bargaining." Amer. J. of Economics and Sociology 30: 383-393.

WALCOTT, C. and P. T. HOPMANN (1975) "Interaction analysis and bargaining behavior." Exper. Study of Politics 4.

WALL, J. A. (1975) "Effects of constituent trust and representative bargaining orientaion on intergroup bargaining." J. of Personality and Social Psychology 31: 1004-1012.

—— and J. S. ADAMS (1974) "Some variables affecting a constituent's evaluations of and behavior toward a boundary role occupant." Organizational Behavior and Human Performance 11: 390-408.

WALL, M. M. [ed.] (1975) "International negotiations." J. of International Affairs 9, 1.

WALTON, R. E. (1970) "A problem-solving workshop on border conflicts in East Africa." J. of Applied Behavioral Sciences 6: 453-489.

—— and R. B. McKERSIE (1965) A Behavioral Theory of Labor Negotiations. New York: McGraw-Hill.

WEICK, K. (1965) "Laboratory experimentations with organizations," in J. G. March (ed.) Handbook of Organizations. Chicago: Rand McNally.

WENK, E. (1972) The Politics of the Ocean. Seattle: Univ. of Washington Press.

WHITAKER, A. P. (1961) Spain and the Defense of the West. New York: Harper & Row.

WINHAM, G. R. (1977a) "Complexity in international negotiation," in D. Druckman (ed.) Negotiations: a Social-Psychological Perspective. New York: Halstead.

—— (1977b) "Negotiation as a management process." World Politics 30.

—— and H. E. BOVIS (forthcoming) "Report on the Slobbovia Negotiations."

WINNEFELD, M. and C. BUILDER (1971) "ASW—now or never," U.S. Naval Institute Proceedings 97: 18-25.

WOLFE, T. W. (1975) The SALT Experience Report R-1686-PR. Santa Monica, CA: Rand.

WOODWARD, E. L., R. BUTLER, and M. LAMBERT [eds.] (1949) Documents on British Foreign Policy 1919-1939). London: HMSO: 2.

WRIGHTSON, M. (1976) "The documentary coding method," in R. Axelrod (ed.) Structure of Decision: the Cognitive Maps of Political Elites. Princeton, NJ: Princeton Univ. Press.

YOUNG, O. [ed.] (1975) Bargaining. Urbana: Univ. of Illinois Press.

—— (1968) The Politics of Force. Princeton: Princeton Univ. Press.

—— (1967) The Politics of Force: Bargaining during International Crisis. Princeton: Princeton Univ. Press.

ZAGARE, F. C. (1977a) "Deception in 3-person games: an analysis of strategic misrepresentation in Vietnam," Ph.D. dissertation. New York University.

—— (1977b) "A game-theoretic analysis of the Vietnam negotiations: Preferences and strategies 1968-1973." J. of Conflict Resolution 21, 4.

ZARTMAN, I. W. (1977) "Negotiation as a joint decision-making process." J. of Conflict Resolution 21, 4.

——— [ed.] (1976) The 50% Solution: How to Bargain Successfully with Hijackers, Strikers, Bosses, Oil Magnates, Arabs, Russians, and Other Worthy Opponents in this Modern World. New York: Doubleday Anchor.

——— (1975) "Negotiations: theory and reality." J. of Inter. Affairs 9: 69-77.

——— (1974) "The political analysis of negotiation." World Politics 26: 385-399.

——— (1971) The Politics of Trade Negotiations Between Africa and the European Economic Community. Princeton: Princeton Univ. Press.

——— and M. BERMAN (1979) The Practical Negotiator.

ZECHMEISTER, K. and D. DRUCKMAN (1973) "Determinants of resolving a conflict of interest: a simulation of political decision-making." J. of Conflict Resolution 17: 63-88.

ZUETHEN, F. (1930) Problems of Monopoly and Economic Warfare. London: Routledge & Kegan Paul.

INDEX

Allison, G. T., 77, 100, 176, 225
anthropology, 13
approach-avoidance, 170
arbitration, 35, 38, 41, 53, 100, 197-201, 212, 222
Arrow, K., 68, 225
Aswan Dam negotiations, 92f
Axelrod, R., 11, 69, 84, 181, 183f, 225

bargaining chip, 144
Bartos, O. J., 8-10, 13, 15, 25, 58, 73-76, 80f, 89-91, 150-153, 157, 172-174, 225
Bernstein, B. J., 77, 225
bilateral monopoly, 7, 72, 95
bluff, 38, 45, 49, 51, 53, 65
Boulware, L., 30f, 40, 50
Braithwaite, R. B., 75, 225
Brams, S. J., 69, 73, 119, 124, 127, 129, 132, 225
Brazil, 146
British Eastern Committee, 179f, 184-188
Burton, J., 85, 226
Bush-Mosteller model, 150, 226

Canada, 146f
Carr, E. H., 68f, 226
Caspary, W., 150, 226
Chicken Game, 73, 201, 210
China, 123f
coalition, 69, 71, 73, 103, 116f
Coddington, A., 71f, 74f, 89, 94, 226

commitment, 55, 57, 63
concessions, 10, 12, 21-26, 34, 36, 42, 47-50, 53, 55, 57, 61, 71, 73-86, 89-91, 93, 95-100, 108f, 120, 137, 148, 150-152, 157, 177, 194-201, 205f, 208, 210f, 216f, 219f, 222
Conference of the Committee on Disarmament (CCD), 140f, 153
conflict, 8, 13, 15, 19, 24, 33, 57, 69, 71, 85, 104, 106, 150
Contini, B., 53, 226
Cooper, C., 57, 227
cooperation, 13, 20, 33, 40, 57, 69, 71
costs, 40, 59, 137, 200
Cross, J. G., 8, 10, 73, 84, 137, 177, 194, 197
Cuban Missile Crisis, 77f, 159, 178
Czechoslovakia, 95, see also Munich

Dahl, R., 68, 227
deadline, 63, 75, 79, 205, 207, 210, 212, 214, 220
DeCallieres, F.,7, 57, 73, 227
decision-making, 7f, 10f, 30, 68-72, 83, 117f, 178, 192, 194, 196, 198
deFelice, F. B., 57, 73, 227
definition, 12, 23f, 30f, 33, 55f, 70, 88
determinance, 7, 74f, 84f, 151-153
Deutsch, M., 8, 59, 72, 81
disarmament, 15-19, 21, 26, 34, 56, 89, 92, 100, 136, 138, 143, 156, 169

237

Douglas, A., 7, 57, 62, 75, 227
Druckman, D., 9, 56, 72, 84, 88, 90f, 95-98, 103, 109, 227

economics, 7f, 10, 31, 72f
endgame, 49, 75, 81, 83
equilibrium, 14f, 39-42, 59f, 91, 108, 151f
European Economic Community (EEC), 53, 212
exchange, 34f, 151, 197, 205, 208, 215, 217, 220
expectations, 10, 17, 20f, 23, 35, 38, 40, 42-53, 55, 58f, 61-63, 78, 81-83, 89, 94-97, 99, 104, 108f, 135, 194-196, 205f, 208, 210, 223
experiments, 8, 21, 53f, 56, 65f, 80-82, 90-92, 95-98, 103-108, 136, 150-153, 172-174

Farquharson, R., 119, 228
Fermeda workshop, 80
formula, 10, 12, 76f, 79-86, 100-108, 110, 137, 151-153, 173, 177, 205-208, 211, 216, 220
Forward, N., 77, 228
Frye, A., 137, 228

game theory, 7, 9-11, 15, 38, 41, 73, 95, 112-132, 194f
George, A., 10, 228
Germany, 179f, 182-191

Hamermesh, D. S., 72, 80, 229
Hicks, J. R., 7, 54, 229
Holsti, O. R., 77, 229
Homans, G. C., 8, 14, 18, 23, 229
Hopmann, P. T., 11, 73, 92f, 97, 100, 109, 151, 153f, 156, 173

ideology, 106, 185
Ikle, F. C., 8, 94, 135-137, 229
information, 7, 18, 35, 42, 45, 52f, 64, 98, 109, 119, 126, 128, 132, 135, 138, 144, 177, 201f, 223
interagency bargaining, 88, 99-109, 137, 139f, 164f, 176, 178
Iran (Persia), 95, 180
Italy, 146

Janis, I. L., 178, 229
Japanese National Security Committee, 179f, 184-191
Jensen, L., 22, 25, 151, 169, 230
Jervis, R., 194, 201, 230
judication, 69-71
justice, 10, 14-16, 18, 20-24, 26f, 35, 61, 76, 98, 137f, 145, 148

Kakutani Kexed Point Theorem, 39
Kelley, E. W., 70, 230
Kissinger, H. A., 112f, 121f, 126, 129f, 135f, 138, 230
Kuhn, T. S., 67, 230

Lall, A., 8, 230
Lamdsberger, H. A., 75, 230
learning, 8, 10, 29, 41, 44-50, 52, 57, 74, 200
Levy Strauss, C., 14, 230
Lewin, K., 57, 59-61, 230
Lindbloom, C. E., 178, 231
Love, R. L., 91f, 231
Luce, R. D., 41, 231

Malinowski, B., 14, 231
March, J. G., 177f, 231
Markov chains, 150
Marshall, C. B., 77, 231
Maus, M., 14, 231
Maxwell, G., 56, 231
McGrath, J. E., 56, 231
Middle East negotiations, 57, 79
minimums, 135
Mittelmark, M. B., 106, 231
mixed motives, 32, 63, 71
Munich negotiations, 179f, 182-191

Nash, J. F., 9, 15-20, 24, 40f, 76, 84, 231
needs, 57-60, 63, 65f
Neustadt, R. E., 177, 231
Newhouse, J., 88, 100, 231
Nicolson, H., 7, 57, 73, 231
Nixon, R. M., 120f, 125, 129-131
North Atlantic Treaty Organization (NATO), 213, 215
Nuclear Test Ban Talks, 11, 25, 92, 149, 153f, 156f, 169-174

Index

opening moves, 11, 18-20, 24, 26, 52, 57, 81, 133-148, 177
outcomes, 8, 16-20, 23-25, 33f, 36, 39f, 47, 55, 61f, 120

Pareto optimality, 40f
Pecquet, A., 73, 232
Pen, J., 72, 232
perception, 10, 51f, 62, 155f, 158, 166, 171, 173, 207
Perry, S. E., 88, 232
personality, 10, 27, 55, 57f, 60-63, 65f, 71, 154
phases, 8, 11, 62
political science, 10, 111, 135
power (persuasion, influence), 10f, 25, 30, 32, 36-38, 40-44, 46f, 54-57, 59, 61, 63-67, 69-74, 78f, 84f, 93, 98, 103, 108, 116f, 119, 175, 177f, 184-192, 221
prediction, 25, 38, 74, 78, 104, 152, 164, 166
preferences, 21, 113-116, 118f, 122-135, 142, 177
Prisoners' Dilemma Game, 56, 73, 91, 201
process, 7, 9-13, 20, 46-50, 56, 61, 63, 70, 72f, 76, 84, 97, 108, 110, 150-153, 195, 200, 222-224
propaganda, 143
psychology, 8-10, 21, 55f, 58-61, 66, 71f, 76, 85, 88, 136

Quandt, W. B., 79, 232

Raiffa, H., 41, 75, 231f
Ramberg, B., 11, 232
Rapoport, A., 68, 73f, 84, 232
reciprocity, 60, 150f, 153-156, 171-174, 184-187
regress, 51, 74, 195f, 201
retraction, 37
Richardson, L. F., 11, 92, 149-151, 154-156, 158f, 161, 163, 169, 171-174, 232
Riker, W. H., 69, 232
Rokeach, M., 57, 232
roles, 61f
Rubin, J., 9, 56, 65, 72, 232
rules of the game, 31, 33, 35, 38, 50, 117f, 198

Rusk, D., 138

Saaty, T. L., 150, 232
Sawyer, J., 9, 136, 233
Schelling, T. C., 7, 8, 32, 57, 84f, 99, 157, 169, 194
Seabed Arms Control Negotiations, 11, 134, 139-148
search, 34f, 64, 153, 176f, 199, 202
security point, 31, 52, 135, 203, 223
Sheehan, E.R.F., 79, 233
Siegel, S., 53f, 73, 81, 233
signals, 63f, 135
Smoker, P., 150, 233
Snyder, G. H., 194, 233
sociology, 8-10, 14, 20
Spanish-American base negotiations, 11, 202-222
Spector, B. I., 56, 61, 64f, 72, 80, 85, 93, 154, 233
split the difference, 15, 17, 21, 38, 44, 201
stalemate, 58, 61f, 71, 74, 96-98, 113, 117, 120, 122, 132, 137, 145, 154, 199, 211, 213, 221
statistics, 8, 11, 165-170, 176
Stech, F., 91, 233
Stein, M., 65, 233
Stevens, C. C., 8, 135, 233
Strategic Arms Limitation Talks (SALT), 25, 27, 34, 110, 136, 138f, 153
strategy, 8, 11, 36, 38-42, 46, 65, 98f, 112-122, 124-126, 128, 131, 138f, 143, 151, 169, 194f, 203
strikes, 30, 33, 52, 54
Strotz, R. H., 42, 234
structures, 8f, 11, 107, 195-201, 205f, 209, 220-222
sums, zero or positive, 10, 12, 19, 30, 69-71, 85, 134
Swingle, P., 72, 234
symmetry, 17, 44, 50f, 72, 74, 85, 136, 154
Szulc, T., 112, 234

Terhune, K., 56f, 60f, 234
terms of trade, 35
threats, 30, 32, 36f, 40, 52, 57, 63, 65, 98, 157, 178, 221

time costs, 10, 38f, 46f, 92f, 138, 145, 148, 202, 207, 210, 223
timing, 45, 52, 54, 84f, 148
tough/soft, 19, 21, 26f, 61, 64, 74, 82, 89f, 93, 95-97, 150, 157, 171-173, 210
Tracy, B., 11, 70f, 74, 84, 107, 194, 234
trust, 8, 21, 26f, 45, 53, 63, 70, 130

USSR, 25f, 53, 92, 123, 126, 136-148, 153, 156f, 160-164, 166-168, 170, 172f, 179, 203
United Kingdom, 146, 153, 179f, 182-191
United Nations, 140f, 143
USA, 25f, 53, 92, 112-132, 136-148, 153, 156f, 160-164, 166-168, 170, 172f, 179, 202-222

Vietnam negotiations, 11, 78, 111, 132, 221

wage bargaining, 7f, 31, 33-35, 40, 53, 56, 73, 80-82
Wall, J. A., 77, 235
Walton, R., 8, 80, 88, 134, 235
Winham, G., 80, 88, 101, 235
Wolfe, T. W., 88, 110, 235

Young, O., 8-10, 70, 72, 78, 85, 194, 235

Zagare, F. C., 11, 235
Zartman, I. W., 9, 57, 59, 61, 70f, 78, 80, 85, 95, 101, 107, 109, 111, 131, 151-153, 172-174, 194, 199, 207, 236
Zechmeister, K., 100, 236
Zeuthen, F., 7, 78, 236